Corporate Social Respon
Social Justice and The Gl
Food Supply Chain

Food is a source of nourishment, a cause for celebration, an inducement to temptation, a means of influence and signifies good health and well-being. Together with other life-enhancing goods, such as clean water, unpolluted air, adequate shelter and suitable clothing, food is a basic good which is necessary for human flourishing. In recent times, however, various environmental and social challenges have emerged, which are having a profound effect on both the natural world and built environment—such as climate change, feeding a growing world population, nutritional poverty and obesity. Consequently, whilst the relationships between producers, supermarkets, regulators and the individual have never been more important, they are becoming increasingly complicated.

In the context of a variety of hard and soft law solutions, with a particular focus on corporate social responsibility (CSR), the authors explore the current relationship between all actors in the global food supply chain. *Corporate Social Responsibility, Social Justice and the Global Food Supply Chain* also provides a comprehensive and interdisciplinary response to current calls for reform in relation to social and environmental justice, and proposes an alternative approach to current CSR initiatives. This comprises an innovative multi-agency proposal, with the aim of achieving a truly responsible and sustainable food retail system. Because only by engaging in the widest possible participatory exercise and reflecting on the urban locale in novel, material and cultural ways is it possible to uncover new directions in understanding, framing and tackling the modern phenomena of, for instance, food deserts, obesity, nutritional poverty and social injustice.

Corporate Social Responsibility, Social Justice and the Global Food Supply Chain engages with a variety of disciplines, including, law, economics, management, marketing, retailing, politics, sociology, psychology, diet and nutrition, consumer behaviour, environmental studies and geography. It will be of interest to both practitioners and academics, including postgraduate students, social scientists and policy makers.

Hillary J. Shaw is Visiting Professor in the Department of Politics and Public Policy at De Montfort University, Leicester, UK. His research spans sustainable economic development, CSR and the integration of global and local food systems. He is the author of many journal articles, essays, reviews, reports and books, including *The Consuming Geographies of Food: Diet, Food Deserts and Obesity* (Routledge, 2014).

Julia J. A. Shaw is Professor of Law and Social Justice in the School of Law at De Montfort University, Leicester, UK. Her research is interdisciplinary and publications include *Jurisprudence* (3rd edition, Pearson 2018) and *Law and the Passions: Narratives of Feeling in the Administration of Justice* (Routledge, 2019).

Routledge Studies in Management, Organizations and Society

This series presents innovative work grounded in new realities, addressing issues crucial to an understanding of the contemporary world. This is the world of organized societies, where boundaries between formal and informal, public and private, local and global organizations have been displaced or have vanished, along with other 19th century dichotomies and oppositions. Management, apart from becoming a specialized profession for a growing number of people, is an everyday activity for most members of modern societies.

Similarly, at the level of enquiry, culture and technology, and literature and economics, can no longer be conceived as isolated intellectual fields; conventional canons and established mainstreams are contested. **Management, Organizations and Society** addresses these contemporary dynamics of transformation in a manner that transcends disciplinary boundaries, with books that will appeal to researchers, student and practitioners alike.

For a full list of titles in this series, please visit www.routledge.com

Corporate Social Responsibility, Social Justice and The Global Food Supply Chain

Towards an Ethical Food Policy for Sustainable Supermarkets

Hillary J. Shaw & Julia J. A. Shaw

LONDON AND NEW YORK

First published 2019 by Routledge

2 Park Square, Milton Park, Abingdon, Oxon, OX14 4RN
605 Third Avenue, New York, NY 10017

*Routledge is an imprint of the Taylor & Francis Group,
an informa business*

First issued in paperback 2020

Copyright © 2019 Taylor & Francis

The right of Hillary J. Shaw & Julia J. A. Shaw to be identified
as authors of this work has been asserted by them in accordance
with sections 77 and 78 of the Copyright, Designs and Patents
Act 1988.

Library of Congress Cataloging-in-Publication Data
A catalog record for this book has been requested

ISBN: 978-1-138-93553-2 (hbk)
ISBN: 978-0-367-78686-1 (pbk)

Typeset in Sabon
by Apex CoVantage, LLC

Contents

Figures and Tables

Figures

Tables

Introduction
Why Do Companies Exist?

Limited liability companies have come to dominate most aspects of life in the Global North. They provide almost all our daily needs, from food and water to clothes, housing, transport entertainment and other luxuries. Most people also work for such an organization, depend on it for their income and, later, their pension. Why do we gain our livelihoods this way, when we know that we are not fully recompensed for the value of the labour we put in, and we do not receive the full value of our payment for the goods we buy from them? The answer is embodied in the very term 'company'; this word derives from the Latin *cum panis*, meaning 'those who break bread together'. The corporate word 'company' shares the same etymology as the term 'company', meaning a group of friends; the origin of the limited liability company lies in organizations such as the Hudson Bay Company or the East India Company. People form sociable 'companies' because of synergy; three together can accomplish more than three people each working alone, because together they can share skills, debate ideas and defend property. Therefore, communities with 'companies' can provide a wider range of goods and services than those where only sole traders exist. There is therefore a social bargain between community and companies; companies are allowed to extract profit from the community in exchange for the provision of goods and services that the community cannot provide on its own.

A major step in the evolution of companies was to grant such associations of people working together with the protection of limited liability. Such protection was granted as far back as the 15th century to English monasteries and trade guilds. This ensured that investors could not be liable for any more than the money they had put in, although even then there were concerns about immoral and illegal actions, such as fraud, damages from pollution and injury to third parties being unpunishable. Under the law, the limited company became a legal 'person' with the capacity for making contracts, taking out loans, owning property and much else. This is known legally as the 'veil of incorporation'; third parties to the company 'see' it as an entity in its own right and have no concern with the investors behind the company,

As companies grew bigger, concerns arose about their increasing impact on society and the environment. The US government "assumed responsibility for correcting social behaviour of large corporations as early as the 1890s and it passed laws on child labour, safety at industrial sites and on workers' rights to form trusts", and in 1906, the US Supreme Court declared that "the corporation is a creature of the state" (Mullerat, 2013: 14). The relationship between state and company is distinctly two-sided; the state sponsors and protects companies, but also seeks to regulate and restrict them. The earliest companies, such as the Hudson Bay Company, were quasi-colonial adventurers as much as businesspeople seeking profitable trades. In more recent times, companies have lobbied the government to change laws in their favour, whilst flouting laws that restricted their profits wherever they could. The efforts by British supermarkets to get Sunday trade legalized are a good example of this. Companies have benefitted from state legal protection at home whilst undermining administrations abroad (notably in 19th century China with the infamous Opium Trades). Where the external effects of corporate operations have become too intolerable, societally or environmentally, companies have sought to buy off criticism with philanthropy; witness the beneficence of large Victorian British companies with model towns for workers, educational grants and the like, whilst operating huge mills with worker conditions we would deem rather exploitative today. When, in recent times, corporate social responsibility (CSR) became a selling point in its own right, rather than something companies did to brighten up any tarnishing of their name that might have occurred through worker conditions or socio-environmental externalities, large companies have sometimes sought government legislation to force all companies in that sector to adopt certain CSR initiatives. That way the original CSR mover can get credit for societal improvement, but not at the cost of any reductions in its profits vis-à-vis its competitors. In other instances, companies resist government legislation aimed at cleaning up negative corporate externalities.

Ostensibly, a company is about trading, which is a two-party agreement; the company trades wages for labour, and it trades goods for money. In reality, there have always been two further parties to this trade; the government and the wider socio-environmental range of stakeholders. The true 'trading' situation of a company is illustrated in Figure 0.1.

The significance of the 'trading arrows' in Figure 0.1 has waxed and waned over time, depending on the company and the historical context. The growing knowledge-economy sector has less need for physical resources from the environment, although it is very dependent on the capacity to generate electric power sustainably. People in less-developed rural economies may have few connections to a remote government to whom they pay very little taxes and receive scant protection from, but as

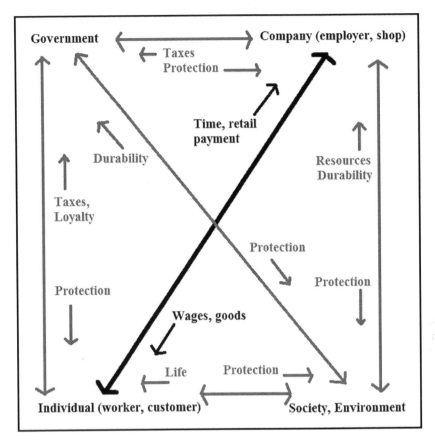

Figure 0.1 The Four-Way Relationship Between Companies, Individuals, Government and Society/Environment. The Direction of the Smaller Arrows Illustrates What Is 'Bought' by Each Party from Another.

the economy moves into industry and services and becomes urbanized, people have more dealings with their government.

Historically, food was a locally produced good where the main governmental concerns were if famine produced food riots or if malnutrition undermined the capacity of the military or reduced the health of army recruits. In pre-industrial times, people, households, produced much of their own food and might even make their own agricultural implements, so the corporate arrow was perhaps absent altogether except for the small percentage of the population who lived in cities. The environment/society arrow was always significant, of course; climatic disaster, disease or war could seriously diminish food production. The era of a largely corporate-based diet for the majority came about when the two major revolutions of firstly the UK and then the rest of the world occurred: the Second Agricultural Revolution of the 18th century,[1] paving the way for the Industrial Revolution of the 19th century. The UK's population went from being 25% urban in 1780 to 75% urban in 1900, a trajectory followed by many other countries soon afterwards. The majority of the population became divorced from the means of production of the most basic good of all, food—the very stuff we are made of.

For most countries, the divorce between the production and consumption of food has been over four stages (Shaw, 2014: 7–8). Industrialization saw people leave the farms for the cities, and then globalization saw the locale of food production move far from the site of consumption, as the UK began to obtain its fruit from the tropics and its meat from Argentina and New Zealand. The third 'divorce' was supermarketization, when we gave up the intimacy of the local corner shop for the cheapness, convenience and range of the anonymous supermarket. All three of these stages carried an increasing reliance on the environment, to provide the energy necessary for these lengthening food chains, and an increasing societal impact, from slavery in the Caribbean to the devastation of Latin American indigenous peoples, from rampant food adulteration in Victorian Britain to the steady rise of sugar in foodstuffs. The fourth stage of divorce, still underway today, is the separation of the consumer from any recognizability of the food we consume. We have ready meals with completely unknown ingredients (unless you happen to be an industrial chemist); we have processed meats that no anatomist could determine the animal of origin from; we have desserts that resemble nothing found in nature at all; in fact, they greatly outdo nature in terms of bright colours, smooth textures and sweetness. We are still separating ourselves from recognizable food in that it has been speculated, in 2018, that within two generations, Britons may no longer know how to cook (Temple, 2018).

The irony is that just as the link between what foods we buy and the organization that originally produced those foods becomes weaker, the links illustrated in Figure 0.1 that run between government and society, environment and the corporation and the individual become more important. It would not take much to disrupt our global food chains: a climate shift, an oil shortage, an IT crash or a war in the wrong place. Meanwhile, the societal cost of a poor diet is rising, as obesity and the diseases and disabilities it produces, from arthritis and cancer to diabetes and blindness, bear down more heavily on health costs, especially in times of austerity and government spending cuts. The old socio-environmental problems of the food chain have not gone away; we still have exploited farm labour, from Lincolnshire to Liberia, and we still face uncertain and unknowable ingredients in our food. Additionally, we also face a range of new food production–related issues, from antibiotic resistance in animals to oceans choked with plastic. With fragile food chains, a damaged environment and increasing food-related illnesses, it has never been more important that the giant corporations, which have a virtual oligopoly of food retailing in every developed country and are rapidly gaining this position in less-developed countries too, do not just sell us food at a profit but also behave in a socially responsible manner. It cannot be the role of consumers alone to ensure that this happens, although they can exert considerable influence on supermarket policies. The government, along with other organizations, such as non-governmental organizations (NGOs) and the media, has a crucial role to play. If we allow supermarkets alone to decide what CSR initiatives they will adopt, we will end up with a damaged society, poor health and, ultimately, perhaps a collapsed food system. This book explores what CSR issues exist in the food chain, what further CSR issues we need to implement and how we might ensure the optimum balance of CSR, along with the provision of healthy, sustainable and affordable food for all.

Note

1. The First Agricultural Revolution was the transition from hunter-gathering to agriculture some 10,000 years ago.

1 Feasting Cavemen and Responsible Giants

1.1 The Eternal Modern Feast of Supermarkets

The slogan 'Just Eat', which was once 'Don't Cook, Just Eat' (YouTube, 2012), appeals to our inner Neanderthal; some of us may cook in postmodern kitchens, but we all consume like prehistoric cavemen. Pre-industrial humans, like all species in nature, lived Malthus-style perpetually on the edge of famine, breeding up their numbers when times were good and suffering the loss of the most vulnerable when food became scarce again. Our bodies were well-adapted for such an environment; every time food was plentiful, we gorged on it, because it would be famine tomorrow. Our biology ensures we are very good at absorbing and storing calories, and we only use up those calories at the very minimum necessary to maintain life once the plentiful times are over. This is precisely why it is so easy to gain weight and so hard to lose it. Prehistoric cavemen would have feasted on whatever large animal they managed to kill; eating quickly not just because their bodies said, "Store calories now!" but because if they didn't consume it, other organisms would, from vultures and rodents to bacteria and fungi. If by extreme good fortune they managed to kill a second large animal tomorrow, that too must be quickly eaten. Fridges were scarce out on the savannah 20,000 years ago. The equivalent now of that large animal kill are the bright shining aisles of our supermarkets, and if feast tomorrow follows feast today, we still overconsume because your body can never be sure that famine won't return. In fact, when 'famine' does briefly return in the shape of a whole day's closure of the supermarkets for a public holiday, witness the frantic food buying as if prepping for some disaster, the terrifying prospect of no easy access to cheap plentiful food for a whole 36 hours.

1.2 The Growth of the Supermarkets

For some, it was more of a disaster when the supermarkets opened in the first place and then gained such market dominance that in many developed countries, just five large retail corporations often now sell over three-quarters of total food consumed. The obvious front-line casualties of supermarket expansion are the smaller retail players, many of who whom have either closed down or been absorbed, taken over by giants such as Tesco. The secondary effects on other small retailers caused by supermarket expansion are discussed in Chapter 3. These effects may include the closure of shops, such as ironmongers, that, whilst not directly competing with the supermarkets, nevertheless depend on High Street footfall generated by smaller everyday grocery shops now stripped from traditional retail areas. This denudation produces 'clone' or 'zombie' High Streets; retail areas that are either strings of identical banks, chemists, takeaways, jewellers, etc., or are populated by only the fringe retailers that peddle trades the supermarkets are not interested in, such as charity shops, gambling shops, vaping shops, personal grooming salons, cheap discount '99p stores' or 'Dollar stores' and the like.

One measure of market dominance is the Concentration Ratio (CR), which is simply the sum of the percentage market shares of the largest companies, usually the biggest three, four or five of them. Australia is an exceptional case where just two supermarkets, Woolworths and Coles, control 80% of the grocery market between them. Larger countries, by area, tend to have less concentrated retail markets because distance protects from competition. However, even in the USA, the number of retailers accounting for 20% of sales fell from 33 in 1980 to just 7 in 2005. In 2005, Walmart alone took 9% of the US retail market and the share of the top three retailers, or CR3 (Concentration Ratio 3), was 13%. Walmart is so large that in 2006, with total sales of US\$ 312.5 billion, it accounted for over 10% of total US imports from China (Zhen, 2007: 37). In European countries, the retail CR3 for 2005 was over 50%, rising to over 80% in the smaller-population Nordic countries of Norway and Sweden (Zhen, 2007: 11).

Table 1.1 gives the grocery market CR for selected countries and how this CR has evolved over time. A consistent measure of CR between countries over time is not possible because different countries use different CR numbers; as noted earlier, for Australia, a CR2 ratio is appropriate because just two supermarkets command the market there, whereas in many European countries, there are four or five major players. The other confounding factor as regards comparison over time is the rapid expansion of the discount chains Lidl and Aldi in many countries since 2000. Because these chains were small or non-existent in many national markets, but have now expanded to capture 10% or more of the market, the CR4 or CR5 in many regions has fallen; however, this can scarcely be taken as a retreat of the dominance of the supermarket phenomenon in general.

The interpretation of CR(n) figures is complex, especially when new smaller entrants are rapidly gaining ground, but the overall trend of these figures is that in all these countries, the supermarkets have a dominant and generally growing market position.

Table 1.1 Grocery Supermarket CR in Selected Countries; Changes Over Time

Country/Year	Ca. 2000	Ca. 2005	Ca. 2010	Ca. 2015
Australia			71% (2)[2011]	80% (2)[2015]
Austria			82% (3)[2009]	87% (3)[2015]
Belgium	72% (5)[2000]		71% (5)[2011]	71% (5)[2015]
Brazil	62% (5)[2000]	64% (5)[2005]		
Canada			75% (5)[2011]	
Czech Republic			63% (5)[2010]	70% (5)[2015]
Denmark	84% (5)[2000]		80% (5)[2009]	
Finland			88% (3)[2011]	80% (2)[2015]
France	83% (5)[2000]		65% (5)[2009]	80% (6)[2015]
Germany	76% (5)[2000]		85% (4)[2011]	85% (4)[2015]
Hungary			55% (5)[2010]	57% (5)[2015]
Ireland		81% (5)[2006]		89% (5)[2018]
Italy	31% (5)[2000]		40% (5)[2009]	51% (5)[2015]
Japan				65% (5)[2014]
Netherlands	95% (5)[2000]		65% (5)[2010]	55% (2)[2015]
Norway	84% (5)[2000]		81% (3)[2011]	96% (3)[2016]
Poland			34% (5)[2010]	47% (5)[2015]
Slovakia			64% (5)[2010]	70% (5)[2015]
Spain	51% (5)[2000]		70% (5)[2009]	50% (5)[2018]
Sweden	95% (5)[2000]	95% (4)[2006]		80% (4)[2015]
Switzerland			76% (3)[2011]	
United Kingdom	71% (5)[2000]	74% (4)[2004]	76% (4)[2011]	85% (5)[2015]
USA	28% (4)[1999]	35% (4)[2006]	43% (4)[2010]	55% (4)[2014]

Source: Adapted from Bell & Cuthbertson 2004; Nicholson & Young, 2012; Ezeala-Harrison & Baffoe-Bonnie, 2016

Number of firms in CR is in brackets. **Non-European Union (EU) countries (2018) in bold.**

Notes: (1) Some CRs have fallen due to market capture by Aldi and Lidl and (2) Methodology not necessarily consistent between years.

The growth of the supermarket as the primary means by which most people in developed countries, also an increasing number in less-affluent nations, purchase their food, has been well-documented already, but from a CSR perspective it is worth reviewing the multiple dimensions of the one principle that has been central to this expansion: economies of scale. The basic premise of 'economies of scale' is simply that as an enterprise doubles in size, many of its costs rise by considerably less than that, if at all. A payroll system that can handle 100 employees can probably just as easily handle 200; a shop-floor manager can oversee 20 staff with not much more difficulty than she can manage 10. Some costs may even fall as the company doubles in size. Advertising becomes less necessary because the corporation and its products are already well-known, and the physical premises become its own advertisement as it creates a bigger physical footprint on the landscape. Perhaps the most significant cost to fall as size rises is raw materials costs, because in general a bigger customer can negotiate (force, demand) a lower price from suppliers. To an extent, supplier's costs will fall as the order size increases because they too enjoy economies of scale—a more insidious discount arises when the order size is so large a monopsony situation arises. The supplier may become a 'commercial colony' of the corporation, dependent on it for all its trade, but lacking the support that a true subsidiary of the corporation would enjoy.

Worldwide, the top-30 supermarket chains control 33% of all global food sales (GRAIN, 2014).The top-ten chains alone have annual global sales in excess of US$ 1.3 trillion, sold through over 106,000 outlets, as Table 1.2 illustrates.

However, one interprets the figures, the message appears to be that a very few supermarket companies with massive economies of scale, less than one per thousand farmers, control most of the developed-world food sales and therefore possess huge commercial power. They are adept at using this power, as the rest of this book shows, and it is then essential that such power is harnessed for the good of wider society (a concept further explicated in Chapter 3) rather than left in the hands of a few huge private corporations.

The essence of gaining economies of scale is that unit prices of production fall, and therefore a virtuous circle (virtuous from the company's point of view, at least, but perhaps not so good for society and the environment) can be set up whereby lower prices leads to further capture of market share, leads to further corporate growth, leads to more economies of scale and still lower prices. Economists recognize that there may be a point when economies of scale become diseconomies; administration

Table 1.2 The World's Largest Supermarket Chains; Sales and Number of Outlets

Supermarket chain	Sales (US$ billion, 2013)	Number of outlets (2017)
Walmart	446.24	11,695
Carrefour	149.01	12,300
Tesco	104.51	6,800
Metro Group	102.27	750*
Seven&I Holdings	95.89	46,000**
Kroger	93.23	2,800
Lidl	86.28	10,000
Costco	85.38	740*
Auchan	79.36	3,050
Groupe Casino	74.61	12,000
(Total)	1,316.78	106,135

Source: Adapted from GRAIN, 2014

*   Metro and Costco are both cash and carry warehouse type outlets with fewer and very large outlets.

** Seven&I controls the Seven-Eleven convenience chain, with many smaller convenience outlets.

becomes more complex as the company expands into different territories with varied currencies, customs, market demands, employee and customer theft rises, management becomes bloated and complacent, the corporation becomes so big it loses the capability to react swiftly to changing demand and is outmanoeuvred by smaller nimbler leaner competitors. To an extent, this has already happened with the largest supermarket chains such as Tesco losing ground since around 2005 to the German deep discounters Aldi and Lidl. British customers have also changed shopping habits, due to exogenous societal changes, such as more people living singly and in smaller homes, and a shift in attitudes away from planning ahead for the week towards a lifestyle of shorter time horizons and last-minute meal decisions. This has driven supermarket shoppers away from big out-of-town sheds towards both online ordering and smaller local shops; in response, the major supermarkets have heavily penetrated the convenience store market with chains such as Tesco Express and Sainsbury's Local. Information communications technology (ICT) has drastically pushed back the frontiers of economies of scale, perhaps to the point where for many industries, the inflexion point, where diseconomies of scale kick in, effectively no longer exists because such a magnitude is beyond the size of planet Earth itself. Supermarkets have been outstandingly successful at giving consumers lower food prices, at least at the till. Of course, as we shall see, the till price is not the only price we pay for cheap food. ICT has enabled the supermarkets to gain economies of scale at the smaller end of the stores' size range, whilst operating multiple small local neighbourhood convenience branches.

Food purchasing generally presents the consumer with a classic trilemma: a situation where any two desirable characteristics out of three must be chosen, thereby excluding the third, but one wants all three. In the case of food, the three characteristics are convenience (speed and ease of preparation), price and healthfulness. Taste or palatability is also important, of course; this is linked to healthfulness as discussed below. Convenient cheap food is usually not healthy; cheap healthy food usually takes effort to prepare, and healthy food that is convenient is usually not cheap. It might seem odd that consumers usually prioritize low price; if we are choosing an accountant or an architect to design a home extension, we would usually go for the best not the lowest price. Yet food *is* us; we are what we eat, so for our own bodies, we pick the cheapest (Shaw, 2014: 13). This is our inner Neanderthal kicking in again; we have short time horizons. See a large animal and kill it now with the minimum effort possible, no point in pondering whether the tribe already has an excess of meat that in the absence of refrigeration will soon rot, or if it even an edible animal or how dangerous it is, by the time Neanderthal man has worked all that out, the prey has long gone, or eaten its human hunter.

The equivalent attitude today is asking someone whether they would choose a prize now of £1,000 or wait a year and pick up £1,200; 90%

of the people you ask will take the £1,000 now, despite the fact that they have effectively turned down an investment opportunity paying 20% interest over one year. If you point this financial short-sightedness out, people reply "I might not be here in a year; you might not be here", or, more tellingly, "Well, I'd rather just enjoy the money now". Interestingly, this attitude of 'satisfaction now over gain later' seems to vary on several parameters. The already wealthy are more likely to bank and wait, whereas the less affluent will take the £1,000 now (even if they could in fact defer for a year and being less wealthy should value the chance of a strong financial reward more). As the percentage return rises, from, e.g., 10% to 20%, the willingness to defer rises at a time when interest rates are miserably low and savers do well to find an account paying even 2% per annum. Also, as the original sum rises, say to £10,000, the willingness to defer rises, because the future rewards of patience are so much higher: £2,000 instead of £200. Translate this into healthy eating now to prolong life and health later or indulgence now, and one could infer that as we eat several times a day, thousands of times a year, meals and snacks, we see each meal as a small 'sum of money', more like the £1,000 than the £10,000. Yes, we know that a sugary sweet isn't good for us and may bring health problems in later life, but, just one more dessert now, can it make so much difference? Also, perhaps those of us who are poorer, more financially stressed, are also more hedonistic now. As George Orwell wrote in *The Road to Wigan Pier*, "A millionaire may enjoy breakfasting off orange juice and Ryvita biscuits; an unemployed man doesn't". Foregoing a fatty, salty indulgence meal for a bowl of salad seems to bring a very small potential return on health in return for that missed moment of pleasure.

1.3 Food Hedonism

With food, we, therefore, tend towards short-term hedonism, and once again, it is down to the caveman heritage. We love the deadly trio of salt, fat and sugar. This made perfect sense, biologically, in the days when most of the available food was plant-based. Salt is vital for health, but may be rare in plants. Sugar is a significant short-term energy source, and fat is how our bodies store energy for long-term growth and healing. Meat and fish are excellent sources of all three of these nutrients, but these three become poisons when consumed in excess. As Paracelsus said in the 16th century *"Alle Dinge sind Gift, und nichts ist ohne Gift, allein die Dosis macht dass ein Ding kein Gift ist"*, which translates to, "All things are poison, and nothing is without poison, the dosage alone makes it a poison or not". In other words, a basic principle of toxicology, nothing is poisonous in tiny quantities, and, significantly for food, every nutritional substance is poisonous in excess quantities, even vitamins, water and oxygen.

Our problem with hedonistic taste and healthfulness is that in our modern food environment of abundant salt, fat and sugar, what is tasty for us is frequently inversely related to how healthy it is for us. Chocolate, burgers and crisps sit at one end of this spectrum, but we should be eating broccoli, sprouts and unsalted nuts. Crucially, this health versus hedonistic taste opposition has been partially set up by the food industry itself, as dominated by the supermarkets. We saw earlier why the hedonistic taste but low health end is so appealing, but why is healthy food so unappealing for many? Like the history of supermarket growth, this is a well-researched area; the basic problem is how our food tastes are formed from birth or even before. Humans have a useful biological adaptation; we are genetically endowed with just two fundamental tastes, a linking for sweetness and an aversion to sourness, because nothing sweet in nature is poisonous but bitter things generally are. However, we detect pungent flavour molecules from what our mothers eat, even whilst we are still in the womb, and as babies, we continue to taste such molecules in our mothers' milk (Shaw, 2014: 51). This means we grow up liking whatever our family, tribe or nation generally eat, which is just as well for a growing hungry infant. The problem today is that sugar has become very cheap, for historical and commercial reasons (Shaw, 2014: 18), and today's children are likely to be growing up in a sugar-rich, vegetable-poor food environment, especially if they are from poorer families, partially because sugary, fatty, salty processed foods are so cheap. Cheap sugar has laid the foundation for our obese society, and the supermarkets are enthusiastically building on that foundation.

1.4 The Growing Obesity Epidemic

Obesity has become one of the most significant health concerns of the early 21st century in the developed world and is rising fast in the developing countries too. In fact, the 'thrifty gene' theory of obesity suggests that as cheap, fatty, sugary foods have, over the course of just a few years, become widely available in countries where hunger and under-nutrition were until recently the norm, we may see an extremely rapid rise in obesity amongst the younger populations of these countries. This is because the 'thrifty gene' theory (Shaw, 2014: 31–2) suggests that unborn infants in the womb can detect if the mother is underfed or not, for example, by her low blood sugar, and adjust their metabolisms to cope. These infants grow into people who are very efficient at hoarding whatever calories they consume, which is not a good biological strategy in an obesogenic sugar-rich world. In countries such as Brazil, China, Egypt, India and Mexico, where a cultural appetite for all (food) things 'Western', that is, from the USA, thrives, the emerging supermarket corporations in these developing countries may come to bear a heavy social responsibility for any rising obesity epidemic.

Obesity causes a wide range of diseases, which cascade on from the initial health issue of diabetes. Obesity-generated diabetes starts because the body becomes desensitized to insulin, especially the insulin 'spikes' produced by periodic bingeing on sugar-rich foods. The resultant raised sugar levels in the blood cause inflammation, especially of the smaller capillaries, which then damages the eyes and peripheries of the limbs, which leads on to blindness and amputations. In other medical cascade effects, raised bodyweight produces arthritis and sleep apnoea, which in turn creates daytime fatigue and raises the risk of accidents with vehicles or machinery. Obesity may also predispose people to certain types of cancer. From a societal point of view, the main issue with the diseases mentioned earlier is that they cripple, not kill straightaway; they are chronic conditions that create years of costs, medical and social care, which, again, the developing countries, as they enter the obesity epidemic, are in no position to bear.

The costs of obesity on society that developing nations like China or India may face is predicted by the costs already facing countries such as the UK or USA. In the UK, the cost of obesity to the National Health Service (NHS) alone is estimated at £6.1 billion and expected to rise to £9.7 billion by 2050, even as the NHS faces other cost pressures from an ageing population and more expensive drugs and other treatments (UK Government, 2017). This is just the cost borne by the NHS; there are other costs to society, including private medical treatment, care costs (both formal and informal) and lost productivity. The UK government estimates total obesity costs now as UK£ 27 billion, rising to £49.9 billion by 2050. In the US, the total costs of obesity are estimated at US\$ 150 to 210 billion per year. There is an interesting financial congruence here with the private cost of eating healthily: the so-called health premium. Although with a little ingenuity and some time to spare, it may be possible to eat healthily and cheaply by going to street markets and learning some cooking skills, for many working people, this is not a practical or desirable option. Healthy produce at supermarkets is generally costlier than unhealthy high sugar, fat and salt foods, by as much as 50% over the same number of calories in cheaper foods. In the US, the cost of healthy eating over an unhealthy diet has been estimated at US\$ 1.50 per day per person (Imamura et al, 2015). With a US population of 325 million people, the private cost to consumers of healthy eating equates to US\$ 1.50 × 365 days × 325 million, or US\$ 178 billion. In other words, there is both a financial incentive for the US government to promote healthy eating and a financial need to help many hard-pressed US families to fulfil this objective of eating a better diet. Without some cash transfer, which would ultimately be self-financing, the costs of obesity to the US will grow. The problem is, this is a long-term issue, and governments now do not like to spend on initiatives that will only bear fruit some years or decades down the line.

Regarding future health costs, childhood obesity is a major concern, because obese children are very likely to become obese adults. It is also far more likely for a healthy-weight child to become an obese adult than vice versa; our biologically ingrained calorie-hoarding habits, in a calorie-rich environment, make the trip from normal weight to obesity very much a one-way affair. Tables 1.3 and 1.4 suggest a rising obesity epidemic within the UK that will create large societal costs for decades to come (UK Government, 2017).

Meanwhile, worldwide, there are (2017) 124 million obese children, 7% of them (up from 13 million, less than 1%, in 1975), as the Western diet is copied around the world.

Losing weight is far harder than gaining it, so the focus needs to be on obesity prevention rather than cure. Because obesogenic foods are so attractive (in price as well as taste), we cannot simply aim for a shift in consumption towards fruit and vegetables. Rather, we need to involve multiple agencies from, *inter alia*, education, government, NGOs and the private sector (Parish, 1996: 21–2). We need to tackle the so-called obesogenic environment, a multi-faceted concept that includes neighbourhoods where car use is more attractive than walking, cycling and public transport. Workplaces could encourage exercise, such as substituting stairs for the lift, walking rather than email. Schools could incorporate more home cooking lessons and even food production on site. Although a focus on food consumption alone is not enough to reduce obesity, the supermarkets must bear a significant responsibility for the condition of our waistlines for three reasons: (a) they sell the bulk of the food we buy, (b) they have a societal role that goes far beyond simply selling food and

Table 1.3 Absolute Numbers of Overweight and Obese Children (5- to 19-year-olds) in the UK, 1975 and 2016

	1975	2016
Overweight and obese	2,660,000	4,530,000
Obese	360,000	1,130,000

Table 1.4 Obesity Breakdown, UK Population, Various Ages, 2015

Age group	Normal or underweight	Overweight	Obese
4 and 5 year olds	78%	13%	9%*
10 and 11 year olds	66%	14%	20%*
Adults	37%	36%	27%**

*   Twenty-eight percent of all children aged 2–15 were overweight or obese.
** Twenty-four percent were 'obese' and 3% 'morbidly obese'.

(c) they owe a moral debt to wider society, which has in numerous ways facilitated their growth and success.

1.5 The Multiple Dimensions of Economies of Scale in Supermarkets

Physical size was an early dimension of economies of scale exploited by the supermarkets, as they left their original High Street locales for large sheds on the edge of town. The average size of a food supermarket in the UK rose from 260 metres^2 in 1974 to 700 metres^2 in 1980 and 1,300 metres^2 in 1994 (sales area of shop; importantly, this excludes any storage area behind the shop). Between 1974 and 1983, the average size of a new store being opened rose from 1,100 metres^2 to 1,900 metres^2. Over the same period, the average size of a store being closed, probably because it was too small, rose from 150 metres^2 to 450 metres^2. In other words, the average size of a store being closed in 1980 was larger than the average size of a store operating in 1974 (Shaw, 2003: 35). Meanwhile, the average size of a UK Tesco store grew from 500 metres^2 in 1972 to 2,600 metres^2 in 1992, and the average size of a Tesco under construction in 1992 was 4,000 metres^2 (Wrigley et al, 2002: 77).

From the 1990s, the focus of new store openings in the UK shifted from larger out-of-town stores back to the urban areas, as Tesco and Sainsbury opened their 'Express' and 'Local' shops on High Streets and in suburban locations. At the same time, Aldi and Lidl were also opening small supermarkets in suburban areas. However, size was not the only dimension of economies of scale exploited by the supermarkets; longer opening hours and product diversification have also occurred. The exploitation of these alternative dimensions of scale has been highly dependent on exogenous technologies and/or political developments. For example, the supermarkets have benefitted from legal developments such as the progressive abolition of Resale Price Maintenance (RPM) in the UK, starting from 16 June 1964, as lobbied for by Tesco. RPM was originally a measure originally intended to protect smaller retailers from 'unfair' price undercutting.

The supermarkets have extended their opening hours later into the evening and into Sundays, eroding a key competitive advantage of small independent 'open all hours' shops. Sunday opening was largely outlawed in the UK by the 1950 Shops Act, a measure designed to protect the welfare (leisure time) of shop workers. Only shops selling 'perishable goods', a class which included fresh produce and periodical journals, could open on a Sunday, along with pharmacies. However, this led to legal absurdities, such as pornography magazines (periodicals), being available for sale on a Sunday, whereas Bibles (books) were not. The UK has become a markedly less Christian country since 1950, and Sunday openings by the large food retailers began just before Christmas 1991 in the UK, in defiance of the law but with the tacit support of a large section of British consumers. The UK Home Office sought guidance from the attorney general, Sir Patrick Mayhew, who advised against prosecution. Instead, the Conservative Government of John Major enacted the 1994 Sunday Trading Act, after pressure from the Sainsbury supermarket, allowing openings by the major chains for up to six hours on a Sunday. Sunday supermarket trading has been now legalized in countries once staunchly opposed to any violation of the Christian 'day of rest', including Catholic Italy in its tourist areas.

Meanwhile, the major supermarkets have greatly diversified their product range out of their original purely food offerings. Tesco, started selling petrol in 1974, as more car-borne customers started arriving at their new out-of-town sites. A large Tesco Extra store will now stock electrical goods, beauty products, entertainment goods, cookware, clothes, pharmaceuticals, white goods and financial products. This has greatly widened the range of High Street shops that are vulnerable to supermarket competition and has left some former core retail areas as 'zombie centres', hosting only the fringe retailing that Tesco didn't want to get into, as these lines offer scant economies of scale. This has turned former thriving retail streets into twilight retail zones, where no everyday items such as meat, vegetables, medicines, bread or household goods can be found; instead, there is a parade of sandwich bars, betting shops, charity shops, hairdressers, coffee bars, takeaways and vape lounges. Interspersed with these may be the 'shadow' supermarkets for those too poor to buy a full value household item, such as Bright House, also smaller white goods and electronics retailers like Euronics. But all those with cars have driven out to their nearest large retail park where the supermarkets are sited. Economic factors hastening this trend include the problems of car congestion and parking, and the squeeze on local council finances as globalization has eroded the high-earning tax base of central government, leading local administrations to restrict and charge more for High Street parking, whilst out-of-town retail centres offer free parking. The retail abandonment of the High Street is typified by the US city of Atlanta, Georgia, where city centre retail sales as percentage of total city sales fell from 39.1% in 1954 to 15.1% in 1977; as a percentage of total metropolitan area sales, city centre sales fell from 28.9% to just 4.0% over this period; the decline being down to the growth of out-of-town retail areas dominated by large-box retailers (Davies, 2004: 90).

From a CSR perspective, this product diversification has taken the supermarkets into whole new areas of upstream supply chain ethics, such as the employment conditions of clothing factories in south Asia; this is discussed further in Chapter 5. The supermarkets have also diversified into new international markets. China and India have been targeted by all the major supermarket corporations because they comprise a large market with a growing middle class with surplus income to spend, and both countries have been liberalizing their economies, opening up to foreign investment. Eastern Europe post-1990 and South America have also been targeted by the major supermarket chains, with the big retailers doing best in regions not too culturally dissimilar from their home territory. Hence Walmart from the USA has expanded heavily into South America, but done less well in Europe, with the exception, of course, of Anglophone Britain, where it took over Asda.[1] Meanwhile, the UK's Tesco has focussed more on Ireland and Eastern Europe, and France's Carrefour has entered large swathes of Europe, North Africa, the Middle East and South America.

Again, there are several CSR angles to be considered here, from respect for non-Western cultural norms and values to the obesity issue mentioned earlier, to the ethics of selling obesogenic foods to large populations both culturally and biologically unprepared for these. Access by the supermarkets to countries such as China, India and Thailand has been facilitated by a global liberal free trade ethos promoted heavily by the US since 1980, with entry into Eastern Europe largely due to the continued economic and political integration of the EU. Meanwhile, infrastructure developments from the big container ports of Felixstowe to key international links, such as the Channel Tunnel, have facilitated the globalization of the food trade, which has brought about considerable environmental implications for the supermarket food trade. Supermarket CSR must now consider issues as diverse as carbon emissions from shipping, damage to the rainforest, agricultural worker wages and conditions across the world, as well as accurate consumer information as to the origins of food.

Supermarkets may argue that they simply 'sell what people want', but their size and market dominance makes them more akin to gatekeepers, even dictators, of what people 'want'. The concentration of market share amongst a near oligopoly (for the consumer) or effective oligopsony (for the farmer) of supermarkets has been noted earlier. The power of the UK supermarkets is illustrated by Nicholson and Young (2012: 5), whose report illustrates the 'hourglass' structure of the UK food chain. Here, 7,000 suppliers must funnel their produce through just four supermarket chains that in 2012 controlled 76% of the UK grocery retail market of 25 million households. A more detailed breakdown, for an earlier year, stated that the UK's food chain consisted of 3,827 fishing-related enterprises (11,000 jobs; 2.87 per enterprise) and 311,000 farm holdings (541,000 jobs; 1.74 per holding), with the farms being supplied by 1,646 agricultural suppliers (26,000 jobs; 15.80 per supplier). Agricultural wholesalers accounted for further 3,136 enterprises (22,000 jobs; 7.02 per enterprise) and food and drink manufacturing and processing comprised almost 17,700 enterprises (429,000 jobs; 24.24 per enterprise). All this output reached the final consumers, people, though a catering sector of 111,620 enterprises (1,394,000 jobs; 12.49 jobs per enterprise) and a retail sector of 61,100 enterprises, or 102,000 stores (1,184,000 jobs; 19.38 jobs per enterprise). Catering accounted for consumer expenditure of £71 billion and retailing £77 billion. Note the very small mean size of these enterprises, with average employees in the low double figures or even single figures (Defra, 2006: 10). Yet in 2004, the Big Four UK supermarkets (Asda with 165,000 employees, Morrison with 132,000 employees, Sainsbury's with 182,000 employees and Tesco with 476,000 employees) between them controlled some 74% of the retail groceries market. At the loosest interpretation of the Department for Environment, Food and Rural Affairs (Defra) figures (ignoring any sales in catering of the Big Four supermarkets), just four giant retail corporations sold almost 40% of the output of over half a million enterprises employing over 3.5 million people.

The same supermarket nexus exists in all developed countries; in the US, Walmart had 61,000 suppliers in 2010 and served about one-sixth of US households; large consumer goods manufacturers and processors like Dial, Del Monte, Clorox and Revlon sell 25% to 30% of their goods through Walmart (Chandler & Werther, 2014: 56). In all these countries, thousands of suppliers must reach millions of customers through a few supermarket giants whose numbers can be counted on the fingers of one hand. At the global level, a 'typical supply chain' is given by Macfadyen et al (2015) as comprising, in downstream order, "13,000 farmers, 1,300 processors, 300 distributors, 5 supermarket chains, 880 retail outlets, and 3.3.million consumers". Worldwide, there are an estimated 570 million farms, of which 4% are in high-income countries and 47% are in upper-middle-income countries. The 'upper-middle' countries include states such as Argentina, Brazil, South Africa, Romania, Russia and Turkey; all these are developing or already have a largely supermarketized food retail economy. Naturally, almost all the high-income countries are supermarketized, excepting some of the smaller island states where local retailers may survive, protected by monopolies of distance. Therefore, one can conservatively estimate that some 200 million farms worldwide depend largely on the supermarkets for access to the consumer (Lowder et al, 2014).

Therefore, supermarkets owe a significant debt to wider society for their success, which has seen companies such as Tesco and Carrefour regularly featured in the list of the world's largest companies. Table 1.5 briefly summarizes the various dimensions of supermarket growth and the wider societal factors which have enabled this expansion. Supermarkets, therefore, also owe a duty, as 'gatekeepers' not just of consumer demand but also of socio-economic conditions, from animal welfare and the environment to farm labourer wages and consumer health, to act responsibly to repay the benefits they have reaped from societal development and change. The fact that supermarket corporations both depend on such a wide range of societal technology and infrastructure, and have

Table 1.5 Supermarket Growth and Enabling Factors

Dimension of scale of Supermarket operations	Supermarket dependence on technology	Socio-political changes (enabling factors)
Increasing physical size (and migration from High Street to out of town)	Lorries, container ships	Creation of enterprise zones (leading to large out-of-town retail parks). Increasing popularity of car ownership. Congestion, parking charges, cash-poor councils
Product diversification (including financial services)	Motor car, shipping	New roads, financial deregulation
Longer opening hours	Motor car (mobile customers, e.g. late evening)	Sunday trading legalized (e.g. UK, Italy)
International expansion	ICT	Globalization, lower trade barriers
Format diversification, local stores, online sales	ICT, refrigerated delivery vans	Decline in pubs, etc., making local premises available

the capability to greatly and adversely affect our health and our environment through the products they sell, means they must bear some CSR towards the society they operate in.

The oligopsonic supermarket supply chain nexus can magnify and propagate food scandals, such as contamination issues, in a way never possible in the 1950s era of small retailers sourcing locally and selling in very limited geographical areas. A good example of this amplification is the 2010 dioxin scandal. This scandal originated with Ukrainian dioxin-tainted maize finding its way into organic chicken feed from the Netherlands, which was fed to hens in Germany, contaminating organic eggs there and resulting in a significant decline in organic egg sales in Germany ((Hall, 2016: 143). In Germany, Aldi, Rewe and Lidl were forced to throw away millions of eggs, as dioxin fears reached as far as Belgium and the UK, where contamination of cakes was feared. Then in 2017, history repeated itself when eggs from Dutch farms were feared to be contaminated with the insecticide Fipronil, which is banned from being administered to animals destined for human consumption (Boffey, 2017). Again, affecting predominantly the major chains Aldi, Rewe and Lidl, this incident ultimately spread to Belgium, France, Germany, the Netherlands, Sweden, Switzerland and the UK—seven countries with a combined population exceeding 260 million people. Ultimately, the systemic cause of these scandals was the relentless supermarket quest for cheap food, resulting in unreliable feed suppliers cutting corners and inadequate resources being given to monitoring the integrity of the food supply chain. In Britain, there was the 2013 horsemeat scandal, when Aldi, Asda, the Co-op, Iceland, Lidl, Sainsbury and Tesco all had to discard tonnes of meat because horsemeat of unknown origin had entered the food chain. Only the UK's upmarket chains Waitrose and Marks and Spencer (M&S) were untouched by the affair.

We often forget that the till price is not the only cost we pay for our food. When buying cheap meat, for example, we 'pay' five times, once at the till and then through tax in the form of subsidies to farming operations. Thirdly, our taxes also go to maintain the infrastructures heavily used by the food chain, such as the shipping, airlines, ports and main roads their delivery systems depend upon; vehicle owners pay road tax, but this does not cover all the damage transport does—for example, noise and pollution from road, air and sea transport. Major transport hubs such as Heathrow or Felixstowe may charge for their use but these facilities also impose major environmental costs such as erosion, pollution and congestion. Fourthly, there is an environmental cost, and fifthly, we pay through deteriorating health for cheap unhealthy food. One quantified estimate of these extra four costs, amounting to the same again as the till price for food, is provided by the Sustainable Food Trust (Fitzpatrick & Young, 2017: 4). They estimate (tax-funded) farm support costs as 2.5p per £1 food till price, regulation and research costs (also taxpayer funded) as 2.7p, and the costs of imported food on society as 7.8p. Additionally, there are environmental costs of 'natural capital degradation' at 25.7p, and biodiversity loss at 10.6p, per £1 till price. Diet-related ill health is costed at 37.3p per £1 the consumer spends on food. There is no costing for infrastructure use such as road usage or Internet bandwidth taken. Some of these costs are borne by society as a whole or by the taxpayer, such as NHS care for obesity-related illnesses; some are borne by the consumer themselves, such as the taxes they pay or in private health costs.

1.6 What Is CSR?

A general principle that wealth accumulated by corporations should be utilized for the benefit of society was expressed by the 19th century steel baron and philanthropist, Andrew Carnegie, who said, "He who dies rich dies thus disgraced". The duties of companies towards a wider set of stakeholders were further developed in 1953 with the publication of Bowen's '*Social Responsibility of Businessmen*', recognizing that corporations have duties beyond simply making profits for their shareholders. In 1991, B. Carroll proposed a Maslow-style pyramid of CSR, with the base as 'economic responsibilities' and higher layers successively as 'legal responsibilities', 'ethical responsibilities' and at the top 'philanthropic responsibilities' (Carroll, 1991). In 1954, Maslow developed a hierarchy of human needs, with physiological needs (food, water, covering) at the bottom, then security (shelter, property), then companionship (friends, family, partner), then esteem (confidence, achievement, respect) and, finally, at the apex, self-actualization. Here Maslow puts morality, creativity, problem-solving and 'reaching one's full potential'.

As with Maslow, viable corporations must first fulfil the lower layers, but then aim for compliance with the higher levels too. The apex level of Maslow is not dissimilar to the qualities a fully socially responsible corporation should display, solving the problems its activities create in the external environment and society, and reaching its full potential as, not just a profit-making machine for the shareholders, but as making a full contribution to the welfare of the communities in which it operates and upon whose existence it depends for survival. However, as regards the 'duties' of which Bowen wrote in 1953, the key questions of, firstly, 'duty to whom?' and secondly 'what duties, what is a duty?', still remain open to debate. Legislation on product safety, for example, varies across national jurisdictions, yet people everywhere have the same biology, so how far should a company go in warning customers of low-level, but individually catastrophic, health risks, such as a product that may cause cancer in one in a million users, in countries where such warnings are not legally required? What if a product may, in the opinion of some but not all scientists, cause harm to the environment not now but in a century's time? What if, like the supermarkets, some of the products you are selling may cause an obesity crisis in 10, 20, 30 years' time, but you are by no means the only possible contributor to that impending but distant crisis, and in any case, you didn't make these products, you just sell them? And the public really want them?

In 2010, the International Organization for Standardisation (ISO) published the ISO 26000 guidelines on CSR, stating that CSR is the responsibility of an organization for the impact of its decisions and activities on society and the environment, through transparent and ethical behaviour that (1) contributes to sustainable development including the health and welfare of society, (2) is in compliance with applicable law and consistent with international norms of behaviour and (3) is integrated throughout the organization and practised in all its relationships. This definition, however, seems to reward corporations just for 'complying with the law'; in contrast, we seldom reward private citizens for such compliance, rather we punish them if they do not comply. However, one should distinguish between hard law and soft law, both in the case of individuals and corporations. Hard law is what one can get penalized by the judicial system for contravening, for walking out of a shop without paying for the goods in one's bag, maybe just because you don't like the demeanour of the staff. However, soft law is more like the social mores of society; there is no legal penalty for contravention, although social ostracism may result for non-compliers, perhaps a custom to be nice-mannered to the shop staff even if you dislike something about the shop itself. Individuals of working age also are generally expected to try and support themselves whenever possible, rather than relying on hand-outs and charity—a 'commercial duty' to create wealth for society rather than simply consuming it.

One possible classification of the obligations of corporations might be, similarly, commercial obligations, hard law and soft law. Commercially, companies must make a return for their investors. They also have an obligation to obey the laws of the jurisdiction in which they operate; this 'hard law' is obligatory and non-negotiable (although supermarkets can lobby hard to change this law, as in the case of legalization of Sunday trading for example). Then there is 'soft law'—a moral obligation to act conscionably, for example, to respect neighbours' environment in terms of noise and visual impact, or not push unhealthy foods towards minors, or to minimize the use of materials that harm the environment. The obligations of hard and soft law, and commercialism, often blur together. For example, it is illegal (hard law) to discriminate against staff or job applicants on religious grounds, but making job adjustments so that Jews can fast on Yom Kippur, or to enable Muslims to fast for the month of Ramadan, is more of a soft law moral issue. However, in areas with a significant Jewish or Muslim population, it makes commercial sense, both from a recruitment and sales viewpoint, to make such allowances in the company work schedule. Equally, reducing carbon emissions by, for example, more efficient heating or vehicle use fulfils a soft law commitment to combat global warming; it also makes commercial sense to economize on fuel consumption. Then one might ask, as with rewarding a company for obeying the (hard) law, should a company get CSR credit for doing something that it would want to do commercially, reducing its energy costs, albeit helping to preserve the environment at the same time?

Unlike an individual who breaks hard law and can be imprisoned for serious breaches, and made to perform community service for minor infringements, the sanctions that a company can face for breaking hard and soft law are not dissimilar to those for breaking commercial imperatives. Short of criminal action against the directors, the main legal penalty a company can face is a fine, or restriction of trading; in other words, financial curbs on its profits. Similarly, a company that fails to protect the environment may face a customer boycott, a financial penalty again. Companies are seldom ordered to close down for even serious legal infractions, the equivalent perhaps to the death penalty, because that would harm the employees now made redundant. This lack of a range of more serious sanctions on corporately irresponsible companies can be a problem for those who would like to see companies be more accountable to wider society; as we shall see later, perhaps the best target to aim at in order to achieve better CSR is not the company, but rather government, NGOs and the consuming public.

1.7 'Provisions' as a Fourth Bottom Line: Why We Need Enhanced Supermarket CSR?

The obligation of companies, to society and the environment as well as to shareholders, has been described by Elkington as the triple bottom line; the 'three P's' of People, Planet and Profit (Elkington, 1997). Elkington's 'People' covers the fair and just treatment of all persons affected by the operations of a corporation. Not just Christians but companies too need to obey Jesus's command to "treat people as you would want to be treated". Meanwhile, 'Planet' covers any corporate activities that degrade, diminish pollute or reduce the carrying capacity of any part of the Earth's environment for its inhabitants (human and non-human), either now or in the future. As regards corporations in the food business, however, we may need a Fourth Bottom Line, 'Provisions'. Food, as noted earlier, is a peculiar good in that people may desire unhealthy food even though over the long run it is bad for them, and the provision of adequate food for all, whilst a vital and laudable aim, may also be damaging to the environment if achieved in the wrong way. Enhancing food supply now without regard to the future environment is a trap many earlier civilizations have fallen into and perished in war and famine as a result, as far back as the ancient Mesopotamians of 6,000 years ago (Seymour & Girardet, 1986: 26–7). In the scientific 21st century today, we should be able to manage things better. In the food supply chain, often what seems good and vital, even in the short run, may be disastrous in the long-term.

The concept of a Fourth Bottom Line has been proposed by Cambridge Leadership Development as well as by the New Zealand government (Cambridge Leadership Development, 2013). This fourth line as currently conceived generally has a non-financial human element, such as spirituality, happiness, ethics or human fulfilment or purpose. 'Why are we doing this'. It attempts to capture the element of well-being or cultural integrity that can be eroded by inappropriate or intrusive development, such as an oil pipeline through indigenous lands, or the touristification of Uluru (Ayers Rock) Australia, or Venice, even though that development may bring jobs and money. The Wellington government has defined the Fourth Bottom Line as 'culture', to ensure the inclusion of Maori culture in the people-, profit-, planet-oriented development of New Zealand. Alternatively, the concept has been utilized to differentiate between private and public returns, as in the case of an airport development that benefits airline companies but may also bring economic returns to the local community, but also disbenefits in terms of noise, congestion and detriment to the environment. The Fourth P has also been defined as 'perspective' (Kenney, 2009), introducing a time element to the concept of sustainable development.

Food is an intensely cultural good; food is 'noisy' (Smith & Jehlicka, 2007: 397) in that it speaks about the 'socio-natural relations of production', the cultures of consumption and social relationships under which it was consumed. Food is us, "you are what you eat"; as we have seen earlier; therefore, food carries significant long-term implications for our health and well-being, as well as costs for society. Therefore, it is suggested that in the case of supermarket CSR, the Fourth P to go alongside People Planet and Profit should be Provisions. In fact, the general goal of a healthy, sustainable, inclusive and accessible diet for all is somewhat absent from much supermarket CSR, despite all the colourful superficial 'noise' found on their websites about the environment, health and exercise, community and much else. Many supermarket CSR websites appear to comprise much 'sound and fury' but relatively little hard content. The following section of this chapter now critically analyses existing supermarket CSR publicity to see whether it is really 'fit for purpose' or is more of a publicity exercise, written for the benefit of its authors and owners rather for than general society.

1.8 Is Anything Wrong With Supermarket Corporate Social Responsibility?

Social concerns about corporate activities have by no means stayed constant over time. In the early 19th century, a British MP was concerned about the fragmentation of the countryside due to the proliferation of canals (Sutcliffe, 1816) and a few decades on many landowners protested about the smoke, noise and visual intrusion of the new steam engines, railways and viaducts crossing hitherto unspoilt valleys. Nowadays the canals, the steam railways and Victorian construction feats such as the Ribblehead Viaduct are loved and preserved as nostalgic remnants of a bygone age of elegance and engineering, a place tourists flock to see. Whether the 20th-century equivalents, the Westway or Spaghetti Junction motorway flyovers, across which many people's food has travelled a few days before they bought it ever achieve such valued heritage status is yet to be seen. Like the Ribblehead Viaduct, they do at least possess graceful curves. However, CSR concerns do not always take 200 years to change. In the 1980s, as the migration of supermarkets to out-of-town greenfield sites next to the new ring road was in full swing, the Campaign to Protect Rural England (CPRE) was concerned about the loss of green space. The 1980s huge sheds have not been demolished and indeed have, as the CPRE and others feared, promoted further residential and commercial development to the point that many of the open ring roads that attracted the supermarkets, with their promise of easy access for deliveries and shoppers, are now becoming congested again. Yet now we accept such sheds as part of the urban periphery landscape; we also love the lower prices and choice they offer, although the advent of the Internet since 2000 as a commercial channel is now taking business from these sheds just as they took business from the old High Street shops.

Supermarkets have moved on, and as noted earlier, the emphasis from the 1990s shifted to local branches of the main chains. In 2002, Tesco bought the T&S Stores chain, which owned the One Stop and the Day and Nite chains. Subsequently, Tesco converted many of the One Stop fascia stores to its Tesco Express fascia. In 2004, several such stores in Hampshire, a generally affluent rural county of southern England, were so converted (Wrigley, 2007). From the point of view of the rural communities these shops served, in locations such as Four Marks, New Alresford and Whitchurch, the Tesco makeover greatly improved the offering of fresh produce and many local households took advantage of this by reducing the number of trips they made to more distant larger supermarkets in urban centres like Winchester and Basingstoke. Local people also perceived some deleterious aspects of the new store regime, principally an increase in large lorry deliveries (in rural lanes, where, for example, a church suffered obstructions to funeral traffic), also the threatened loss of some cherished architectural features of the old shops, such as an old 'Hovis' sign, and, finally, the loss of the old Post Office, which One Stop had hosted. Tesco wanted to maximize the retail return on its shop space; however, many local people were of pensionable age and unfamiliar with the Internet as a means of accessing government services.

The problems with Tesco's larger lorries, and the threatened Hovis sign over the Tesco Express in Whitchurch, Hampshire, are illustrated in Figure 1.1.

Figure 1.1 Tesco Lorry in Whitchurch Hampshire, 2005

The three CSR issues here were resolved in different ways. The Post Office was retained by Tesco and is still (2018) recorded as existing there, although a similarly converted One Stop store in Alresford Hampshire did see the Post Office move to another store (which subsequently closed and the settlement was without this facility, until the Co-op supermarket offered it a home). The lorry issue has not gone away, and Google Street View pictures of the site in 2009 show an identically parked Tesco lorry. However, we have perhaps become inured to such congestion problems as the general volume of traffic has grown. The Hovis sign was retained and is present on Google Street View 2009 and 2011 shots—but has vanished in the 2016 view. Over the decade since 2005 the population of Whitchurch will have changed considerably and the awareness of this locally historic sign will have faded. Likewise, the Post Office has lost much of its significance with the rise of email and online government sites, in a generation more accustomed to online services, computers and the Internet. This small case study illustrates that as society changes we perhaps come to accept the once unacceptable, like ubiquitous CCTV, Trump as US president and stringently enforced parking charges, what was once objected to become a part of the fabric of everyday life. Perhaps ominously for those who would keep a watchful eye on the less-corporately responsible activities of supermarkets, this suggests that an organization only has to persist with some policy long enough and it becomes normalized; the fight against it becomes too onerous; the fighters fade away. If large companies are to be made truly accountable for any harmful actions against society of the environment, we may need an alternative watchdog, perhaps government or NGOs, operating through sustained media campaigns to keep public awareness alive.

CSR publicity is a relatively new feature of corporate activities, with the number of companies across the globe publishing CSR reports up from virtually none in 1992 to 267 in 1996 and to 2,235 in 2006. (Jones et al, 2007). In 2010, some 4,000 companies across the world disclosed information on their environmental, social and governance performance, and this rate of increase did not slow in response to the global financial crisis that began in 2007, the so-called Credit Crunch (Mullerat, 2013: 17–18). Although these numbers document a significant increase, it has to be kept in mind that reporting companies still constitute only a small share of global business, with its roughly 82,000 multinational enterprises and over 23 million SMEs.

By 2016, it had become virtually obligatory for even small and medium-sized enterprises to have a CSR element in their web page. However, the voluntary and unregulated nature of these pages means there is very little consistency or pattern to them, Lidl's CSR page contains barely 500 words (Lidl, 2017), by contrast, Tesco's online CSR publicity runs to many hundreds of linked web pages. Such large CSR offerings contain a huge range of initiatives, proffered in many different media forms, including texts, videos, PowerPoint slides, photographs, personal statements, press releases, graphics, music, audio commentaries, statistics and external links—in fact, just about every form of communication technically possible on a computer with screen and sound. A kaleidoscopic mix of every colourful image and sound and words imaginable, and like a kaleidoscope the mix changes every year. Local community initiatives start up and after a year or so are supplanted by something else. A national crisis, poverty, drought, famine, hits the headlines and some supermarket will start a programme to alleviate the suffering, until another national catastrophe supersedes. Even environmental issues change over the years, with the issue of plastic pollution having suddenly shot up the agenda since the TV programme *Blue Planet II* highlighted the damage being done to marine organisms across the globe in 2017.

However, like a kaleidoscope, the ever-changing patterns all start to look the same after a while. Behind all the variety the big UK supermarkets CSR reports are all rather similar in content, covering what Khan and Kakabadse (2014) call "eight oligopolistic common themes"—namely,

1. Recycling, waste reduction and energy efficiency
2. Transportation
3. Regeneration
4. Supply chain improvements
5. Packaging and labelling
6. Animal/nutritional welfare
7. Charitable donations or schemes
8. Marine/water footprint (which would now include, since 2017, the impact of plastic on marine life)

CSR reports all use very similar metalanguage, with striking colourful images and videos, with soundtrack and commentary, frequently championing certain very specific causes—for example, palm oil or Fairtrade bananas. The viewer may get so immersed in the sound and visuals that they forget the specificity of these causes and that many other related issues are not being publicized. For example, there are many endangered species of animal and plant, not only the photogenic Indonesian primates whose habitat is at risk from palm oil plantations. Equally, the range of Fairtrade products, although broadening from the original tea, coffee and bananas into fruit, vegetables, wine and some other foodstuffs, is still absent from the majority of lines sold in large supermarkets. CSR is frequently presented as target driven, with targets either set by the government or the corporation itself (the latter, somehow, always met). It might be preferable to have general principles, linked to wider socio-environmental issues, such as overall global de/re-forestation, the problems with this, maybe some climate change figures, some overall data on tress cover and the contribution made by the company, but this seldom materializes on the website. CSR is also often inward looking, using language such as, "Our business, our customers, enhance our operations, manage our risk, impact of legislation on our business" (Khan & Kakabadse, ibid). Perhaps we need less, but better—better co-ordinated CSR, more long-term programmes, more monitoring and dissemination of results, more engagement with stakeholders outside the supermarket corporations, both forward looking (what do they want in the future) and backwards looking (what did they think to what was done), backed up by consistently presented data.

As we saw earlier, CSR activities tend to be short term, and companies tend not to align their efforts with what other companies, still less their direct competitors, are doing. The most they do is compare efforts to the extent that they can say "we are better than them in this (specific, limited, but gaudily presented) aspect of CSR" In fact, CSR can be simply greenwashing, promoting a planet or society-friendly image in one area whilst continuing with damaging activities across the main part of the business. CSR messages are often rather simplistic, such as "we plant X trees for everyone used in/for every number of kilometres we drive our vehicles". To properly evaluate this sort of claim, we need to know, *inter alia*, what sort of trees (conifer monocultures or broadleaf deciduous?) or what land is being taken (was it smallholder farmland, with rich species and crop diversity?). There are seldom any maps to indicate where those trees are being planted; are jobs being destroyed as areas become woodland as opposed to small-scale croplands, what happens to those trees (industrial forestry, tourism, wildlife sanctuary, private forests for some oligarch?) and what associated infrastructure goes with all those new trees (logging roads, tourism burden, industrial sawmills, docks)? Instead, the CSR message frequently includes older people walking by massive ancient oaks, with butterflies and beetles, and idyllic forest mountain scenery. Of course, such scenery cannot be created by man or nature in less than centuries, far longer than any supermarket has been in existence, let alone issuing CSR reports, and within a year or so, a different product will be on the market, a different CSR initiative, a different corporate website will be uploaded, a different idyllic couple or group of skipping children or contented wildlife/happy farm animal. Continuity and specific accountability are notably absent, or if present at all, drowned out by colourful eye-catching statistics and images.

1.9 The Need for More Accountable, Comparable and Long-Term CSR

Supermarket CSR publicity often presents an eclectic mix of general promises, such as "unsold food in our stores that is still safe to eat can now be donated to local community organizations *where possible*" (italics added), along with the opposite, very specific, numerical statistics that are so precise and narrow that they begin to lose context with the wider picture, such as "single carrier bag usage is down by 80%" (both quotes, Morrisons, 2018). Frequently used slogans such as '100% British' do not tell us how this was verified, whether it means reared in the UK or just imported for final processing, or even if this the most environmentally sustainable means of production. From a global social welfare perspective, it might be better to give employment to farm workers in Africa rather than use British labour. From a (British) national productivity perspective, robots might be best, and from a rural economic viewpoint, British workers would be used to maintain the rural economy and services. These subtler comparisons are seldom made on CSR pages. The time element is also missing from many CSR pages, with little comparison with what was attempted last year or before and how much of this was actually achieved. The 'units' in which CSR contributions are given may also be vague, for example, "last year we donated a million meals to XYZ charity". At three meals a day, we may eat 1,100 meals a year, so does a 'million meals' equate to feeding 900 destitute people for a year? Or to providing one hot meal a day for 2,800 people? Or to alleviating 'holiday hunger', when poor pupils do not receive free school lunches in school holidays, maybe 120 days a year, to 8,000 deprived pupils? These are all very different social initiatives and outcomes. Where a time element does appear, it may be devoid of context or verifiability, such as, "We don't just buy from the farmers we work with; we work with them to improve their business and ours. To do this more effectively, we established an expert-led programme in 2009" (Morrisons, 2018). What experts, working for whom, achieving what? Meanwhile, Waitrose's CSR report (Waitrose, 2018a) contained the following section of exciting prose:

> Looking beyond compliance, and focussing on our key supply chains, both divisions have made significant progress in the key programmes they have established to address the most salient risks. . . . Working with the Wilberforce Institute, completed risk assessments on 13 sites in the UK, Spain and Italy growing mushrooms, leeks, cabbages, salad crops, tree fruit and tomatoes. Working with suppliers to drive improvements and share best practice across the supply base. Developed new strategy for the Waitrose Foundation to align it with the business's sourcing, ethical and technical priorities, address salient human rights risks, and expand to more sourcing countries by 2020. Extensive stakeholder consultation over 2016/17 and attained Management Board sign-off.

Few people will get very far with checking that, let alone evaluating and comparing with other supermarkets and with what really needs to be done, however praiseworthy, sincere and effective the Waitrose/John

Lewis Group is with combatting modern slavery in its mushroom and leek supply chains.

The website Business Respect did praise a ten-point CSR programme by Tesco, saying, "Tesco's ten point plan, typically, are (sic) focused on real substance and have targets attached to them". The ten points are as follows:

1. Halve energy use by 2010,
2. Double customer recycling by 2008,
3. Ensure all carrier bags are degradable by 2006 and carrier bag use cut by 25% over the next two years,
4. Introduce nutritional labelling on all 7,000 Tesco own brand products by 2007,
5. Launch a healthy eating and nutritional education programme for families in deprived areas,
6. Get 2 million people running, cycling or walking in events in the run-up to the 2012 Olympics,
7. Reduce the frequency and noise of deliveries to Express stores,
8. Increase local community consultation before building new superstores,
9. Help small suppliers by holding open days across the UK,
10. Improve local sourcing by introducing regional counters into stores and improve labelling to highlight local produce. (Business Respect, 2006).

Some of these are indeed specific targets and checkable too, such as 1— but did anyone go back later and check? Even if they did, few enterprises are the same 'business' as they were even 12 months ago. Supermarkets open new premises, close old ones, with different levels of energy efficiency (e.g. insulation), change suppliers, alter food chains and routes travelled, so any change up or down in energy use is hard to compare, like with like, with an earlier point in time.

Aims 2 and 6 are less checkable, as they involve knowing how private consumers behave, and 6 is by no means as precise as it appears—run how often, how far, and how long is this routine kept up for?

Aim 7 is vague. What noise levels? And like much CSR would financially benefit the company (fewer larger lorries, less drivers.

Aim 8 carries no commitment. Will the community's wishes be acted upon once 'consulted'? Even Aim 10 is unquantified. What is 'local'? Twenty miles, 50 miles, same country, within Europe? 'Local' may vary according to the venue the produce is sold at; for an inner city market, the radius of production would need to be wider than for a rural market town, and for a coastal city, one should increase the radius by 42% over an inland venue. Unfortunately, much CSR material is presented in this rather vague manner, leaving actual verifiable quantifiable action to help the planet or people somewhat thin on the ground.

Leach (2016), in the Gather report, highlights a major flaw in the collective CSR outputs of the UK's supermarkets: "There is a need to have a stronger and more coherent story at the heart of each report to successfully link the report together". The Gather report highlights the over-long nature of some CSR statements, and the fact that at heart many CSR initiatives link back to the financial viability of the business. There is an underlying emphasis on maintaining supply chains so customer sales can be kept up, or on reducing energy use, so the fuel or electricity bill can be minimized. There is also a lack of any internationally accepted common standard of CSR, which allows every company to publicize what it chooses, what gives it the most green credit and, in all the profuse detail given by the larger corporations, any omissions will be hard to spot. There is a general business adage, "What gets measured, gets managed"; we need an equivalent, a measurable CSR standard akin to GAAP (Generally Accepted Accounting Principles) for social responsibility statements. A Generally Accepted Responsible Social Principles code, or GARSP code, might contain at least minimum standards on emissions per value of corporate sales, or percentage of materials consumed that originate from sustainable sources, or proportion of suppliers whose employment conditions meet International Labour Organization (ILO) standards. Then we could benchmark companies as to how far they exceed, or fail to meet, these basic global standards. This could be one way to avoid our age of globalized capitalism being the last 'GARSP' for the environment, perhaps.

The EU, one of the largest economic and political blocs in the world with a population of over 500 million (third behind China and India) and a gross domestic product of 17 trillion US dollars (second, very close behind the USA), and "the first continent that became a convert to the CSR movement" (Mullerat, 2013: 5), is becoming the regulatory capital of the world. Bradford (2012: 1) describes

> the unprecedented and deeply underestimated global power that the European Union is exercising through its legal institutions and standards, and how it successfully exports that influence to the rest of the world. Without the need to use international institutions or seek other nations' cooperation, the EU has a strong and growing ability to promulgate regulations that become entrenched in the legal frameworks of developed and developing markets alike, leading to a notable "Europeanization" of many important aspects of global commerce.

Even large US companies such as Microsoft, Google and Facebook set their ethical standards by EU regulations (ibid: 3). This is a global version of the California Effect versus the Delaware Effect. Although US companies have a fiscal incentive to locate in Delaware because that state offers the lowest tax requirements, incentivizing cheapness and a race to the bottom, the counteracting California Effect persuades US companies to raise their ethical standards to those demanded by California, because California is a large wealthy state that business wish to have a presence in its domestic market, a 'race to the top' (ibid: 5). In terms of economic equity, this could be undesirable, with poorer regions of the world ending up with the polluting, worker-exploiting, corporate operations that are out of sight of the consumer, whilst the wealthier regions get the cleanest most environmentally friendly corporate activities and the most desirable workplaces. It then becomes the role of activists and other NGOs to draw the wealthy consumers' attention to these poorest regions so standards can be raised there too.

Instituting a major supra-national bloc, such as the EU as global CSR regulator would have several major benefits. Firstly, attempts to develop a higher shared common standard of CSR may be undermined by the refusal of one market player to participate. This then leads to other players opting out, as they perceive the first non-participator to be gaining a financial advantage. As discussed later in this book, there are two opposite effects here. In a very price-competitive market like supermarket food, where market share and economies of scale are of paramount importance and any financial failing is swiftly punished by the shares market, no retail chain wants to voluntarily put itself at a disadvantage (Fox & Vorley, 2004). On the other hand, if the CSR initiative is valued by consumers, the first mover to adopt this policy can gain good publicity (and hopefully gain customers as well) and force its competitors to adopt the same social values. This has happened in the UK with the store chain Iceland and its corporate policies on sustainable palm oil, for example. If a supra-national authority were to encourage the simultaneous adoption of CSR policies by all market players at once, this gaming would come to an end.

Secondly, a common 'GARSP' standard would reduce consumer confusion as to who is the greenest. The UK chain Iceland has pioneered social responsibility policies on palm oil and plastic waste, but is ranked by *The Good Shopping Guide* in the lowest tier of a threefold 'traffic light' ethical classification (Good Shopping Guide, 2018). Thirdly, a common internationally adopted set of CSR standards would facilitate tracking of progress by supermarkets towards (or away from) some agreed Gold Standard. Comparisons between the currently variegated and uncoordinated CSR policies of various firms would become much easier. This would be rather like the current competition for market share between, for example, Sainsbury's and Tesco, except that here every player could aspire to attain 100%.

As of now, major societal and environmental problems connected to and caused by our food chain operations still persist. We still have the obesity crisis, and the numbers of overweight are rising in many countries. Poor working conditions in food production and processing still exist, and producing our food continues to create major environmental and sustainability problems. Persuading people to eat healthily, to demand less processed sugary, fatty, salty food which precipitates expensive health issues years after consumption is still difficult. Of course, we cannot expect private profit-making corporations to achieve, on their own, a Utopian society free from poverty and food-related illness; as Jesus said at Matthew 26:11, "The poor you shall always have with you". However, the continuation of many social, economic and health problems connected with our globalized food industry, where the supermarkets play a key role at the crucial nexus between producers and consumers, suggests that all is far from well, far from satisfactory, in the supermarket CSR arena.

1.10 The Need for Other Actors in the Realm of Supermarket Corporate Social Responsibility

Individual purchases exert a negligible influence on large corporations but collective consumer choices and action (e.g. boycotts) can change the policies of even the largest multinational companies. This collective action only occurs when some other organization, probably a newspaper or other media channel, or a charity or other NGO, picks up on a cause and creates mass publicity so that hundreds of thousands or even millions of consumers all switch buying habits simultaneously. The decision by the major UK supermarkets to first charge for disposable plastic bags then to start to eliminate them entirely was driven by the UK newspapers and the CPRE. The issue in the early 2010s was the increase in unsightly rubbish in the countryside, roadside verges strewn with plastic detritus and bags caught in tree branches. The anti-plastic bag campaign then received a further massive boost with the TV series Blue Planet II where David Attenborough highlighted the damage discarded plastic was doing to the world's oceans and their marine wildlife.

Consumer-driven CSR can sometimes be misguided; a notable case was the boycott of Shell petrol stations over the Brent Spar case in 1995, when Greenpeace asserted that a redundant oil platform to be sunk in the North Sea by Shell still contained considerable amounts of crude oil and other chemicals that would eventually escape and harm the environment. The platform was eventually recycled on land, but Greenpeace's assertions about the harm that would have been done by a deep sea sinking were retracted. In the supermarket food sector, some 'common-sense' intuitively correct environmental initiatives may also turn out to be mistaken. Two examples are the notion that warm-climate produce, such as tomatoes grown in Spain and flown into Britain, is worse for the environment than growing this produce in Britain; in fact, the energy used in continuously heating the greenhouses may exceed the one-off fuel used by the aircraft to fly them in. A second fallacy may be that glass bottles are better than plastic; in fact, glass has to be heated to high temperatures to recycle it, and plastic bottles, if collected efficiently, can be shredded and made into a wide variety of other products; glass is also heavier to transport than plastic.

Devinney et al (2006) has suggested the acronym $C_N SR$ as the deliberate consumer choice to make or abstain from purchases based on personal and moral beliefs. Properly informed consumer social responsibility could also adopt a version of the 4-P Quadruple Bottom Line, where the 'P' for Profit would now stand for 'Parsimony'. The need for proper information to direct this $C_N SR$ implies that both state and non-state actors, governments and NGOs have a significant role to play in persuading the public to influence corporations. The state is a major player and stakeholder in the food chain, and influences diet and health in several ways. The government of the day enacts laws and regulations, imposes taxes and directs local government agencies, state agencies such as schools, hospitals, the armed forces and prisons are major food purchasers, and the costs of a poor diet heavily impact on state finances in terms of NHS costs and lost productivity. The state has significant information resources and can exert significant influence via a range of media channels on people's food choices.

Government policies on food and CSR will always be coloured by the prevailing political climate, but charities and other NGOs are also seldom free of 'political' agendas either. Ideally, then, we need a combination of all these parties acting to inform and persuade public purchasing pressure on companies, exerting checks and balances on each other. Following Devinney, one might term these initiatives $C_S SR$, state social responsibility. A wide variety of methods could be employed, from information releases to nudge theory to fiscal influences, taxing ecologically or socially harmful corporate practices more heavily and rewarding with tax rebates when companies act in the wider socio-environmental interest. The possibilities for such variants and extensions of CSR are explored more fully in Chapter 7. Meanwhile, the next chapter of this book, Chapter 2, explores in more detail the moral, legal and ethical principles of a theory of comprehensive CSR that truly benefits people, community and the environment.

Note

1. In 2018, Asda merged with another UK chain, Sainsbury's; the role of Walmart in this new company has yet to be clarified.

2   Food Justice as Social Justice

Towards a New Regulatory Framework in Support of a Basic Human Right to Healthy Food

2.1 The Need for Regulatory Reform to Address Food Injustice

Food is a source of nourishment, a cause for celebration, an inducement to temptation and a means of influence, and it signifies good fortune and well-being. Together with other life-enhancing goods such as clean water, unpolluted air, adequate shelter and suitable clothing, food is a basic good which is necessary for human flourishing. Accordingly, when we reflect on the deprivation and suffering which arises from the conditions of, for example, austerity and poverty which lead to hunger and malnutrition, we inevitably experience a sense of injustice. Yet the demands of markets and powerful corporations who determine the shape of our food systems have often worked against the best interests of people. Recent research by the *World Food Programme* suggests that 815 million people worldwide go to bed on an empty stomach, and one in three suffer from malnutrition (2018). At the same time, constituting a 'double nutritional burden', inadequate food provisions and a lack of healthy food lead to an even greater number of people becoming obese. Accordingly, "not only do the consequences of not enough—or the wrong—food cause suffering and poor health, they also slow progress in many other areas of development like education and employment" (World Food Programme, 2018).

Issues of food equity span a variety of social, economic and political structures which determine processing, distribution, marketing, retailing and consumption. Yet, founded on monetary values, the prioritizing of accumulation has resulted in a series of economic, social and environmental externalities that are devastating local economics, harming individuals, families and communities. Such profit-first food strategies have not only damaged the planet, but oppressive and largely unregulated corporate practices in this area have also resulted in the rising incidence of food injustice. In addition, a prolonged period of global fiscal austerity, which has called for massive reductions in spending on social programmes, has not only dominated political discourse but has had an adverse impact on the health and well-being of the poorest members of humanity. It is evident, therefore, that our current food system, from agricultural production right through to the shop sales till, fails to meet the essential criteria of social justice—namely, freedom from want, freedom from oppression and access to equal opportunity.

This chapter addresses what is one of the greatest challenges facing society today—widespread hunger, malnutrition and obesity, particularly in low-income populations—by investigating a series of alternative approaches to food injustice and seeks to articulate an alternative basis for regulatory reform. Questions such as (1) should there be a fundamental human right to healthy food; (2) if so, what would an ethico-legal food system look like and (3) how might it be enshrined and supported in law will be explored according to the ideals of social justice and moral philosophy, and the modification and extension of existing legal provisions.

2.2 Hungry for Justice: The Right to Nutritional Food and a Healthy Diet

Eradicating hunger and malnutrition are two of the great challenges of our time. The 'right to food' has been recognized in the 1948 Universal Declaration of Human Rights; the 1966 International Covenant on Economic, Social and Cultural Rights; and in the non-binding declarations of, for example, the World Food Summits of 1974 and 1996. The promotion of good health, nutrition and access to healthy food are also goals of the UN's 2016 *New Urban Agenda*, which accords with the UN's earlier 2030 *Agenda for Sustainable Development*, which aims to "end poverty and hunger, in all their forms and dimensions, and to ensure that all human beings can fulfil their potential in dignity and equality and in a healthy environment" (UN General Assembly Resolution, 2015: A/RES/70/1). These and other legal instruments recognize the obligation of the state to respect, protect and guarantee adequate living conditions for each one of its citizens. Whilst such recent proposals refer to food security, the food supply and the availability of sufficient food, they also stipulate the right of access to healthy and nutritional food provisions as a basic good. However, the commodification of the food system has played a big part in militating against the perception of food as a public good and as evidenced by excessive pricing, patents and private land use regulations, which seek to promote and protect private or corporate interests.

Food is viewed as a commercial commodity, subject to free competition, consumer purchasing power and the maximization of profit for growers, producers and retailers, rather than as a universal human right. Unlike gold, steel or Brent Crude, however, food comprises more than simply an opportunity to create another lucrative commercial enterprise. Rather, the primal right to survive makes food a matter of social justice and moral economy. Food is, therefore, the proper object of a fundamental right which calls for the assumption of ethical responsibilities that express the equality of all, especially the poorest. Otherwise, in the words of Adam Smith

> [a policy that] hurts in any degree the interest of any one order of citizens, for no other purpose but to promote that of some other, is evidently contrary to that justice and equality of treatment which the sovereign owes to all the different orders of his subjects.
>
> (1981: 271)

The right to an adequate supply of nutritious food is, therefore, not only indispensable for the realization of human rights, but it is also inseparable from social justice as an equitable vision of society. This is a society in which every member is given access to the necessary resources to allow full participation in all aspects of communal life. As suggested by Allen in *Mining for Justice in the Food System*, "no other public issue is as accessible to people in their daily lives as that of food justice. Everyone—regardless of age, gender, ethnicity, or social class—eats. We are all involved and we are all implicated" (2008: 159).

Although access to healthy food is not perfectly correlated with public health outcomes, those with limited access to nutritional foods often suffer most acutely, because individuals who live in areas with access to a retailer selling fresh fruit and vegetables tend to be less obese than those who live in a 'food desert' (Shaw, 2014: 28). Healthy food access has also been associated with less obvious social benefits, as diverse as improved educational performance and crime reduction. Consequently, to promote a more favourable attitude towards the consumption of healthy food, there has been a series of public information campaigns in the UK aimed at encouraging the consumption of fresh fruit and vegetables. Initiatives, such as '5 a Day' and *Change4Life*, a social media campaign launched by the Department of Health in 2009, were initially popular; however, it was suggested that the long-term effects on behaviour or attitudes towards a healthy diet were limited (Croker et al, 2012: 404). One of the biggest food system challenges currently in the UK is the proliferation of fast food outlets, as their meals are typically higher in salt, sugar and saturated fats. A recent report by *Public Health England* found that England's most deprived areas are also fast food hotspots, with five times more outlets found in these communities than in the most affluent (PHE, 2018). The data indicated that chip shops, burger bars and pizza places account for more than a quarter (26%) of all eateries in England, excluding Indian and Chinese takeaways and kebab shops. In recognition of the scale of the problem and the extent to which the local environment has a major impact on individual behaviour (in that streets heaving with fast food retailers can influence our food choices), some local authorities have produced planning policies which aim to restrict the growth of new takeaways and fast food outlets. These local plans have focused on issues such as the proximity to locations where children and young people congregate such as schools, community centres and playgrounds, and restricting new outlets where there is already an over-concentration and clustering within a particular area. The role that schools can play in promoting healthy food is further explored in Chapter 7.

Although these government-backed initiatives by local planning authorities are useful, it is suggested that they fall short of adequately addressing the wider challenges posed by obesogenic environments. For example, a set of contingent relationships—between particular individuals, food, culture and urban space—create communities with specific characteristics and constitute our foodscapes. However, the "relational constructedness of things" is often ignored or not fully appreciated by policy makers (Massey, 2005: 10). Rather than address the phenomena of food deserts and their consequences, such as obesity, as societal problems—necessitating a holistic and collective approach involving producers, retailers, marketers and law and policy makers—public health promotion pedagogies and strategies tend to hold the individual responsible. In which case, and notwithstanding socio-economic factors which inhibit access to healthy food, individuals are urged to monitor, manage and control their own bodies, and are held accountable for making the 'right' decisions to ensure their future health. The corollary of this approach is that people are complicit in perpetuating their own misery and ill health due to making poor lifestyle choices.

Such reasoning ignores the influence of, for example, 'adaptive preferentism', whereby poverty and adverse social circumstances tend to distort one's preferences, and so undermine the impetus for projects intended to maximize their health and well-being. For Bartky, adaptation is subtle and outside the control or awareness of the individual; it leads to 'deformed desires' which

> fasten us to the established order of domination, for the same system which produces false needs also controls the conditions under which such needs can be satisfied. 'False needs', it might be ventured, are produced through indoctrination, psychological manipulation, and the denial of autonomy; they are needs whose possession and satisfaction benefit not the subject who has them but a social order whose interest lies in domination.
>
> (1990: 42)

Whilst the politics of social hierarchy and inequality may cause individuals to conform to particular norms, beliefs or options which are presented as being the only ones available to them, adapting to their predicament does not preclude taking advantage of an opportunity to strive for change. That is to say, there is no reason to believe that individuals who have adapted to reduced circumstances would not be amenable to improving their life choices, should such alternatives be available to them. After all, they are still suffering the ill effects of deprived conditions, but as rational decision makers have chosen to cope to the best of their ability and derive what limited advantage they can from a bad situation. A just institution would recognize and address the need to reduce or remove any barriers to a nutritious diet and healthy lifestyle, by first acknowledging the material conditions which prevent access.

2.3 Social Stratification, Poverty and the Unequal Burden of Family Health and Nutrition

Government initiatives, such as the Department of Health's 2009 *Change4Life* campaign, often focus on 'improving family health', which invariably means the responsibility for effecting change is placed on the shoulders of women, as occupiers of the traditional caring role in the home. This gendered approach aligns with food marketing in advertisements which commonly depict women as the chief food providers regardless of an increase in single father households, due to *inter alia* increasing numbers of women entering the workforce. So although women are often pressured into taking control of the family diet, as well as dealing with other often onerous family normative burdens, in fact children are increasingly likely to be cared for by someone other than their mother. Such behavioural beliefs also appeal to a model of responsibility which is bound to a particular conception of moral agency, in which individuals are implicated in their actions according to "a linear chain of relations between free will, knowledge, voluntary action, causality, responsibility and blame" (Barnett et al, 2005: 25). Consequently, in modern popular and legal discourse, the caregiving relationship is continually associated with physical proximity, which focuses on the "relations of responsibility that exist between actors, rather than the [nature and form of the] responsibility that is placed upon them" (Colls & Evans, 2008: 628).

In addition to applying a particular cultural conception of a woman's role in the household, class is another significant factor. The UK Department of Health's *Healthy Weight, Healthy Lives: Consumer Insight Summary*, on which *Change4Life* was based, stated that families defined as having low socio-economic status considered poor diet and low physical activity levels to be a low priority, if not unimportant (Department of Health, 2008: 11). The report continued:

> Adopting a healthy lifestyle was seen as hard work, stressful and unrealistic. It was also strongly linked to 'middle class' values and activities—yoga classes, gym membership, buying organic food. Many priority cluster families saw healthy living as the preserve of stay-at-home mums who can afford not to work and instead spend their time exercising and shopping for, and cooking, healthy meals.
>
> (DH, 2008: 12)

Yet, in common with Michelle Obama's 2010 US Internet-based *Let's Move!* campaign to end childhood obesity, structural inequalities were disregarded, and mothers were held to be solely responsible for their family's unhealthy diet and ill health. The campaign comprised a typical neoliberal discourse which conformed to the cultural notion of the 'good mother' and appealed to a class, race, able-bodied and gender biased ideal of citizenship. Working-class women, and particularly mothers, were characterized as both the problem and the solution, letting them shoulder the blame for the nutritional poverty and obesity of their own families, and for societal health in general. For example, in the Department of Health's *Healthy Weight, Healthy Lives: Consumer Insight Summary*, under the heading "Promoting Healthier Food Choices: making cooking fun", mothers and children were encouraged to "learn to cook together in cooking clubs" by "using school recipe books comprising recipes created by other mothers" (Department of Health, 2008: 54). Both *Let's Move!* and *Change4Life* aspired to reconfigure familial relations to fit an idealized standard with middle-class overtones, whilst at the same time concealing this objective.

Such campaigns assume a relatively privileged population of educated and reasonably healthy citizens who are more likely to be already participating fully in society, yet people who are classified as living in poverty are often described as being undernourished or malnourished, uneducated, lacking in basic life skills, suffering various levels of deprivation and are generally excluded from social life. In addition, our relationship to food, knowledge of nutrition and mastery of culinary skills is complex, and determined by a range of factors. As 13th-century Persian poet Rumi observed, "The satiated man and the hungry man do not see the same thing when they look upon a loaf of bread", paraphrased in the 1920's prohibition era by American gangster and businessman Al Capone, "When I sell liquor, it's called bootlegging; when my patrons serve it on silver trays on Lake Shore Drive, it's called hospitality". Research into the psychology of food and food cultures has demonstrated the profoundly relative nature of how everyone thinks about food and eating (Shaw, 2014: 42–5). By assuming what amounts to a general, and ultimately untenable, ideal for those families who are likely to need the greatest help in accessing healthy food (and in implementing a healthy diet and regular exercise regime), both campaigns functioned to further marginalize the most disadvantaged members of society.

In modern times, human beings no longer gather their own food or kill what they eat; rather, they survive on a diet of processed food such as ready meals, particularly those of the meat variety, fatty fast food and salty snacks (Shaw, 2017: 210–2). So it is hardly surprising that children and many adults are ignorant as to where their food originates or how it is produced, let alone which foods are more nutritious than others. A recent UK poll of 27,500 school children, cited in *The Consuming*

Geographies of Food, found that "one in ten thought tomatoes grew underground . . . one in three believed cheese grew on plants, and . . . one in five children had never visited a farm" (Shaw, 2014: 127). A further point is that since the costs of a food-literate citizenry would almost certainly be prohibitive in terms of having to adhere to a broader set of ethical standards, the prevailing ignorance is useful, if not essential, to the food retail industry, which makes more profit from processed foods than from raw fruit and vegetables.

Social class is, for many sociologists, fundamental to the cultural context within which food practices, rituals, routines and preferences are created. Food not only shapes individual and collective identities but also functions as a medium for the reproduction of class and gender habitus (Bourdieu, 1984). The still widely held perception of a typical—relatively affluent, educated and middle-class—household, with the central figure of a 'good mother' as the facilitator of a healthy lifestyle and wholesome diet for her family, is therefore dangerous. It ignores gross social inequalities in life opportunities and the relative capacities of disadvantaged groups to engage in healthy food practices of their choice, and so militates against the ideals of social justice. The deprived and impoverished are often considered to be not doing enough to lift themselves out of poverty. Perceived as disreputable and unworthy, they are not only often blamed and shamed but also frequently blame themselves for their 'moral and personal failure', in the belief that they 'count for nothing' (Shildrick & MacDonald, 2013: 293; Lister, 2015: 139). However, the more pertinent question arises in relation to the nature of such otherwise affluent societies, whose economic and political systems are responsible for perpetuating so much poverty. The great disparity between the richest and poorest, for example, is understood by many to be a moral problem, if not a moral crisis, for society as a whole. If it is accepted that food is more than a commodity and is a fundamental condition of human flourishing, then a social contract in relation to healthy food rightfully encompasses and requires an enhanced collection of interdependencies. This would rightly appeal to an ideal of social justice which is grounded in a pluralist conception of well-being to be enjoyed by every individual within multiple domains of life.

2.4 A Rawlsian Approach to Alleviating Food Poverty as a Fundamental Principle of Social Justice

The current crises of obesity, malnutrition and food poverty are all issues which relate to public policy and social justice, but it is suggested that they would also benefit from being contextualized within a philosophical framework. This is not least of all because many philosophers have explored the notions of equality, fairness and justice, and have attempted to set out what constitutes a good life, and much has been written on the ideal conditions for human flourishing or *eudaimonia*. Although food ethics as a specific concern of social justice has been given little attention by classical philosophers, Plato, Epicurus and the Stoics all recommended a good diet as necessary for well-being and intellectual activity, and Voltaire and Hume both refer to the sociality of good food. Later work related a lack of food to revolution, for example, the "golden age of English food riots" (1740–1801) began when grain prices doubled or tripled which led to more than 600 food riots across England and Wales (Bohstedt, 2010). For Marx, capitalism could be defined by contrasting agrarian life with industrialization. In each case, it is clear that food plays a constitutive role in social, cultural and political life.

Recognizing the utility of alternative approaches to the prevalent neoliberal trajectory (that asserts a successful and just society can be achieved through the free market with little or no state intervention), recent research has applied a diverse range of philosophical and moral theoretical frameworks to difficult modern social issues, such as the increasing levels of homelessness (Watts, 2014) and healthcare (Daniels, 2001; Cruickshank, 2012). In support of such alternatives to existing 'considered judgements', Nussbaum argued that "without an account of the good, however vague, that we can take to be *shared*, we have no adequate basis for saying what is *missing* from the lives of the poor or marginalised, or excluded" (1992: 229). Furthermore, the possibility of informed critique is diminished when there is no adequate means by which to justify or interrogate the claim that a particular embedded practice or policy is unjust. Consequently, theoretical applications have produced a deeper understanding of, for example, the redistributive obligations that exist between various actors. They have also helped to elucidate a more holistic framework for addressing current policy gaps and for use in mapping the necessary conditions for promoting a healthy diet and access to fresh fruit and vegetables for all, as primary social goods.

John Rawls was arguably one of the most influential 20th-century thinkers in the fields of ethics, political philosophy and the philosophy of law. In the landmark 1971 *A Theory of Justice*, he presents what is one of the most comprehensive normative egalitarian arguments, setting out why it is important to care about poverty and social justice. He advanced a classical liberal position and resource-oriented account of well-being and justice, which went beyond the fair distribution of material resources to include a wider set of primary social goods to which all individuals were entitled. The primary goods comprised basic rights and liberties, freedom of movement and freedom of choice between a wide range of occupations and access to positions of influence and responsibility, including wealth and income. Although such resources were not considered to be ends in themselves and only means, Rawls conception of a just society requires that all individuals start out with equal access to this set of primary goods. Having the resources for sustaining a good standard of healthcare and access to a regular supply of nutritional food, for example, is the basis for 'normal functioning', which, in turn, renders life-enhancing opportunities available to everyone (Daniels, 2001: 2).

These flexible, multi-purpose primary goods, consisting of basic rights, liberties and opportunities, wealth and income, were augmented by the incorporation of a set of social goods comprising 'the social bases of self-respect'. For Rawls, the importance of self-respect underpinned his idea that a person has an inherent dignity, and intrinsic value, that basic institutional structures should not be allowed to violate, because

> the primary subject of justice is the basic structure of society, or more exactly, the way in which the major social institutions distribute fundamental rights and duties and determine the division of advantages from social cooperation. By major institutions I understand the political constitution and the principal economic and social arrangements. Thus the legal protection of freedom of thought and liberty of conscience, competitive markets, and private property in the means of production . . . are examples of major social institutions.
>
> (1971: 7)

Since the basic structure of society is considered to be 'institutional', all major political and social institutions would be held responsible for maintaining a nurturing social environment, within which all citizens would have a sense of self-worth and the confidence to carry out their life plans (Rawls, 2001: 58–9). This would require designing institutions in such a way that they were able to address 'deep inequalities', rather than only shallow inequalities such as those relating to individual actions and choices. It would also mean devising strategies to meet basic social inequalities, such as those relating to health and nutrition, especially when all such competing needs cannot be met.

2.5 The Reciprocal Influence of Egalitarian Institutions as a Basic Requirement of Social Justice

Rawls' ground-breaking insight was that the construction of a just society ought to be accomplished without regard to what socio-economic position individuals would occupy within it. Consequently, fundamental structural inequalities such as being born into a less advantageous social position, with compromised and unequal life chances, would not be allowed to inhibit or determine an individual's future life prospects. Behind what he termed the 'veil of ignorance', policy makers would not know (or would bracket out their knowledge of) what position they occupied in the social hierarchy and would, rather, seek to choose to develop a society in which each citizen enjoyed a complete set of basic economic rights and benefits (1971: 5). Furthermore, justice requires social collaboration amongst 'equals' for their mutual advantage, and for Rawls, this could be realized by increasing the levels of participation of those most affected by poverty in the political processes of decision making, on issues which have a fundamental impact on their life conditions (Rawls, 1971: 14).

As moral agents, for Rawls, all citizens are rendered indistinguishable from one another, and each person must have the capacity to determine "how they are to regulate their claims against one another and what is to be the foundation charter of their society" (Rawls, 1971: 11). This also means, although there is a variety of variables to be completed, taking a broad view of Rawls account of 'fair equality of opportunity', "those with similar abilities should have similar life chances" (Rawls, 1971: 63). 'Similar' would be best translated as 'approximate', because there are elements of well-being (such as happiness and knowledge) which individuals can acquire without depriving others of the same. Realizing the fair equality of opportunity account does not, therefore, necessitate the levelling down of all differences between individuals within the context of each exercisable opportunity they may have in life. Rather, "opportunity is equal for the purposes of the account when certain impediments to opportunity are eliminated for all persons" (Daniels, 2008: 60). So, in cases where individuals have particular skills but their prospects are threatened by, for example, an inferior, or lack of, education, institutional involvement to help advance their prospects would not only be justified but also necessary. Poor health and nutritional poverty would also be possible sources of inequality of opportunity according to the Rawlsian model. Consequently maximizing the possibility of human flourishing or simply 'normal functioning' entails an intention to remove significant obstacles to personal progress, as an appropriate aim and obligation of social justice and a just society.

In a less than perfect world, Rawls ideal theory assumes a reasonable level of social benefits for all—aiming to ensure fair equality of opportunity and the fair distribution of social goods—so that every individual has both the necessary freedom and resources to enable them to pursue their personal idea of the good life. This means nobody should suffer from deprivation, such as hunger and malnutrition, which may impair their capacity for moral reasoning. Rawls called for a radical rethinking of the collective mythology in some societies which adheres to the notion of self-reliance; for instance, the perceived divide between good citizens who work and pay their taxes versus socially undesirable dependents who rely on charity and state handouts. This myth disregards the reality that human beings are vulnerable to illness, injury and disability; it also ignores the effect on people of their environment. Accordingly, he rejected the classical utilitarian account, which ignores the needs of 'minority' groups for the sake of 'maximising utility' for the majority and undervalues the unequal distribution of benefits and burdens in society.

Rather, he preferred Immanuel Kant's categorical moral imperative to treat people as ends in themselves and not merely as a means to collective ends on the basis that

> [e]ach person possesses an inviolability founded on justice that even the welfare of society as a whole cannot override. For this reason, justice denies that the loss of freedom for some is made right by a greater good shared by others. It does not allow that the sacrifices imposed on a few are outweighed by the larger sum of advantages enjoyed by many.
>
> (1971: 3)

For Rawls, simply because an individual was born into a rich family, for instance, does not in itself provide any justification for that person to be treated favourably by social institutions. So-called accidents of birth, ethnicity, sex, or having particular talents and abilities are considered to be morally arbitrary characteristics, in that there is no special entitlement to societal goods and privileges because of them. Rather, Rawls focusses on the poorest members of society in the belief that freedom from poverty, as a baseline, is necessary to enable each person without exception to have the capacity for self-determination. Within his conception, individuals should be allowed to compete for influence, wealth and other goods only when competition takes place in the context of fair conditions, because the prevalence of unfair conditions permits vast accumulations of wealth and power to be concentrated in the hands of the few. To this end, his 'difference principle' requires that social and economic inequalities be reconfigured to provide the greatest benefit for the least advantaged, so that "the least favoured person can be identified and his rational preference determined" (Rawls, 1971: 77). The 'least favoured person' at the heart of Rawls 'difference principle' refers to a class, rather than an individual, which means that absolute priority to the interests of the least advantaged is given only in situations where their collective shared interests are in conflict with those of the rest of the population. Although a definition of the most deprived members of the population is not provided, it seems clear that Rawls envisioned this group to be sizeable, perhaps comprising up to one-third of the population.

Rawls distributive theory of justice has been accused of being incomplete or overly simplistic, for example, in failing to allocate appropriate weighting to different primary social goods; although, he resolves this latter issue by referring to a broadly measurable 'core' of primary goods (1971: 93). He asserted that income and wealth were already sufficiently correlated with primary goods as 'impersonal' social goods—alongside the more 'personal' civil rights, political rights and liberties—and thus able to realize and maximize a specific welfare function. Importantly, his account of primary goods originates from the conception of the citizen as free and equal, reasonable and rational. Primary goods were considered to be essential for developing and exercising the two moral powers—"a capacity for a sense of justice and a conception of the good"—and for pursuing a wide range of specific and individual conceptions of the good life.

Notwithstanding his critics, from a seemingly impossible position of irreconcilable divisions, Rawls work imaginatively explores the possibility of public consensus and universality, by first questioning what is social unity, whether a just and stable society is a credible aim in our diverse and homogenous modern environment, and, finally, he explicates the conditions under which social unity may be realizable. Moreover, his recommendations for socio-economic affirmative action, in addressing the issues of fair equality of opportunity, resource maximization and the eradication of involuntary disadvantage, are still relevant to today's society, where an increasing number of citizens live in nutritional poverty with a lack of adequate institutional intervention. This current state of affairs goes against one of the main ideas behind Rawls conception of justice, which is good governance by a properly administered community— within which each member enjoys meaningful autonomy in developing their institutions and, in turn, this endorses the manner in which these institutions influence them. In this way, the reciprocal influence of society and individuals enables the social institution to function as a self-sustaining system. A Rawlsian conception of a well-ordered and just society, therefore, requires that all "its major institutions are arranged so as to achieve the greatest net balance in satisfaction summed over all individuals belonging to it" (1971: 22).

2.6 Between Theory and Reality: From Moral Law to Soft Law Solutions

Even if, in the modern globalized world, the economic prospects of individuals cannot be tied solely to their institutions or to the productivity and co-operative abilities of societal members, in *A Theory of Justice*, John Rawls demonstrates that an egalitarian understanding of liberal democracy—whose actual expression we can already see in the world to some extent—can be internally consistent. It is suggested that his approach to justice can be used to create new ways of thinking about the development and impact of modern food policy in relation to food poverty and the food retail environment. A Rawlsian account of corporate governance, for example, would not confer a position of privilege and dominance on shareholders vis-à-vis other actors who also share an interest in an organization's activities. Consequently, the fight for social justice for people living in poverty, without access to life-sustaining affordable and healthy food, could not be waged without their active involvement. It would be ineffective, just as recent policy initiatives have failed, due largely to the poverty debate being framed by politicians and the media. Even the World Bank has conceded that "the poor are the main actors in the fight against poverty" (2001: 12). Rather, the success and very existence of the company would be dependent on serving the interests of multiple stakeholders. In the form of a combination of general laws and modified legal principles, hard and soft regulation, CSR initiatives, and those of other actors such as NGOs, academics and social scientists, all subjects would be entitled to the same level of consideration and be capable of receiving the same level of rights. Furthermore, all companies would be held accountable to a set of duties and obligations that extended their scope of responsibility, to embrace a wider set of stakeholders and their interests. The scope and necessity for involvement of multiple agencies and stakeholders—especially NGOs and the media—in improving the food system, is explored in the concluding chapter, Chapter 8, of this book.

In the wake of large corporate takeovers and mergers (such as Asda UK and Sainsbury's), and as the reach and influence of multinational enterprises grows, there are increasing calls for corporations to be more transparent and assume more responsibility for the wider impact of their activities. Despite a recent push to 'harden' formerly self-driven 'soft laws', however, there is still no consensus as to the basic definition of social responsibility in relation to companies (Berger-Walliser & Scott, 2018: 170). Soft law mechanisms are attractive because of their flexibility, and CSR—as a kind of corporate soft law—appeals to private corporate actors for that reason, and because of its voluntary and non-enforceable nature. The perceptions and attitudes of CEOs to CSR also vary, depending on a large number of quantitative and qualitative factors; for example, the organizational context and form, and how contextual conditions and motivations influence the company's adoption of, and the extent of their engagement with, CSR initiatives. More often than not, CSR tends to be viewed as either a philanthropic gesture that has ethical and normative dimensions or a business strategy that has an instrumental dimension (Porter & Kramer, 2006). This ad hoc approach means it is often difficult to understand the specific underlying processes and conditions under which corporations are able to deliver sustainable outcomes for health, society and the planet.

A variety of sustainability-related accounting models—such as the well-known, triple-bottom-line philosophy of economic, social and environmental performance (Elkington, 1997), further finessed as the '4 Ps', profit, people, planet and provisions (see Chapter 1)—have been suggested as useful yardsticks. However, the disparities in how CSR is defined and measured often go beyond semantics to deeper construct-level differences, ranging from philanthropy to ethics, to health and safety issues, to more composite measures assessed by external rating agencies (Aguinis & Glavas, 2012: 942). What is significant is that the choice of priorities, privileges and appropriate implementation of any guidelines and directives is determined by the company, which can decide how to evaluate the conditions, and whether to devise incentives for compliance and determine a set of punishments for non-compliance. However, to allow corporations to consider CSR as simply another means of value creation ultimately undermines its impact and efficacy. Importantly, in the absence of hard law or statutory regulation, the activities of socially responsible businesses can make the difference between a thriving and healthy community and one dogged by ill health and poor life chances. For that reason, there is a strong public interest in the establishment of particular standards and initiatives, also in the continuing promotion and support of those norms which have already been agreed upon.

The widening gap between shareholder primacy and stakeholder theory is illustrated in a recent report published by the Joseph Rowntree Foundation entitled *Poverty in Wales*, which shows that, in the UK, Wales has a higher rate of poverty than England, Scotland and Northern Ireland (Barnard, 2018). There is a healthy-life expectancy gap of around 15 years amongst those who live in the most deprived parts of Wales, such the Valleys, compared to those in far less deprived parts, such as rural Monmouthshire, just a few kilometres away from Valleys towns like Ebbw Vale and Merthyr Tydfil. At the GCSE level in Wales, there is also a substantial attainment gap between those who are eligible for free school meals and those who are not, meaning the former are less likely to achieve five or more good grades (Barnard, 2018: 26–7, 32). Consequently, the schoolchildren who rely on free meals have a greater likelihood of long-term unemployment and an inability to avoid poverty in adulthood. Although the Welsh government has introduced the Abolition of the Right to Buy and Associated Rights (Wales) Act 2018 to protect existing social housing stock, the current shortage of affordable and good-quality homes with ease of access to local affordable healthy food retail outlets by low-income households continues to exacerbate the detrimental effects of nutritional poverty and food insecurity more generally.

In some of the UK's biggest cities, developers are planning huge new residential developments which contain little or no affordable housing. London councils, for example, have granted property developers planning permission to build in excess of 26,000 luxury apartments, priced at more than £1 million each, despite fears that there are already too many half-empty investment properties, or so-called posh ghost towers, in the capital (Neate, 2018: 3). Planning documents show that in Manchester, none of the 15,517 homes granted planning permission by the council's planning committee in the last two years are set to be affordable, which contravenes the council's own rules and policies. Some of these enormous new developments comprise in excess of 1,000 apartments, containing swimming pools, tennis courts, cinemas, gyms and concierge facilities. Of a further 19 developments comprising 850 homes granted planning permission by Manchester Council, only 136 will be allocated as social housing. In Sheffield, only 97 homes out of 6,943 (1.4%) approved by planners in 2016 and 2017 met the UK government's affordable definition, and in Nottingham, where the council has pledged that 20% of all new housing will be affordable, only 3.8% of units approved by council planners met this definition (Pidd, 2018: 15). Many of these new developments will be built in city centres, with the danger that only those on high salaries will be able to afford to live near the myriad amenities and enjoy all the advantages of city centre living, leading critics to accuse council planners of social cleansing. The UK's supermarkets are also starting to build housing above their sites (Chapter 3). Although some of this provision is 'social' or 'affordable', many of these units are more likely to be luxury-end apartments, with facilities aimed at the wealthier buyer.

The boom in developments of luxury apartments is taking place as the UK's cities face a growing crisis in the availability of affordable housing. A process of redevelopment and revitalization means low-income residents are being replaced by high-income dwellers, thereby transforming the character of many neighbourhoods. Often displaced to the peripheries, poorer residents from the city centres are shunted into cheaper areas further from the metropolis. In turn, the buying power of the new residents of these revitalized and gentrified neighbourhoods attracts a new and different selection of retailers in the commercial corridors; for example, the high-quality supermarket chain Waitrose is found in wealthier areas in the UK, and Macknade Fine Foods caters to the residents of affluent Faversham in Kent. The increased housing and tax revenues, changing community institutions and modified cultural composition lead to a variety of supermarkets, independent shops, fresh food retailers, delicatessens and branded chain stores, creating new and exclusive spaces. Rather than alleviating poverty, the displacement and relocation of low-income, long-term residents inevitably leads to the polarization of the urban environment and only serves to highlight the socio-economic gap between the rich and poor. The new neighbourhoods of the latter group are more often characterized by a glut of fast food outlets, charity shops, betting shops and a lack of retail outlets offering healthy, fresh and affordable food choices.

In the final parts of *A Theory of Justice*, Rawls emphasises the importance of human dignity and respect: the idea that a person has dignity and intrinsic value that social structures should not be allowed to violate. Clearly, whilst the mainstream CSR movement has promoted extra-legal strategies ostensibly in the public interest—for example, by accepting external monitoring and committing to socially responsible investing policies—these often have a limited impact. This is because CSR tends to be conceptualized as a type of self-government which co-exists alongside the public system of governance but without any clear strategic relationship. If it can be agreed that corporate directors ought to give priority to serving the interests of non-shareholders and society in general, as well as aiming to maximize shareholder value, the basis for such a shift of priorities may appropriately be based on a more philosophical school of thought. Otherwise, if businesses lack accountability and the capacity to address matters beyond bare economic interests, this has an obvious impact on important societal matters such as public health.

Making the collective good a legitimate aim of business not only entails companies voluntarily assuming an albeit market-embedded moral responsibility for the flourishing of society in general, but may also require the imposition of certain legal duties. Accordingly, the scope of responsibility for the consequences of an unhealthy diet extends beyond the individual to global corporations, the government, local authorities, food producers, food marketers, the mass media and food retailers. In determining a collective approach to the problem of healthy food access, it is suggested that a new set of ethical priorities be formulated, under-pinned by an appropriate regulatory framework, which would impose a series of formal duties and obligations by extending existing public and private law principles. To this end, the following section considers the possibility and configuration of such a legal framework, which would be capable of providing the basis for corporations to maximize the likeli-hood of their businesses serving, broadly defined, the collective interest.

2.7 The Potential and Limits of Corporate Social Responsibility

For each citizen, proper nutrition is vital for optimal development, physi-cal growth, general health and a feeling of well-being, as well as playing an important role in reducing the risk of chronic illnesses such as heart dis-ease, diabetes and some forms of cancer. With full health, their life chances and opportunities for human flourishing are maximized. For the state, an inability to access healthy food adversely impacts on worker productivity, educational achievement, infant mortality and a country's national income. In which case, ethical and impartial social policies that most closely align with a model of the just society and promotion of the common good have many benefits and advantages for all actors. Yet the separation between markets and politics has produced a fragmented approach to primary social goods, which aligns with Freidman's maxim that "the social respon-sibility of business is to increase its profits" rather than engage in activities to increase social welfare (1970: 122). So whilst governments administer public policy, corporations are encouraged to undertake social duties on a voluntary basis, which may or may not complement governmental acts by filling institutional and legal voids, which constitutes a "dichotomous view of CSR and government" (Moon & Vogel, 2008: 304).

In both historical and relative terms, governments have always been able to exert some level of influence on CSR activities, by, for example, incentivizing companies to promote particular training and employment policies through the allocation of funds, or by threatening to impose an alternative legislative measure on their industries. However, as corporations have grown and become global, or at least transnational, individual states no longer have the power to regulate them across all their activities. It has also been argued that the proliferation of CSR box-ticking exercises has assisted corporations in claiming liberal credentials whilst effectively concealing the exploitative behaviour at the core of many of their activities. This contention underpins recent claims that CSR is a myth (Doane, 2005: Shaw, 2019) in as much as the central concept of the 'corporate conscience' or, more commonly, the caring 'corporate citizen', is flawed; yet people are persuaded by the promises given in the narratives of CSR statements of vision, mission and values. Even though companies possess many of the same rights and duties as individuals, to paraphrase 18th-century poet and Lord Chancellor Edward, First Baron Thurlow, the non-natural corporation has neither "a body to be kicked nor a soul to be damned". In *The Corporation: The Pathological Pursuit of Profit and Power*, the legal 'personhood' of the corporation was interrogated, asking, "What kind of a person is this?" (Bakan, 2005). In his book, and the accompanying documentary, Bakan concluded that the average corporation was greedy, devious, arrogant, self-serving and, most of all, psychopathic.

The problem with assuming corporate institutions can "do well while at the same time doing good" is that this is not the way in which markets operate. In reality, most CSR initiatives promoted by large corporations are actually attempts to legitimize their power and increase their profit margin. For instance, the growing consumer demand for ecological or 'green' goods and vegan and vegetarian meal options in the UK allows corporations to sell such products and business practices as socially responsible when in fact they are simply looking to capture a larger segment of the conscientious consumer market. Even when the intention seems laudable, a corporation often lacks an overview of the bigger picture, being invested in its own sphere of business activity narrowly conceived. For example, McDonald's decided to sell apples—'Apple Dippers', accompanied by a packet of sugary caramel dipping sauce with each portion—in its US outlets to address the challenge of increasing levels of obesity; however, the company's drive for economies of scale, uniformity and the guarantee of continued supply resulted in a loss of biodiversity in apple production, as they favoured only the 'Cameo' variety (Younge, 2005: 15). This, and other well-documented CSR failures, indicates that an ethical and environmentally sustainable basis for developing fair and just food policies which encompass the entire food supply chain is arguably best achieved through a genuinely democratic process, which reaches beyond the often-misleading CSR rhetoric to encompass a wider range of stakeholders.

In *The Devil's Dictionary*, a corporation is described as "an ingenious device for obtaining individual profit without individual responsibility", and responsibility is "a detachable burden easily shifted to the shoulders of God, fate, fortune, luck or one's neighbour. In the days of astrology it was customary to unload it on a star" (Bierce, 1911). Providing the conditions for promoting trade and retailing policies and practices that serve people and their right to safe, healthy, ecologically sustainable and affordable food cannot be left solely to the corporation. Furthermore, having CSR 'stand in for law' undermines democratic accountability and is no substitute for the assumption of control by a responsible government over the proper function of economies and institutions through which essential goods and services are delivered and social needs are met. Whilst the CSR movement has achieved some success in advancing environmental and social practices—for example, restricting the use of plastic packaging, reducing food waste and supporting local charities, such as food banks—it is argued that there are limits to improving corporate conduct without the intervention of more extensive and effective government regulation.

2.8 Beyond CSR, Soft Law and Traditional Regulatory Models

There is clearly scope for markets to generate some social and environmental benefits through CSR measures, but the market alone is unlikely to achieve the kind of progressive outcomes which are necessary for human flourishing. There are, however, various advantages to regulation, for example, certainty, predictability and, in many cases, innovation—due to allocating resources to speculative research and development in pursuit of long-term goals—beyond the profit motive. Traditional regulatory models would also impose mandatory rules, along with punishments, to ensure that the company acts in a socially responsible manner. As philosopher Reinhold Niebuhr suggested, "All social co-operation on a scale larger than the most intimate social group requires a measure of coercion. While no state can maintain its unity purely by coercion, neither can it preserve itself without coercion" (1961: 3). Although forcefully resisted by business, social and environmental progress may be more readily achieved through direct regulation rather than relying on the free market to implement policies which have little obvious financial return. One such area is health and safety in relation to food provisions.

It is now mandatory for nutrition information to be declared on pre-packed food to comply with the *European Food Information to Consumers Regulation No 1169/2011* (FIC) and the *Food Information Regulations 2014* (FIR). Their requirements are binding on food business operators (FBOs) at all stages of the supply chain, where their activities relate to the provision of food information to consumers. The aim of the new rules is to "serve the interests of the internal market by simplifying the law, ensuring legal certainty and reducing [the] administrative burden, and benefit citizens by requiring clear, comprehensible and legible labelling of foods" (FIR: Recital 9). Local authorities must enforce these regulations across the UK. In the case of infringement, an 'improvement notice' will be served in the first instance, noting the areas of 'non-compliance', and it may be necessary to remove products from sale until the terms of the notice have been satisfied. Failure to comply with an improvement notice constitutes a criminal offence, and an FBO found guilty of an offence under the FIR will be liable to a substantial fine under Section 85 of the *Legal Aid, Sentencing and Punishment of Offenders Act* (LASPO) 2012. The comprehensive nature of the legislation and uniformity of application renders it more useful, and successful, than any previous soft law initiative in this area, such as the 2006 'Guideline Daily Amount' (GDA, now Reference Intakes) scheme, or 'traffic light labelling', which was introduced by the UK government as a voluntary scheme in 2013. The current legislation also means food labels are now much clearer for consumers, with improved nutritional and allergen information. However, considerable difficulties yet remain in relation to implementing a fully informative and accurate system of food labelling, as discussed in Chapter 5.

In the context of various emergent environmental and social challenges—affecting both the natural world and built environment—such as climate change and feeding a growing world population, the relationship between, for instance, the major investors, producers, retailers and regulators is becoming more complicated. Consequently, more research is being undertaken on the broader social effects of, in particular, privately owned assets which impact on essential networks and infrastructures, with a particular focus on the legal structure and obligations of the corporation as a major infrastructure provider. According to US author and former Harvard Business School professor David Korten, companies which serve a well-defined public purpose must be subject to strict rules of public accountability; there is no legitimate reason to give "a group of private investors a legally protected right to aggregate and concentrate virtually unlimited economic power under unified management, to pursue a narrow private interest without regard to broader social and environmental consequences". He concludes that "the private-benefit corporation is an institutional anomaly, a creation of monarchy that properly shares monarchy's historic fate" (2015: 26).

Although the current position in Western legal systems is that companies have a primary 'duty of care' to their shareholders, which means profit maximization is the norm, social enterprises such as 'fair trade' companies have chosen to operate according to a social benefit model. Learning from their successes, new institutional models have been suggested which move social purpose from the periphery to the heart of the company's operations. The international, multi-stakeholder initiative *Corporation 20/20* (Raskin, 2018) is one such model and is based on the following principles:

1. The purpose of the corporation is to harness private interests to serve the public interest.
2. Corporations shall accrue fair returns for shareholders, but not at the expense of the legitimate interests of other stakeholders.
3. Corporations shall operate sustainably, meeting the needs of the present generation without compromising the ability of future generations to meet their needs.
4. Corporations shall distribute their wealth equitably amongst those who contribute to its creation.
5. Corporations shall be governed in a manner that is participatory, transparent, ethical and accountable.
6. Corporations shall not infringe on the right of natural persons to govern themselves, nor infringe on other universal human rights.

Launched in 2013, this initiative enshrines social responsibility from the founding of a company, with the aim of motivating the types of enterprises that might be better able to respond to societal challenges, such as food insecurity, nutritional poverty, climate change or protecting biodiversity. Whilst the proposal was well-received and garnered positive publicity, some years later, it remains to be enacted into law. Similar proposals have been put forward by the coalition on corporate accountability (CORE), in relation to the UK. They aim to hold corporations to account by "promoting a stronger regulatory framework, higher standards of conduct, compliance with the law, and improved access to remedy for those harmed by the activities of companies" (CORE, 2018). The coalition recently attempted to influence the scope of the updated Criminal Finances Act 2017, by calling for the introduction of a general offence of "corporate failure to prevent economic crime", which would require companies to prove they have the correct preventative procedures in place. Although this additional measure was rejected, an amendment to expand provisions of the Proceeds of Crime Act 2002 to those companies complicit in human rights abuses was successful.

All such approaches have in common the desire to hold company directors responsible for a legally sanctioned and comprehensive duty of care, which would extend beyond their obligations to shareholders to other stakeholders. They would be required to identify and take into account the circumstances of this wider group and act in a way that mitigates any destructive effects of their activities on individuals and communities that may be considered likely to be negatively impacted. A duty to report, by providing a public account of the corporation's activities and the consequences of its actions at regular intervals, would act as an aide-mémoire and may help to avoid the violation of an implied social contract. In short, if CSR and corporate governance are to combat the effects of social inequality and environmental degradation, then they must be more than simply a placebo which generates only a feeling of goodwill and fair outcomes.

In suggesting an alternative to hard or soft regulatory solutions in *The Theory of Moral Sentiments* (1759), Adam Smith argued that a feeling for justice must act as a constraint on the prioritizing of, for instance, economic activity over the welfare of individuals, maintaining that only 'kindness or beneficence' cannot "among equals, be extorted by force" (2002: 81). He further recommended that all judgement be preceded by self-reflection or moral-mirroring, which obliged an examination of

> our own conduct as we imagine any other fair and impartial spectator would imagine it. . . . It is only by consulting this judge within that we can ever make any proper comparison between our own interests and those of other people.
>
> (Smith, 2002: 128–9)

The corollary of this standpoint is that for a corporation to exercise a genuine commitment to enhancing the development and well-being of a community—of which it is a part, in geographical, economic and/or cultural terms—its directors and managers need to want to cultivate a closeness or proximity that prioritizes mutualism, co-operation and a feeling of neighbourliness.

2.9 'Proximity' via Lévinas and the Law of Tort: Social Responsibility Begins in the Neighbourhood

It is easy to forget that human actions only have meaning in the context of society, in which all members create a world of meaning. Individuals as social beings are dependent on the ideal of community, so that if actions are to have any meaning, they must be recognized by others. Since the world is shaped by everybody who lives in it, all undertakings are defined by their relationships with other projects and, therefore, the target of our ethical obligations is our neighbour—in other words, every single individual in the 'neighbourhood'. As stated in Chapter 1, in the Judeo-Christian tradition, the Holy Bible begins by identifying the people who surround us as those with whom we have a necessary and mutually binding obligation of compassionate consideration: "Love your neighbour as yourself" (Leviticus 19: 18). The New Testament parable of the Good Samaritan extends the category of 'neighbour' from a particularist definition (people like us, people close to us) to a universalist reading in which, at least in theory, neighbourly consideration is deserved by, and owed to, all human beings (Luke 10: 27–37). In the later configuration, the idea of the neighbour is neither wholly universal nor specific but is framed by proximity and includes the widest group of unknown or absent others who may be rightfully considered to be within our contemplation. The concept of proximity anticipates danger or harm to another who may be adversely affected by our actions and therefore imposes a duty of care.

The recognition of others, especially the stranger or outsider, is the opposite of single-minded self-interest and separation; rather, it is to actively display care, concern and consideration. This universal extension of consideration means the particularity of each individual—his or her economic position or social status—must be abstracted in order to apply to everyone without distinction. As Kierkegaard explains, "When you open the door . . . and go out the very first person you meet is the neighbour whom you *shall* love" (1998: 50, 51). This broadened scope of personal responsibility, which for Lévinas emerges from compassion rather than calculation, is described as an 'ethics of the Other', which is immediate, non-reciprocal, fluid, open and infinite, and as such can never be satisfied by a lukewarm commitment to an arbitrary goal (1969: 150). Endorsement of the other is an integral part, therefore, of acknowledging the political subject because our identity depends on the recognition of others to the extent that "misrecognition can inflict harm, can be a form of oppression, imprisoning someone in a false, distorted and reduced mode of being" (Shaw & Shaw, 2015: 238). This struggle for recognition continues to be "the master principle of society" because only by being granted a name, a place and a function within a group or institution can the individual hope to escape the "contingency, finitude, and ultimate absurdity of existence" (Wacquant, 2008: 264).

In recognition of the human need for belonging, for fraternity and familiarity, the corporation cleverly avoids calling itself an institution; rather, it routinely represents itself as a person, a friend or a neighbour, as fundamentally benevolent and caring. Many CSR mission and vision statements have adopted an ersatz language of mutual support, referring to themselves as 'families', such as referring to Asda UK as a member of the 'Walmart family' (Shaw, 2008: 8). At the same time, such corporations regularly behave unethically, breaching their purported familial bonds. Situated at the opposite end of the spectrum to often arbitrary laws, rules and self-serving voluntary CSR initiatives—which frequently display indifference to the suffering of others—the demand of an alertness to the endless 'call and command of the other' is impossible to evade, because of their powerlessness and vulnerability (Lévinas, 1969: 89). This raises the practical question of 'who is my neighbour'—namely, how is it possible to properly identify the class of persons towards whom a duty of care, in respect of a wider commitment to the common good of 'the neighbourhood', is owed?

The legal definition of one's neighbour is set in Lord Atkin's formulation of the 'neighbour principle', articulated in *Donoghue v Stevenson* [1932] AC 562 as

> persons who are so closely and directly affected by my act that I ought to reasonably have them in contemplation as being so affected when I am directing my mind to the acts and omissions which are called into question.

The rule which demands "you are to love your neighbour becomes in law: you must not injure your neighbour". Whilst this seemingly lesser level of obligation imposes a negative duty of restraint and abstention from harming one's neighbour, a positive duty is implied, on behalf of corporations providing essential goods and services, in the form of a wider moral obligation to take an active interest in their well-being in order to avoid the violation of an implied social contract. Later in *Donoghue v Stevenson* [1932] AC 571 Lord Macmillan made it clear that it was intended by the courts to introduce the highest standard of a duty of care:

> A person who, for gain, engages in the business of manufacturing articles of food and drink intended for consumption by members of the public in the form in which he issues them is under a duty to take care in the manufacture of these articles. That duty, in my opinion, he owes to those whom he intends to consume his products. He manufactures his commodities for human consumption; he intends and contemplates that they shall be consumed. By reason of that very fact he places himself in a relationship with all the potential consumers of his commodities, and that relationship which he assumes and desires for his own ends imposes upon him a duty to take care to avoid injuring them.

Whilst the neighbour principle has been criticized for being vague, it remains the cornerstone of English tort law of negligence. Following *Donoghue*, an additional two-stage test was acknowledged in *Anns v Merton London Borough Council* [1978] AC 728, where it became necessary to ascertain a "sufficient relationship of proximity or neighbourhood" and whether there was 'reasonable foreseeability' or a lack of 'reasonable contemplation of harm' or 'carelessness' as to the likelihood of causing harm to the injured party. Just over a decade later, in *Caparo Industries plc v Dickman* [1990] 2 AC 605, a further three-stage test was proposed. It was decided that, as well as 'proximity' and 'reasonable foresight of harm', the 'fairness, justice and reasonableness' of the imposition of a duty of care should be considered alongside the application of the traditional neighbour principle. When determining whether a duty of care exists in a given situation, the courts can use their discretion as to whether to admit public policy considerations and drive the further evolution of the tort of negligence accordingly.

The consequence of neoliberal policies on international competition above all other considerations has permitted corporations free access to most world markets, enabling them to eliminate or take over competing businesses. The issue of unfair commercial practices and unequal bargaining power between retailers and suppliers, therefore, is an area of ongoing concern. A variety of remedial measures have been implemented, including the use of contract law, self-regulation, private standards, audits and certification schemes. Within the context of international competition law, for example, Article 102 of the *Treaty on the Functioning of the European Union* creates the offence of abuse of a dominant position, yet few European countries have imposed financial penalties. As discussed in Chapter 1, in most developed countries, only a small number of supermarket chains enjoy almost complete market oligopoly. The tort law system, however, already performs a key scrutinizing role where there are, for example, significant public health risks, such as the harmful exposure to toxic substances, unsafe pharmaceuticals, vaccines and medical devices, defective consumer goods and hazardous substances, such as tobacco. By awarding substantial compensatory and punitive damages—such as in the recent US case against Monsanto in which the San Francisco jury awarded $289 million (£226 million) to former school groundsman Dewayne Johnson who was diagnosed with non-Hodgkin's lymphoma after many years of using 'Roundup' weed-killer—the court has the capacity to redress a wide range of different public harms (Bellon, 2018).

As discussed earlier, food policy and the supply chain is an area of growing concern in the 21st century, especially as the existing food regime appears to be undergoing a period of transition. For example, the new political economy of food—globalization, financialization and industrialization of the food system—has resulted in produce which is less food-like due to *inter alia* intensive growing processes, bio-engineering and genetic modification. Although such changes raise important issues relating to the health and safety of our food supply and affect everyone, higher and volatile food prices have impacted most of all on the poorest in society. With the pending merger between agrichemical conglomerates Bayer AG and Monsanto, and the rise of digital and data-based farming, it is likely that currently independent farmers will be subject to mass data collection and coerced into producing chemically sensitive monocultures to the detriment of biodiversity in the food supply chain. Together, these companies control around 80% of the global vegetable seed market, and a major concern is that the merger will also cause food prices to escalate and put small family farmers out of business.

Clearly, the largely unlimited power of large corporations to control is simultaneously the power to dissemble, reimagine and exclude (Shaw &

Shaw, 2016: 38). In the UK grocery retail sector, a small group of large companies exert immense power over their supply chains, which has led to unethical terms and conditions being imposed on a weakened supply base, and subsequent claims of misuse of power. Legislation, such as the Groceries Code Adjudicator Act (GCA) 2013, has been introduced to address some of these concerns and to curb corporate behaviour which undermines upstream suppliers and acts against the long-term interests of the consumer. However, such measures are still only imposed ad hoc and in specific areas of corporate activity. Yet the broad and all-encompassing nature of the three-stage test, and associated punishments, means the 'duty of care' concept in tort law has the capacity to act as a powerful disincentive to companies that would disregard the wider societal consequences of their behaviour. It is suggested that it may be formally adapted as an extended, broadly conceived statutory measure (which intersects with company and international law) to support and monitor the implementation and delivery of CSR promises. In this way, it would be possible to hold private enterprises responsible across the entire range of their activities—particularly when these relate to the production of public goods such as social goods—so they can be held accountable, both legally and morally.

2.10 Can There Ever Be a Human Right to Healthy Food?

The alarming reality and grave conclusion, revealed by recent statistics, is that poverty and particularly food poverty—including food insecurity and nutritional poverty—is not just on the rise but, in some communities, has become the norm. In the wealthiest societies, almost half of Americans have experienced, or will experience, a prolonged period of poverty at some point in their lives. In the current climate of austerity, welfare reforms, poor employment prospects and rising food and fuel costs, the growing use of food banks by middle-class families in the UK, for example, means that charitable trusts are under increasing pressure. They are having to assist more and more people each week in response to an unprecedented upsurge in the need for emergency food aid, and as Lambie-Mumford and Dowler have pointed out, "there is no sign that increasing uptake in food aid is abating" (2014: 1422). That food poverty exists in developed nations, such as the US and the UK, has not only been a major cause for alarm, but indicates the failure of a complex interplay of social, economic, political, planning, cultural and educational influences.

The response to the urban food crisis—via ad hoc CSR initiatives, food bank collection boxes, recipe advice on healthy eating and clear labelling of high sugar and fat foods, and similar contributions by other actors from voluntary and NGOs—is often uncoordinated, limited to particular locales and time-bound. Such initiatives frequently offer merely temporary transient sticking plaster solutions and fail to address the more serious, complex, wide-reaching and systemic nature of the urban food insecurity, poor nutrition and associated ill-health problems. The enormous and multifaceted task of attempting to ameliorate the current healthy food crisis presents something of a financial hurdle in this era of globalization and centrally imposed austerity measures. It is suggested, however, that crisis situations often present the perfect opportunity to experiment with fundamentally different models in such areas as social innovation, progressive policies and public-social alliances, and should not deter the development of new partnerships and novel regulatory frameworks.

After all, access to healthy food is more than just a privilege; it is a right that ought to apply to every individual so that he or she is able to function, flourish and fully participate in all aspects of social life. In Boswell's 1791 *Life of Samuel Johnson*, the famous essayist, literary historian and cultural critic is quoted as saying, "Where a great proportion of the people are suffered to languish in helpless misery, that country must be ill policed and wretchedly governed: a decent provision for the poor is the true test of civilization" (Boswell, 2008: 446). In relation to urban food access and dietary requirements, neglecting the needs of disadvantaged socio-economic groups is producing a generation of people who are malnourished and food insecure. If governments are to be perceived as civilized and civilizing forces, they must take a holistic approach to addressing the underlying and systemic economic and social injustices which produce inequality, and undertake an appropriately nuanced and reflexive approach to confronting the causes of those inequalities. This requires a coordinated, determined and sustained approach which looks to reform the urban food system at the local level—in terms of accessibility, availability and affordability—and at the more complex level of interaction and collaboration with producers, suppliers, retailers and consumers.

It is not by the application of soft and hard laws, CSR initiatives or via the application of reason or abstract universal principles alone that we may respond to what Emmanuel Lévinas refers to as 'the call of the other'; rather, the voluntary assumption of responsibility for another by an institution and its CEO and chief operating officers in respect of those interests for which they might 'rightfully' assume responsibility is only possible after eliciting the right motivation. Finding a solution that upholds and protects a broader set of public interests—specifically in relation to the human right to healthy food—depends upon a commitment to producing novel methodologies, ideas, carefully formulated hypotheses and, most importantly, a comprehensive and inclusive plan of action. Such theories and policies for social transformation must be both broad in scope and sufficiently detailed to be practicable. This would be achieved, in the first instance, by liaising with local communities, voluntary agencies, 'local' retailers and researchers—those already in close proximity to, and having a vested interest in, the most representative group of 'neighbour' stakeholders—in order to reveal and map the complex interrelationships between food, diet, health and their environments. Only by engaging in the widest possible participatory exercise and reflecting on the urban locale in novel, material and cultural ways is it possible to uncover new directions in understanding, framing and tackling the modern phenomena of food deserts, nutritional poverty and food injustice. The following chapters will address the performance of the major supermarkets—in the UK and elsewhere—in the specific areas of society, employment and the economy, the environment, food suppliers, the local community and consumer health.

3   Food Retailing, Society and the Economy

3.1 From Laissez-Faire to Planning Regulations

In 19th-century Britain, there was little attention given to the externalities caused by retailing. There was a laissez-faire attitude towards houses being converted into shops; anyone who wanted to turn his or her residential premises into a sales area could simply do just that, with no intervention from the authorities (Davis, 1966: 300). These house to shop conversions gave us the old inner city landscape of small convenience stores on street corners and the ribbons of comparison goods shops along arterial routes out of cities, where the shop is a flat-roofed, ground-floor extension over what was the front garden, with the original 18th-century house some yards back. The term 'shop' derives from the German 'schuppe', meaning a workshop where goods were made, and before the Industrial Revolution, these goods would have been sold at periodic fairs in town centres. The Industrial Revolution, and its predecessor the (Second) Agricultural Revolution, produced a large shift of population from the countryside to the city. There they no longer produced their own food from rural smallholdings and, living in cramped terraced housing, entered a fully monetised economy where all their basic needs were bought for cash from their factory wages. It was the proliferation of crowded insanitary terraced housing that helped start the concept of urban planning, with the planned Garden Cities of Letchworth and Welwyn, and the construction of 'Homes for Heroes' after the First World War.

After 1914, there was an increasing recognition that shops create externalities, such as traffic congestion, both through customer visits and deliveries. The increasing scale of shops, especially the food retailers described earlier (Chapter 1), resulted in them moving off High Street into out-of-town centre retail parks and large stand-alone suburban supermarket sites. They have since 2006 moved into smaller Express and Local sites, usually not newbuilds like the supermarkets were, but conversions from other commercial premises. These moves have entailed a number of planning and economic issues. The sheer size of a supermarket implies considerable car and delivery lorry traffic, also other externalities that may annoy neighbouring householders, such as car park lighting, long opening hours extending well into the evening or even 24-hour trading and noise from trolleys being moved. Supermarkets also have a considerable visual impact, with tall corporate logo signs advertising their presence; they want to be seen over as large an area as possible. Economically, supermarkets can become wage setters for the area, often forcing wages downwards because many supermarket jobs are low-skilled, or have been deskilled. They can also drastically alter the retail composition of nearby shopping areas, often denuding the High Street of butchers, greengrocers, fishmongers and the like, in their place come sandwich bars, takeaways, hair and beauty shops, vape shops and betting shops. In some areas, food retailing may continue if there is a large ethnic minority population, but with a somewhat altered range of foods on sale.

The planning system is essentially about balancing competing community and neighbour interests against the desire of the landowner to make the maximum economic return on his or her land; economic development should also create returns for the nation in terms of tax revenue, but the local community may not perceive any benefit from this. The balance of community interests for and against a new supermarket will vary with every planning application, as all communities and locales are unique. On the one hand, this gives supermarkets a great opportunity to show their social responsibility credentials by tailoring every proposed supermarket, its design and product range to the needs of the neighbourhood. On the other hand, it massively shifts the balance of power towards the supermarket, because every site and neighbourhood is unique, lessons from resisting or modifying one planning application may not easily transfer to another, whereas the supermarket simply wants to insert yet another similarly designed large shed and car park. However, a major problem with this 'balancing' is the David and Goliath imbalance of power of any opposition to the supermarkets; Tesco and Walmart are amongst the largest companies in the world, versus local communities and town councils. This is one fight where Goliath often wins.

3.2 Behemoths Versus Boroughs

The large size of a supermarket corporation gives it several advantages in any battle for planning permission. In the UK, as in many countries, there is an oligopoly of just a few large supermarket chains, but there are hundreds of local authorities. The supermarkets have vastly more resources, in terms of money, legal expertise and even time. A supermarket can grind on with repeated applications whilst the local authority cannot be seen to be wasting local taxpayers' money with continual planning enquiries, perhaps even delaying the arrival of a large employer. The local government may also have a much shorter lifespan than the supermarket; it can be voted out whilst the supermarket endures. It does not look good electorally if the local authority seems to privilege the concerns of the wealthy, such as the environment and house values, when the (more numerous) less-affluent voters would appreciate more local jobs and retail facilities within walking distance. Time is also on the supermarket's side in another way; once a supermarket is in place, people come to use it, the opposition dies down, people move away and the community may become accustomed to what it once vehemently opposed.

The planning system also falls into disrepute if it means retail premises stand empty rather than generating jobs, facilities and taxes. There is a perpetual conflict within the planning system between having the categories too broad or too narrow. If too broad, it becomes easy to change the use of a retail premise in a way some in the community may find undesirable: a pub to a Tesco Express, for example, or a convenience store to an undertaker. If the categories are too narrow, retail premises become boarded up and vandalized, and may blight the entire High Street in which they stand, whilst the community is deprived of a retail outlet. In Hadliegh, Essex, for example, Tesco applied for planning permission in 1998 and again in 2004 and 2006. A fourth application in 2010 was turned down by Babergh Council by one vote, on the grounds of 'poor design'; Tesco then made a fifth application in 2012, although by now a large Morrison had been built near the town centre. In 2013, the application was still being pursued, although to date (2018), Tesco has not managed to open a store there. However, Paris has made extensive use of planning restrictions to keep small food shops, the traditional *boulangeries* and *boucheries*, from becoming mobile phone shops. Many older retail premises in that city have clauses to ensure that successive shopkeepers can only sell 'similar products' to the previous operator, a measure approved by the Paris city council in 2005. Of course, Paris has a thriving tourist industry, whose income generation can help pay for the preservation of the traditional shops of the city.

Supermarkets can also utilize their massive resources to persuade councils to grant planning permission through so-called Planning Gain, also known as the Grampian Condition. This term derives from Scottish legal case law; in a case entitled *Grampian Regional Council* v *City of Aberdeen District Council* (1984), it was established that planning permission could be made conditional on the applicant completing certain works beneficial to the community on land that was not theirs. Such works might include improvements to a local park or the road system, or enhancement of a local nature reserve. In Newport, Shropshire, Redrow Homes promised a large grant towards the restoration of the local canal if they were granted permission for some 80 homes north of the town (this application was refused in 2017 after local objections). The practice is also known as a Section 106 Agreement, after the relevant clause Section 106 of the Town and Country Planning Act 1990.

Depending on one's perspective, Planning Gain is either a useful trade-off between the private gains a large corporate applicant would make and the development the community needs, a useful means of getting companies to fund local improvements that would not otherwise have been done, or it is straightforward bribery. The background question of why the government cannot fund the improvements local people want is seldom asked of course. In Hay on Wye, a small market town on the Wales-England border, Gaufron Developments applied in 2012 to build a new supermarket on the site of the old primary school, which was still using 'temporary' buildings erected in 1974 with an expected 20-year lifespan. In return, Gaufron would build a new primary school on what was then the playing fields. Opponents of the supermarket, fearing the erosion of Hay's small independent shop sector, asked why the town should have to accept this development, when the local people had already paid their taxes, which were supposed to fund, *inter alia*, a new school for Hay's children. On the other side of the debate, the less-affluent side, people wanted the new jobs, better access to the range of food a supermarket would bring and the new school buildings too. The outcry over why Hay should have to depend on Tesco for the overdue refurbishment of its primary school was resolved in 2015 when Powys Council did promise to rebuild the school, which is now been accomplished (Hereford Times, 2015). Hay on Wye, with its 1,700 people, remains without a major supermarket beyond its Spar shop in the centre and a co-operative supermarket about half a mile out of town, probably beyond walking distance for many older consumers or mothers with small children.

Supermarkets can also apply for planning permission under another name, exploiting the fact that planning permission is for 'use', not 'user'; it cannot discriminate between business operators. The big UK supermarkets, especially the largest, Tesco, correctly suspect that their arrival may be resisted in certain areas because of their reputation (similar to Walmart in the US) for mass enterprisicide of local retail businesses. In the London Borough of Barnet, Tesco used a nominee company, Carpets 4 Less, to apply to Barnet Council for permission to operate a retail premises there. Barnet Council suspected that Tesco was behind the Carpets 4 Less application and gave permission in 2005, but only for carpet retailing there. In 2007, Tesco then appealed the decision, asking for change of use to A1 (all retailing permitted). Tesco claim Carpets 4 Less was only ever given a short-term lease on the site Tesco bought in December 2004 (a former car showroom) to "stop the site becoming derelict". In 2010, a highly politicized row broke out in Stokes Croft, a Bohemian inner suburb of Bristol, UK, when Tesco applied for permission to open a retail premises under the front name of 'Jesters', which was ostensibly a comedy club, to occupy what had been six smaller premises on Cheltenham Road. Local concerns included the large food delivery lorries making frequent deliveries on the congested urban road, which would not happen with a comedy club as well as the threat to the numerous independent food retailers in the area. The local Green Party councillor said the arrival of Tesco was like "putting a Whisky World in the middle of a Muslim area" (Shaw, 2014: 79). The Guardian took the analogy further, saying, "If Tesco is a Whisky World, then the local mosque can be found in the headquarters of the 'People's Republic of Stokes Croft' ". The battle for retail market share in a suburb of a British provincial city had now escalated in simile to a global cultural clash. In early 2011, protestors from a nearby squat occupied and destroyed the new Tesco Express; the police were called in and found themselves confronted by a large anti-Tesco group. In May 2011, the Tesco Express reopened; it had to, or 'the mob' would have triumphed over a global corporation. The area still features a mural close to the Tesco, saying, "Think Local, Boycott Tesco". Advertising the protestors website, which advertises one product Tesco are unlikely ever to stock a 'Tesco Value Petrol Bomb'. Even anarchists can adopt modern information and communications technology.

3.3 Supermarket Land Banks

As any property buyer will know, the presence of immaterial attributes such as planning permission can add considerable value to any real estate. If land processes are rising rapidly, as they were in the UK in 2000, it makes commercial sense to buy the land sooner rather than wait until it is actually needed. Aside from adding to the total value of the corporation, and hence its share price, supermarkets have a further incentive to buy land and secure planning permission for it long before they have any intention of actually constructing a store there; this land is then blocked for use by any competitor. By the early 21st century, suitable sites within the UK where it was possible to build a large supermarket, with the necessary roads and a suitable catchment population, and not in an area where urban development would be problematical because of, for example, Green Belt restrictions, had become scarce and valuable assets to the retail industry. In 2013, Tesco stated the value of its property holdings as £20 million.

In the early 2010s, the scale of land holdings, or land banks as it was termed, became disturbing to some, with Tesco reported in 2014 as holding 4.6 million square metres of land it had no retail premises on (Guardian, 2014a). This land comprised 310 separate sites, which were reckoned to be capable of hosting 15,000 new homes, at a time when the affordability of housing to many younger people was very problematical. Some of this land was 'invisible' as a land bank; it remained in use as agricultural land, leased to a farmer; however, some comprised unsightly inner-city brownfield sites where the community had been promised a supermarket, yet the land remained as a derelict eyesore, attracting squatters, vermin and vandalism, an unused resource in the busy centre of a town. In one highly publicized case, Tesco bought a large prominent disused hospital site near the centre of Wolverhampton, UK, in 2001. This was the former Royal Hospital, just south-east of Wolverhampton centre, which had closed in 1997. Meanwhile, Sainsbury wanted to move from a smaller site on St Georges Parade, Wolverhampton, dating from 1988, and develop another large brownfield site to the west of the town centre; Wolverhampton councillors believed that the area 'only had room for' one major supermarket, without damaging the central retailing area. Then in 2004, Sainsbury's dropped its plans for Raglan Street, and Tesco did the same for the Royal Hospital site in 2005. This was at a time of rapid transformation within the UK supermarket industry, with the rapid growth and penetration upmarket of the Aldi and Lidl chains, and growth of both online grocery shopping and a shift by households towards 'little and often' last-minute frequent small shops. The concept of large sheds where households would come every one or two weeks for major purchases was beginning to look a little outdated. Tesco subsequently tried to obtain the Raglan Road site and shut Sainsbury's out altogether, until a Supreme Court ruling that stated city councillors acted unlawfully when opting for Tesco. In 2014, Sainsbury's finally opened their Raglan Street superstore, with their former St George's Parade site still standing empty in 2017. Tesco's story was less happy; in 2014, it reaffirmed its intention to develop the hospital site, opening by 2016, but months later in January 2015 pulled out again. This was at a time of scandals and crisis for Tesco with falling market share, troubles over misstated profits and horsemeat contamination of its ready meals, and bad publicity over mistreatment of its suppliers. Tesco was retrenching, closing some stores and ceasing to operate 24 hours a day at others, whilst consumer demand was weakened by the ongoing Credit Crunch. The hospital site saga finally looked to be drawing to a close in 2017 with plans confirmed to build houses on the site, having stood empty for no less than 20 years. A significant part of the blame for such an eyesore having persisted just outside Wolverhampton for so long was laid with Tesco.

Bridgewater, Somerset, and Kirkby, Liverpool, are two further sites where Tesco has pulled out, leaving a large void in the urban fabric; often, the demolition is done, and then the new supermarket plans are cancelled, potentially denying the town a building which could have found other uses, although the St George's Parade and Royal Hospital sites in Wolverhampton lay empty and undeveloped for years despite still standing. In Bridgewater, the Sedgemoor Council received £5.3 million compensation from Tesco for pulling out of the redevelopment plans. In Newport, Shropshire, Telford and Wrekin Council lost £1.2 million on surveys done in anticipation of a Sainsbury store being built just south of the town, which was cancelled in 2015 as an Aldi, and later a Lidl, arrived there; the council may recoup some of these losses if, as with the

Royal Hospital, the site is developed for residential use instead. Supermarkets do not, of course, hold idle land just for spite; they are attempting to maximize profits, now and into a future that is always uncertain. The social dilemma is when there is a better societal use for that land now, especially for affordable housing in early 21st-century Britain, but the supermarket may wish not to sell just yet. The hoarding of land principally to deny retail development opportunities to competitors is private profit maximizing but also societally controversial. Hoarding of vacant land by supermarkets may occur because land prices are weak at a certain point, or because the hoped-for physical supermarket expansion is still anticipated. Some supermarket banked land is unsuitable for housing, as it may be at the side of existing supermarkets that could be extended, or in the middle of commercial retail parks. In 2013, Tesco did begin to sell off some surplus land holdings, a move that forced a write-down in values of £804 million and contributed to a fall in pre-tax profits of over 50% to £1.96 billion (Felsted, 2013).

A variation of land hoarding is when supermarkets choose to make an existing retail space they no longer require unattractive to any potential competitor. The simplest method is to demolish the store before the site is sold, possibly with a covenant restricting any re-erection of a large store there. In 2007, Tesco acquired a former co-operative store in Slough and traded from it whilst it was refurbishing another Tesco store a mile away. When it moved trading back into the refurbished Tesco it demolished the Co-op. The Office of Fair Trading ordered Tesco to rebuild the shop, but instead, Tesco erected five smaller units there, too small to appeal to any competing food supermarket chain. In Linwood, Scotland, there was a combination of premises degradation and applications under a false name. Here in 2001, a firm called Balmore Properties bought Linwood town centre shopping precinct and then allowed all the existing shops to move out without issuing any new leases; the precinct became so run-down it was nicknamed 'Scotland's Basra' (after a city in Iraq heavily fought over during the Allied invasion of Iraq in 2003). Then in 2007, Tesco bought the precinct from Balmore Properties and promised to redevelop it. Tesco even set up a website, www.lovelinwood.com (this website now defunct). However, Balmore and Tesco were closely linked from the beginning, with Balmore being set up by a law firm run by Tesco; Balmore was wound down shortly after the 2007 sale. Linwood was already a deprived area after the job losses caused by the closure of the Hillman Imp car factory back in 1963, but things became worse after the Balmore acquisition of 2001, and now Tesco got the credit for rescuing it as a shiny new Tesco superstore. Today, excepting an Asda superstore on an out-of-town retail park site towards Paisley, Tesco enjoys a virtual monopoly of retailing for the 9,500 residents of Linwood. Similarly, in 2009, the Australian Competition and Consumer Commission had to outlaw the exclusive leasing agreements used by Coles and Woolworths, which prohibited shopping centres from leasing space to competitors (Keith, 2012: 63). Urban demographic changes may work to shield the supermarkets from repercussions as they abandon inner city areas for wealthier catchment area suburban and out-of-town locales; the old inner city location may have an older less-educated population, along with higher crime rates and morbidity levels and lower rates of car ownership (Cameron et al, 2010). The local population is less likely to be able to successfully challenge the supermarkets' actions and to try and overturn any restrictive covenant placed on the vacated premises so they can have a supermarket again. The departing supermarket leaves the area 'food-desolated', and this attracts drug users and other illegal activities, precipitating the neighbourhood into a further spiral of decline.

The supermarkets are not the biggest land-hoarders in Britain; that distinction belongs to the major house builders, who have attracted opprobrium for slowing down the completion of houses and their release onto the market, so as not to depress the price. However, the Labour Party has threatened to legislate against land banking, with proposals ranging from taxes to enforced sales to even confiscation. A Land Value Tax could be imposed, to compensate the community for the expense of, for example, maintaining roads and street lighting to retail park sites that lie undeveloped. Undeveloped sites also create environmental and health costs. Empty spaces in cities force people to travel further to the next facility; the ugliness of such sites means they will probably not walk to cover this extra distance and missing food retail sites help to create 'food deserts', areas where fresh healthy produce is hard to access for the less well off with limited transport options. An unsightly urban landscape can create an 'obesogenic environment', where exercise such as walking is unattractive, or unsafe, and people drive to cover even short distances. It is better if inner urban sites can be converted into a mix of retail and residential, promoting walking along tree-lined streets to the shops, school or work. However, even once a promised supermarket has been built, there may still be planning problems if, as has happened in the past, the supermarket departs from the conditions of what was agreed—a scenario not unknown in the world of residential planning either. These departures and illicit variations are now discussed next.

3.4 Other Supermarket Planning Issues

Planners are keen, as noted earlier, to keep the amount of new supermarket space being developed below a certain level so as not to outcompete existing town centre retailing and cause mass closures there. In Wolverhampton, councillors only wanted one supermarket adjacent to the shopping core of the town. Once agreement is reached to put a supermarket on a certain site, it may come with strict size limitations. Several countries have legal floor area limitations on new supermarkets. In

1998, Ireland limited them to 3,000 square metres, later relaxed to 3,500 square metres in the Dublin area, France's Loi Royer (1973) and Loi Raffarrin (1996) limited them to 1,000 square metres, or 1,500 square metres in towns of population over 4,000, and Japans' Large-Scale Retail Stores Law of 1973was very restrictive, curbing any retail developments of over 500 square metres. Supermarkets, however, are keen to gain more economies of scale by enlarging their floor area, also widening the range of goods they sell and outcompeting both independent shops and other supermarket rivals. Since planning permission did not specify any restrictions on internal alterations once the supermarket was built there were two common loopholes once exploited by UK supermarkets to gain extra sales space.

The first loophole was the mezzanine floor. Many new supermarkets were built with very high ceilings, perhaps 10 metres above the floor. This wasn't just to create an air of spaciousness within the store, but to facilitate the later insertion of an extra floor, the so-called mezzanine floor. This could nearly double the floor sales area. The second trick was to design the supermarket with an unnecessarily large warehouse area. Supermarkets have enthusiastically adopted the Japanese kan-ban, or 'just-in-time' system of deliveries, and have invested considerable amounts in sales-predictive IT and sophisticated weather forecasts to ensure they don't have to keep much spare stock at the back of the shop. Soon after opening, the warehouse would be remodelled to convert most of it to new sales space. For example, in Stockport, Manchester, Tesco got permission for a 9,430 square metre store but then built one 1,665 square metres bigger and retrospectively applied for permission for that. Tesco claimed the extra space was for warehousing, not retail (but this would be easy to convert to retail at a later date). These loopholes were closed in 2003 when alterations materially extending the retail sales area of a supermarket by more than 10% were proscribed. Another tactic to get around the reluctance of planners to grant planning permission to large new supermarkets, because they feared the competition effect on existing retail areas, was to apply to build a small store, with a large number of car park spaces. Later on, an extension to that small store over the car park could be applied for (Blythman, 2004: 29).

In other supermarket violations of planning permission, Southampton City Council halted construction work on a new Tesco Express in Butts Road, Southampton, a conversion from the former Bullseye public house. The store had been given planning permission but without a trolley rack, which would have caused a noise nuisance to the neighbouring houses; Tesco built the rack anyway, also installing a cash machine, which hadn't been permitted and would have attracted more car parking. Although the Express store has a small car park, Butts Road is a busy residential road and increased traffic flow would be dangerous. The issue of small but significant infractions of planning permission by new supermarkets has vanished from the media in recent years; the only supermarkets still opening new premises to any great extent are Aldi and Lidl, who seem always to have been careful to stay within the law. Or perhaps their standardized no frills premises, generally lacking extra features like cashpoints, tend not to incur departures from planning permission anyway. However, a new era in supermarket development could yet cause disputes with neighbours, who may be about to see their local supermarket dramatically rise in height.

After a period of stability in the 1980s and '90s, the UK population has been rising, due to increased immigration, from 57 million in 1990 to over 66 million in 2018. Even with a declining birth rate and Brexit, the UK population is expected to reach the 75 million mark sometime in the mid-21st century. This is the equivalent of another city the size of London, and if we are not to cover more countryside with houses and roads, we must build upwards. People are living longer, and more people are living alone, which further raises the number of homes required, and this is one need the supermarkets are tapping into. Supermarkets are essentially flat single storey (or at most two levels) with a large car park that sits unused for a considerable number of hours a week. The airspace above these premises can be utilized for housing especially cheaper flats, for smaller accommodation suited to single people. An early example of this was at Poole, Dorset, where in a case of Planning Gain the Asda gained building permission by including plans for 64 social housing units above the store.

In one sense, this is just a continuation from the suburban housing estates on the edge of larger towns where the retailing essentially consists of one large supermarket and possibly a few smaller shops in an associated parade; the Tesco Extra in Bar Hill, Cambridge, or the Tesco in Edenthorpe, Doncaster, are good examples of this. In turn, such settlements are essentially 'consumption towns', a 20th-century version of the Victorian 'production towns' like Saltaire or Bourneville, erected with a single employer, a textile mill or chocolate factory, at their centre. It is also a reinvention of the old High Street model of shops at street level with houses above. However, the new housing constructions over supermarkets are likely to be on a very different scale from even the Poole Asda; the Guardian (2014b) carried a picture of the Tesco in Woolwich, south-east London, which is the height of a nine-storey building with 'hundreds of flats' above. Overall, it has been estimated that supermarkets on London alone could host an extra 150,000 homes above if all the 'air rights' above these shops were fully exploited, and in Battersea, the Sainsbury's has partnered with Barratt to build 750 homes plus a new London Underground station (Spittles, 2017). Supermarkets can be rebuilt with flats above, or these flats can be put on stilts above the car park. The more innovative 'beds and sheds' developments include gardens, gyms and leisure centres. Lidl, in 2018, is considering mixed-use developments above its stores, including houses, student accommodation, offices, hotels and even schools (Hipwell, 2018). The store, of course, benefits from a (literally) built-in pool of customers; if the store owns the site it also makes a large return on the flats themselves. The store logo will also be raised higher and visible from much further away. However, if the store is on the edge of town, there are likely to be objections from nearby householders finding themselves overlooked by a new large residential high-rise development. This type of residential development is relatively new and disputes involving light, privacy and visual intrusion probably have yet to emerge.

Supermarkets produce a range of visual and auditory intrusions on the landscape, and are aware of the damage that bad publicity can do to their market share and profits. As discussed in Chapter 1, supermarket development can clash with the community's desire to preserve old historical features such as the old Hovis sign above a conversion to a Tesco Express in Hampshire, or the noise and congestion caused by lorry deliveries. The logistics of fresh just-in-time deliveries, 24-hour opening and Internet order pickers operating at slack times, late at night, may disturb neighbouring householders with the noise and lights of lorries. Acoustic fencing may be installed, but this too is unsightly and may block light and views. In more affluent areas where opposition is likely to be louder and better-organized, the supermarkets make great efforts to preserve local features. In the wealthy London suburb of Richmond on Thames, a new Tesco Express abjured its usual garish blue and red logo for a muted grey and white colour scheme, and incorporated art-deco logos in the shop window and a small 'museum window' commemorating the building's former use, because it occupied the site of a grade-2 listed art-deco café, Mattiae Café and Bakery, which had been vacant for seven years before Tesco moved in in 2015. In fact, the Tesco has become a minor tourist attraction in its own right, attracting business to other nearby retailers. In other locations, less affluent, the population is not only less well-resourced for mounting an objection but may also be more mobile; neighbours change quickly, and the newcomers may accept what was already there before they arrived. In this case, the supermarket can get by with a more profit-oriented, less socially responsible, solution.

3.5 Respect for Other Nations' Laws and Culture

Supermarkets may also be guilty of flouting laws and ignoring customs in other countries, a situation which frequently arises because of inadequate appreciation of the different culture prevailing in a target country from the country of origin of the supermarket chain. In turn, these differences often originate in the very different history of the target country. Henry Ford may have famously said that 'history is bunk'; however, ignoring history can cost companies very dearly when entering other countries.

China, for example, insists that Western companies entering its market do so via a joint venture (JV) operation with a Chinese partner—a requirement due at least in part to China's mistreatment by Western powers in the 19th century as they underwent the humiliation of the Opium Wars and the Unequal Treaties. However, some Western supermarkets have tried to ignore this JV requirement. In 2001, Carrefour was found by the Chinese authorities to be operating all its 27 Chinese stores with 100% Carrefour ownership and in Carrefour was forced to sell 35% of the ownership to a Chinese partner to comply with local JV laws (Zhen, 2007: 145). Carrefour was also careless with its stock control in China, for example, selling bread with three different sell-by date labels on the same pack that was in any case beyond human consumption and was also found to be selling fake CDs. These errors cost Carrefour over a year's delay in further store openings in China.

Crucial cultural differences may also appear in countries much closer to the home culture of the supermarket. In 1997, Walmart started to expand into Germany. On the surface, Germany has many similarities with the USA, both are Western-affluent developed capitalist countries with high levels of car and other consumer goods ownership and an established supermarket shopping tradition. However, Walmart became almost a textbook example of how not to do international expansion by ignoring local culture and preferences. Walmart failed to take account of the strong environmental movement in Germany, a national attribute arising from their love for the forested mountain regions of the country. The USA also has large forested regions; what the USA has not got is the historical reasons for this forest-affection; the defeat of invading Romans in the Teutoberger Forest and the alarm over 'waldsterben' (forest-death) in 1970s Germany due to acid rain from power stations burning low-quality sulphurous coal. German environmentalism translated, for Walmart, into an aversion for large out-of-town sheds attracting largely car-borne shoppers, and this limited their expansion and economies of scale in Germany. Another German cultural attribute is fear of inflation, this dating from a more recent historical event, the hyperinflation of the 1920s that indirectly contributed to the rise of Hitler. Germans also like to store cheap tinned foods with long shelf lives, a further legacy of the war period. This is one reason why Germany was the place of origin of the highly successful international deep discount chains Aldi and Lidl. Walmart discovered that its costlier fresh food could not compete with these established discounters, especially on their home turf.

Furthermore, Walmart tried to impose, rather heavily, a US corporate culture on German workers. This included having all board meetings conducted in English, not so popular in a country that had lost a world war to a mainly English-speaking alliance just 50 years earlier. German managerial staff who had transferred from chains like Interspar or Werkauf found Walmart to be considerably meaner than their past employer with travel expenses, even asking senior managers to share hotel rooms. Whilst Walmart was concerned that German managers were paid higher than their US counterparts, the German managers felt Walmart was underpaying them. The company also tried to distance itself from trade unions, in contrast to the German culture of co-operation between managers and workers, and Walmart found itself beset by strikes and frequently being found to have acted illegally by withholding information from the unions. Walmart tried to make in-depth inspections on conditions at its suppliers' premises, a practice not generally acceptable in Germany. The company banned gift giving between staff and alienated customers by instituting a 'meet and greet policy', which German shoppers found intrusive and annoying; customers also resented the 'baggers', preferring to bag their own groceries, and resenting paying for such unwanted 'service'. Walmart also tried to ban 'flirting' between staff members, ostensibly to protect them from sexual harassment; in 2005, this ban was judged to be a breach of human rights by a court in Wuppertal. Perhaps most cringingly of all, Walmart staff were expected to participate every morning in the Walmart company cheer, "Gimme a W, Gimme an A, an L, a squiggly, an M, an A, an R, a T. Whaddya get?". Some employees even hid in the toilet so as to avoid what they saw as an excruciating daily ritual (Patel, 2012: 240).

In 2006, Walmart finally exited Germany, selling its remaining 85 stores there to Metro, having lost US$ 1 billion on the whole venture. Germany had been exposed to considerable bad publicity about Walmart, including a film released at the Berlin Film Festival entitled "Walmart: the High Cost of Low Price", and by then, anti-US sentiment was growing in Europe over the Gulf War. Walmart cannot be held to blame for US military policy in the Middle East, but in many other respects, its large loss in Germany was down to a string of cultural errors that could, for the most part, have easily been avoided. Supermarkets may fail at competing in other countries due to failure to appreciate the indigenous culture. In the domestic market, they may attract bad publicity for competing too well and driving other shops out of business. In purely business terms, this is what companies are supposed to do, outcompete their rivals, but sometimes the supermarkets do this too well, and we tend to dislike monopolies, especially in fundamental goods such as food.

3.6 Supermarkets and Competition With Other Retailers

Supermarkets, with their wide range of goods, food and non-food, present rigorous competition to nearby retailers in a broad range of sectors. This threat to smaller shops from supermarkets comes in two forms; firstly, directly through selling the same goods as High Street shops (but often cheaper due to huge economies of scale). This range of goods has now expanded to include clothing and coffee retailing so that even local coffee shops may lose business to supermarket cafés. For example, some High Street cafés have complained that Waitrose's cafés are damaging their livelihood, although this has been disputed, with high shop rents and other business factors also blamed. However, the upmarket north-west English supermarket chain Booths had a CSR policy of not opening in-store coffee shops where this might cause the closure of High Street cafés. Waitrose, since it instituted a free coffee policy for *My Waitrose* cardholders in 2014, has become one of the UK's largest coffee retailers and represents considerable competition to High Street cafés.[1] Secondly, unrelated High Street business may suffer, even if they sell goods and services unavailable in the supermarket, as footfall on the High Street declines. Ironmongers and clothing repair shops, for example, suffer as the old retail centre depopulates. A further risk to these small shops is the social degradation of the traditional retail area, as vacant shops find other uses, from takeaways to tattoo parlours. The High Street may begin to look tatty and unloved, crime rises, vandalism raises small shops' insurance costs and makes them unviable, and takeaway food shops may be closed during the day, open evenings only, meaning the shopping parade presents an array of shuttered fronts in daylight hours, further deterring shoppers.

In one sense, this is just supermarkets doing well at their trade, but the elimination of competition may have adverse social effects that damage the reputation of the retail chain. When Tesco tried a foray into the US market under the 'Fresh and Easy' fascia in 2007, they made a commitment to enter 'food desert' areas, districts with poor access to fresh healthy produce. These tend to be deprived areas hosting many unhealthy takeaway outlets, such as pizza and burger bars. However, as the Fresh and Easy venture began to falter, Tesco dropped its pledge to enter areas such as the eastern Los Angeles suburb of Hemet, where many poorer pensioners with limited transport options lived, even as it was still opening new Fresh and Easy stores in more affluent locations like Hermosa Beach. This was at the time when Michelle Obama, wife of the then US president Obama (2009–17), was raising public awareness of obesity and food deserts with her '*Let's Move*' campaign. However, there may also be an ethical argument against new supermarkets entering deprived areas, even with a view to revitalizing the area, as expressed by the small-shop proprietors of Harlem, New York, when a Pathmark supermarket was proposed for the area in the late 1990s. These shop-keepers argued that they had invested in the area when no supermarket would touch it. They resented the government help for Pathmark, as their taxes had effectively paid for a competitor to come in, and there was a racial aspect because many of Harlem's small shopkeepers were black (Wrigley & Lowe, 2002: 145).

The closure of supermarkets, abandoning an entire area as opposed to closing older smaller premises in order to open a larger store close by is relatively rare. It takes considerable time and money to get a supermarket up and running, and abandoning a premises risks leaving an opening for a competitor. However, in some parts of the US, this does happen, because the area is depopulating due to industrial decline. Absolute depopulation of a large area is much rarer in Western Europe, with its more densely packed population and higher land values. There are two states in the developed world that actually have lower populations in 2010 than they did in 1950, former East Germany and West Virginia in the USA. There are many other depopulating regions, from parts of Siberia to districts of Eastern Europe and some more isolated smaller islands in the Caribbean and elsewhere, but these are much smaller territories and less supermarketized.

In January 2016, Walmart closed its doors in Kimball, McDowell County, a depopulating former coal mining area of West Virginia (Pilkington, 2017). The population of McDowell county has fallen from 100,000 in 1940 to just 18,000 in 2016. The nearest supermarket to Kimball is now 12 kilometres away in Welch; the closure also deprived the town of its main social meeting place. Some residents of Kimball will grow their own food but most will face a long drive, or use the Five Loaves and Two Fishes food bank 3 kilometres down the road. Car ownership is low in the area, and life expectancy is similar to Namibia's. The only other sources of food in the town are cheap restaurants serving less than healthy fare. The Walmart site may eventually be occupied by a cheaper-end supermarket, such as Dollar Food, which sells little or no fresh produce. Kimball will suffer in less visible ways too. Other local shops may close as local spending power declines. The local tax base for the council shrinks too. Donations to the local food bank may also fall, just as demand rises; the Kimball Walmart used to donate 200,000 pounds of meat, dairy, pies and bread a year to the town's food bank. The overall feeling of community, the sense of purpose provided by the jobs at Walmart, is lost, as are social contacts with work colleagues. There is a possibility of a hardware and farm supplies store, Rural King, taking over the former Walmart premises in Kimball, which will restore some jobs, but will still leave the town with no easy access to healthy food and groceries.

In the UK, closure of supermarket premises has been blamed for the creation of 'food deserts', areas where people cannot for various reasons obtain a healthy diet with adequate fresh produce (Seth & Randall, 1999: 267). In the case of a rundown shopping centre in a deprived part of Edinburgh, a Scottish court ruled in 1997 that Safeway supermarket could not close a Presto branch it had acquired in Westside Plaza (formerly Wester Hailes Shopping Centre). Safeway had a lease that ran until 2009 but antisocial behaviour, such as drug use, theft, shoplifting and vandalism, meant it was more economic for Safeway to close the store and continue paying the lease than to actually operate the premises as a supermarket. Staff found the working conditions 'intolerable'. However, the court ruled that Highlands and Universal Properties, the landlords of the shopping centre, would suffer unjustly if the anchor store Presto was allowed to close. Since 1990, considerable money had been spent on revitalizing Westside Plaza, which would be wasted if Presto closed, probably taking most of the other shops with it (The Herald, 1997). This legal ruling was only possible in Scottish law; in England, the remedy would have been compensatory damages, and English courts are very reluctant to make rulings of specific performance—an order for the store to stay open.

Unsurprisingly, the issue of access to food retail, of the viability of local shops and High Street success is not prominent on supermarket CSR websites. If present at all, it is rapidly glossed over in a quick-fire sequence of other topics virtually guaranteed to leave the site visitor feeling they have seen something about small shops, but they weren't quite sure what. An example of this is the "Asda Pure Organics Social Film" (Riley, 2014), a short clip of 3 minutes 37 seconds. It begins, over the first ten seconds, "*Over the past century the people of the UK have dramatically changed the way they buy their food, from shopping at local markets and grocers, to getting everything under one roof at the larger supermarkets*". This is a wonderfully free-floating statement that glosses over some three centuries of UK retail change, from pre-industrial town square markets through corner shops to supermarkets, in one sentence. Then over the next 80 seconds, we are swiftly taken through a series of CSR-retail issues, including the environment, profits, climate change, food chain supply sustainability, organics, animal welfare, children, best start for them, health, organics and additive-free food. All the while, a distracting lulling jingle is being played, along with swift-changing images of birds, bees, fruit, crop fields, a tractor and pigs, before moving to a woman in a country cottage with a docile cat. Such sensory overload, by image, word and sound, will create a general feel-good factor but tells very little about the realities of rural-life or small-shops retailing. Or indeed anything very much at all, except that all is well with the world, so long as you rely on Asda to supply your daily bread (even additive-free organic bread). Supermarkets could gain considerable CSR if they helped small High Street independent traders, most of whom are not competing with the likes of a Tesco superstore anyway, by, for example, sharing business tips and expertise, and finding ways the two (different) enterprises could work together, rather than as adversaries.

There is a 'clawback of trade' theory that suggests the arrival of a supermarket might boost the trade of local retailers by bringing in more shoppers to the locality. In theory, if a supermarket opens in a small town, shoppers will no longer travel to the supermarket in a distant larger city. However, this depends on factors such as trip-linking; people may still travel outside the small town to work, and shop on the way home, or take their children to school in the larger settlement and then buy the groceries. In 2005 in Hampshire, several village-location One Stop stores were converted to the Express format after Tesco took over the One Stop chain. There was indeed a small but appreciable shift by shoppers from these villages to using the Express shop, which had a much better selection of fresh produce than One Stop had stocked, away from remoter city-based supermarkets in places such as Winchester, Southampton and Basingstoke. This relocalization of shopping back into village centres also borough environmental and health benefits, as weekly car mileage fell and some consumers shifted from driving to shop towards walking to access at least some of their grocery shopping (Wrigley et al, 2007).

Whether clawback of trade effects outweigh competition effects depend on the exact location of the supermarket and the ease of shopper travel between the two; paradoxically, the closer the supermarket is to the local shops, the more the small shops benefit, as the propensity of supermarket shoppers to also visit nearby independent stores then rises. A supermarket right in amongst the small shops may boost their trade, as in the case of a small butcher in Bramley shopping precinct, north Leeds, trading next door to a Morrison supermarket. The independent butcher sold the unusual cuts of meat, such as ostrich that Morrison did not stock, and the supermarket attracted customers to the precinct. Conversely, a supermarket separated from the small-shops retail area by even a small 'psychological barrier' (something that prevents or deters totally free flow of shoppers between superstore and independent shops) will likely reduce the independent shops' trade. This barrier can be as trivial as a main road with pedestrian lights, or a foot underpass. It may be totally imaginary, as in the case of the Tesco store in Brigg, Lincolnshire, UK, which provided free two-hour parking (with no compulsion to actually use the store). This represented the only free parking in Brigg (other, council-owned, car parks were Pay and Display), and the store was just a few hundred metres from the small shops in Brigg town centre, yet a council survey revealed that Tesco Brigg car park users did not generally visit these smaller Brigg High Street retailers. The reason was that the few minutes' walk involved traversing an alleyway past the backs of older buildings, which were visually uninviting to pass. However, in Shepton Mallet (Somerset), where a Tesco opened in 2007 and was separated from the historic town centre by the A.371 major road, 36% of traders nearest to the new store thought it had been 'good for their business' and 28% thought 'bad'; in the town centre shops furthest from the new Tesco, the proportion approving was much lower at 8.7%, with 43.5% saying 'bad' (Wrigley et al, 2010).

Small shops can provide unique, socially valuable and tailored services to customers in a way the supermarkets cannot. In the days of film video cassettes, a video rental store in a US town with a large number of film buffs employed only staff with a love and knowledge of films, and they were expected to spend some time actually watching the films on rental so they could advise customers on what to take out; a local Scunthorpe (UK) grocery retailer, in an area with many dikes and canals, began specializing in fishing equipment. This evolved into an unlikely suburban-location fishing gear retail centre and attracted customers to other shops in the parade (Shaw & Shaw, 2009: 94). Small village shops may miss the regular visit by a pensioner and act as informal social services alert if she fails to turn up. Small shops can know their regular customers in ways a large anonymous supermarket, or even a high-staff-turnover local supermarket branch such as Tesco Express never could.

In rural areas especially, where a pub or Post Office may be a central hub of the community the closure of these facilities as a new supermarket branch like a Tesco Express moves in may arouse considerable opposition. Issues with rural Post Offices closing as former One Stop stores were converted to Tesco Express shops were noted in Chapter 1. Pubs have also been vulnerable, because many have become precarious, financially, due to a wide range of exogenous factors. These factors include, higher taxes on alcohol, stricter enforcement of drunk driving rules (this especially impacts in rural pubs), rising energy costs (the premises must be kept lit and heated, even if only one or two customers turn up), a decline in social drinking as more people interact online through social media and more onerous business regulations for pub landlords. As with small shops, local villagers do not go by the 'use it or lose it' principle but want someone else to give it enough trade to keep going until the odd occasion when they do go there. Then when the pub does close there are large protests. In Cuckfield, Sussex, the conversion of the former Ship Inn into a Co-op in 2014 sparked anger; villagers bought drinks from a nearby pub and took them into Co-op to socialize there as if it was still a public house; one has to ask if they drank and socialized in there as much when it still *was* a pub. There was already another Co-op just 1.2 kilometre away, and local people felt the new Co-op might threaten the independent village store (Wealden Stores), which sourced much of its produce locally. The protest thereby extended in scope out to the livelihood of local farmers and other businesses.

3.7 Supermarket Competition With Retailers in the Developing World

The supermarket mode of shopping originated in the US and then spread to Western Europe; it is now rapidly penetrating other global regions, especially Eastern Europe, India, China, South-East Asia, Mexico and South/Central America. There is less penetration of supermarkets in parts of the Middle East, Iran, Central Asia, Eastern Russia and Africa, but even in these areas the trolley habit is gaining ground, with Shoprite, South Africa's biggest retailer, now present in 15 African countries. In North America and Western Europe, the supermarkets began serving the less affluent end of the social scale and moved upmarket over time; Tesco began as a pile-it-high-and-sell-it-cheap retailer, and Lidl, in particular, has moved somewhat into Waitrose territory with some of its more upmarket offerings. In the Global South, it has been the opposite story, with supermarkets appealing to the more affluent urbanized middle-class consumers, whilst traditional market and street-side stall retailing continues to be used by the less wealthy. Will we ever see the closure of many of these traditional retail outlets as we have done in Europe and North America?

There is some evidence in India that supermarkets may be about to curb the growth of the traditional small shops, the family-run *kiranas*. Rani and Ramachandra (2015) project that there are 'concerns' over the fate of small independent Indian retailers and that supermarket spending and numbers will grow rapidly. However, Table 3.1 suggests that—for now—small shops in India may just be holding their own.

India is still experiencing both relatively rapid population growth and urbanization. Therefore, even as the supermarkets gain in share and turnover, there is still a growing (in absolute numbers, at least) market share for the *kiranas*. The middle class to which the modern supermarkets cater is still relatively small and urbanized. In a few decades' time, it is likely that India's population will have stabilized and the supermarkets will start eroding the absolute numbers patronizing the traditional *kiranas* and street markets. The growing middle class may by then have begun a flight to the suburbs and near-urban rural areas, which may precipitate closure of some small shops and start the production of food deserts as Britain and the US have now. It is a similar story in Thailand, with a more stable population, where the supermarkets are growing, again from a small base, and small traders are largely holding their own, with some

Table 3.1 Share of Retailing of Traditional and Modern Retailing in India

Year	2008 (actual)	2013 (actual)	2018 (projected)
Sales billion rupees all retail outlets	9,575.3	16,717.8	16,821.1
Number of retailers (all) thousands	12,058.8	12,423.2	12,724.7
Modern retailers, sales billion rupees	163.0	287.2	501.9
Traditional retailers, sales billion rupees	9,512.3	15,884.6	16,319.1
Number of modern retailers (thousands)	6.5	6.0	8.1
Number of traditional retailers (thousands)	12,052.3	12,426.5	12,716.6

Source: Adapted from Rani & Ramachandra, 2015

decline in 'traditional markets' (Schaffner et al, 2005). In Indonesia, too, in 2005, some years after the emergence of supermarket retailing there, 70% of all food and 90% of fresh food were still sold by traditional retailers. In wealthier developing countries, such as Chile, especially in their more affluent regions, the small independent shop sector is shrinking markedly; in urban Chile between 1991 and 1995, 15,777 small shops went out of business, mainly in the capital Santiago, a decline of over 21%. In Argentina between 1984 and 1993, as the supermarket sector took off there, small shops numbers fell from 209,000 to 145,000, a decline of just over 30% (Reardon & Gulati, 2008), although some of this decline can be attributed to adverse economic conditions in those counties.

The lesson seems to be that, as regards supermarket dominance on other players on the food chain, the worst effects as seen in the developed countries have yet to emerge or are just emerging now in the middle-income countries of the world. This gives farmers and small shopkeepers in locales such as India and Chile time to organize into co-operatives to maintain their buying or selling power, and governments in these countries could promote this to avert the day when even their domestic supermarket chains become targets of Carrefour, Tesco or Walmart and these nations find much of their retail profits being sucked out of the country back to Europe or the USA. Otherwise, there could be mass unemployment amongst the many *kirana* owners of India, also many smallholder farmers might become landless and destitute. Measures to protect the small food enterprises, farms and small family retailers might raise *kirana* food prices a little but the biggest price rises would be at the supermarkets, who would enjoy fewer economies of scale. Since in the Global South these supermarkets cater more for the wealthier middle classes, such price rises should be socially bearable.

3.8 Supermarkets and Job Creation

Do supermarkets create or destroy jobs? Supermarkets are large employers. On average a large supermarket has 70–90 FTEs (full-time-equivalent jobs), with more employed outside the supermarket premises as drivers, head office staff, buyers and others. Construction of a supermarket will also create jobs. These jobs can have multiplier effects in areas of high unemployment; if those employed would have been otherwise out of a job, and they spend a significant portion of their wages locally. On the other hand, supermarkets are more efficient at sales-per-employee or sales-per-salary, suggesting that retailing jobs are likely to be lost on balance as supermarkets gain market share unless total consumer spending rises. In the short run, the absolute number of jobs available will rise as a supermarket opens because small independent shops under threat do not close straightaway. All businesses face both fixed and variable costs; fixed costs are those incurred whether trading is done or not, and variable costs are those incurred through trading. A shop's fixed costs include lighting; the premises are lit whether any customers come or not. A shop's variable costs include the wholesale price of the stock that is bought in to sell at a mark-up. Basic mathematics says that a business should trade if it is covering at least its variable costs, because it is then making more money than if it doesn't trade at all; this applies even if the fixed costs aren't being fully covered also. Of course, a business only covering its variable costs, and making a loss overall by failing to cover variable plus fixed costs, will eventually have to close, but most business can weather a period of overall losses, so long as this is not prolonged.

The crucial point here is that small businesses have a larger proportion of their costs as 'fixed costs'; large supermarkets have succeeded in reducing their fixed costs proportion. A small shop with low trading levels will pay rent, insurance and energy bills before any trading is done. The small level of variable (stock wholesale) costs is then marked up by a much larger margin than supermarkets do to cover overall costs. Supermarkets, however, can employ staff on flexible or zero-hours contracts; they can force down the wholesale costs of items not selling well; they can close loss-making stores if necessary whilst continuing to operate the chain overall. Their wholesale mark-up is low, around 5% compared to the 50% or more a small shop must mark-up for its owner to make a living. This means a loss-making small shop can carry on perhaps for two or three years, making an overall loss if it is at least covering the small proportion of its costs that are variable. Small business owners often make quite a low wage from their enterprises and will struggle on until retirement, or the bank pulls the plug. Small businesses have both entry and exit costs; closing one down is not cost free and takes time also. It may be a matter of personal pride to 'own a business' even a loss-making one. So when a supermarket opens, the small shops it may have condemned will not start closing for some years, and these closures can then be attributed to the owner pulling out, or other adverse economic trends that have begun on the last couple of years; it is hard to blame the supermarket directly for any job losses here as small-shop assistants are made redundant.

When considering job creation or destruction it is not just a question of the number of employees; other factors such as the level of wages, the quality and prospects of these jobs, their hours (full or part-time) and their expected duration (permanent, temporary) must be considered. For deprived areas with high unemployment, with perhaps poor transport links and many people without cars, the percentage employed from within the local area is crucial. It does not help poorer areas if a highly paid manager drives in five times a week, especially if she also spends her salary away from the area too. Supermarkets frequently have had a key role in neighbourhood regeneration projects, for example, at Seacroft in

Leeds and Castle Vale in Birmingham, and the promise of creation of jobs for local people is a significant part of that regeneration. These jobs may be treated as 'planning gain' and help the supermarket obtain planning permission; they may also be part of the company's CSR programme.

Supermarkets also participate in the SkillSmart programme, partly funded by the UK government and led by retailers (D. Lloyd, 2013). Large supermarkets are faced with a significant number of employees who, despite having left school, lack any qualifications or even anything more than the most basic level of literacy, are running programmes with local colleges to educate these workers. Some might argue that this is the government subsidizing private-sector jobs training, but it is an accepted responsibility of the state to educate its citizens, and those receiving such education are not compelled to stay with their current employer. In the US, Walmart is offering its 1.4 million employees who have more than 90 days service the option of earning a university degree in business or supply chain management, with Starbucks and McDonald's offering similar packages. Walmart says it may widen the degree options in the future. With tertiary-level education being strongly inversely associated with obesity, this programme may even have some appreciable economic health benefits for wider society. Of course, a better-educated workforce with lower turnover is beneficial for Walmart too.

In Seacroft, the insertion of a new Tesco in a former rundown shopping mall was accompanied by promises to employ local labour. Two hundred and thirty jobs were given to long-term unemployed local residents. The supermarket may promise to employ those who might find it hard to get a job, the long-term unemployed who are out of the work habit, with atrophied and outdated skills, the disabled, those with few qualifications and those recently released from prison. A pertinent question, but one that is seldom followed up, is how long do these employees stay in their posts? If the new employee found it hard to maintain a daily schedule, as some long-term unemployed do, were they given some leeway, or replaced with someone with more retail work experience? Or were their jobs eventually automated away, as, for example, robot tills replace human checkout operators? The *Guardian* reported (Mc Hardy, 2001) that 18 months after the opening of the Tesco Seacroft store, all but 12 of the 230, some of whom were also give training such as literacy courses, were still employed by Tesco. This is an impressive statistic given that turnover in the retail sector is high, estimated at between 40% and 100% annually. Similarly, when Sainsbury's opened in Castle Vale the 'B35' stigma (B35 was the postcode of Castle Vale) was greatly reduced. Previously, employers would barely consider the Curriculum Vitae of a job applicant with that postcode (Wind-Cowie, 2010: 53). Over in New York, the US supermarket chain Pathmark has been credited with the revitalization of a number of deprived neighbourhoods, such as East Harlem and Bedford Stuyvesant in New York (Lavin, 2005), where food deserts were also alleviated by new supermarkets (but note the objections raised earlier in Section 3.6 to Pathmark's presence in Harlem).

3.9 Supermarket Pay Levels

Low wages are prevalent across a whole swath of trades connected with food and retailing, including supermarkets, restaurants, agriculture and the hospitality sector. Retail wages are low for several reasons. Firstly, many retail jobs are relatively low-skill, and employ 'transferable skills'— that is, generic skills possessed by a wide range of applicants from many backgrounds and places. Therefore, job competition keeps wages low. Secondly, the long opening hours of supermarkets, which must span a long time period from before other jobs start until long after they finish, means jobs are part-time variable hours, filled by 'pin-money' workers, such as housewives and students; not being the main household bread-winner may mean willingness to work for a lower return. Thirdly, there has been considerable deskilling even in those retail jobs that did require some skills. By the 1990s, a typical supermarket store manager had been stripped of many responsibilities, such as store layout, what lines to carry, promotions and store budgeting, making them little more than a junior manager for a tranche of unskilled workers (Wrigley & Lowe, 2002: 106). The traditional responsibilities and autonomy of a store manager had been centralized up to head office, and their most onerous responsibility was now managing staff and controlling 'shrinkage'.

It has also been suggested that the uniformity and convenience of supermarket food is deskilling shoppers, who no longer know, because they no longer need to know, the different joints of meat a High Street butcher would sell, or the best ways of cooking such joints. Meat is now an anonymous slab of protein in a plastic-wrapped Styrofoam tray, to be stuffed in an oven or microwave according to the on-pack instructions (Blythman, 2004: 44).

A wider problem with low supermarket wages, as opposed to wages in smaller shops generally, is that the supermarket may become a wage-setter for the whole area, just as supermarkets tend to set the local price for petrol. The presence of a Walmart may lower retail wages across the entire US county it is situated in by 1.5% (Dube et al, 2007), and it has been suggested that Walmart supermarket managers have as one of their stated aims to keep total wage costs below a certain % of sales (Patel, 2012: 240). Meanwhile, from the McDonald's restaurant chain, we have derived the designation 'McJob' to signify a low-paying, low-prestige job that requires few skills and offers little chance of promotion. The food and retail industries often have a very 'flat' employment structure, not pyramidal with a clear career progression path upwards; they have a very high proportion of low-paid staff and not many openings at higher job grades. The UK has a minimum wage, also termed the 'National

Living Wage'; this wage is applicable to employees aged 25 or more[2] and in 2017 stood at £7.83/hour. However, the Living Wage Foundation estimates the true 'living wage', the wage needed for a 'decent standard of living', as £8.75/hour outside London and £10.20/hour in London (Living Wage Foundation, 2017). Especially for workers with children, the legal minimum wage does not cover essential living costs and has to be topped up with tax credits, which means employers paying at this level are effectively being subsidized in their business costs by the tax-payer, because they rely on a continued supply of workers with some basic level of health and education. The labour force cannot reproduce itself with insufficient income. Housing Benefit may also be payable to a worker on low wages, which decouples the housing market, rental and owner-occupier, from any link with what is affordable to many lower-wage workers and again effectively uses the retail sector (and other low wage employers) to subsidize wealthy landlords.

Tesco's workforce received an estimated £364 million tax credits in 2014 and was also accused of paying its staff at its One Stop stores less than at the Tesco-fascia stores. Furthermore, the Tesco-owned stores that retain the One Stop fascia ted to be in less-affluent areas and charge higher prices than Tesco Express does (Hipwell, 2017a). Tesco replied that One Stops have a lower footfall so have "different operating costs and cannot support a higher volume business such as a Tesco Express or Sainsbury Local". Overall, prices at One Stop were 15.4% higher than Tesco Express; staff at One Stop were all paid £7.20/hour, versus £7.24 starter at Tesco Express, rising to £7.67 for longer-served staff. In the US, the fast food giant McDonald's was estimated to have cost taxpayers US\$ 1.2 billion in public assistance paid to their low-paid employees (Taylor, 2013), whilst also in 2013, the US Democrat Party alleged that a typical Walmart supercentre in Wisconsin, employing 300 staff, cost the taxpayer \$900,000 a year (The Economist, 2016). Walmart responds that its wages cannot be excessively low because when it opens a new store it typically gets at least 10 and possibly 100 applicants for each vacancy; 3,000 applicants for 300 jobs in Los Angeles, 8,000 after 525 posts in Glendale Arizona and 25,000 applications for 325 posts in Chicago (Chandler & Werther, 2014: 89). However, Walmart has itself probably both lowered wages elsewhere and reduced job vacancies, so, in a climate of workfare and austerity, these applicants may have little choice; the true test is how long they will stay with Walmart when they have a choice of other jobs to apply for. The social security net in the US is much more threadbare than in Europe, and many jobless in the US get to know true destitution in a way unfamiliar to many Europeans. Also, supermarket wages may be higher than the real wage paid in small shops, where much unpaid labour may be contributed by family members. In 2013, the state of Washington, DC, proposed that a higher minimum wage be imposed on larger retail-ers, because the larger the company the more money leaves the area, and local multipliers are lower (Economist, 2013a). A bill was in fact passed on 10 July 2013 requiring retailers with at least US$ 1 billion in annual sales and stores of over 75,000 square feet to pay a minimum wage of $12.50 an hour, higher than the general minimum wage of $8.25. The effects of this measure were felt mainly by Walmart.

Some supermarkets have recently been increasing the remuneration of their lowest paid employees. In Britain, Morrison's has raised the hourly rate of its 90,000 shop-floor staff to £8.20 from March 2016, above what the Chancellor George Osborne then stated was the 'national living hourly wage', £7.20. This represented a pay rise of 13% for these workers, at a time when both prices and wages in the UK were virtually stagnant. The deal will cost Morrison £40 million over a year. In September 2015, Lidl also raised its lowest pay rate to £8.20 per hour, and Sainsbury raised its minimum remuneration by 4% to £7.36 an hour. In 2018, Sainsbury simplified its job structure and is to pay a 'base rate' of £9.00 per hour, up from £8.00, in order to secure the best staff and compete with Aldi and Lidl, who are rapidly gaining market share. However, this simplified pay structure means paid breaks and colleague bonuses are being removed. In March 2015, the co-operative supermarket committed to raising staff pay by 8.5% over two years, to reach a minimum rate of £7.30 per hour. Higher wages, and good employment conditions, keep employees happy and motivated, and are an important way of increasing efficiency and production. It also means lower staff turnover and higher staff loyalty. The Costco group is said to have very low staff turnover, especially for the retail sector which generally has a high churn rate, because it pays above-average wages (Kaye, 2012).

Previously, Lidl's low wages and poor work conditions had sparked criticism of the chain in places such as Finland and Germany, where such bad publicity undermined the main competitive advantage of Lidl over incumbent traders: its sharply lower prices. Finnish shoppers were made to feel guilty over contributing to poor labour conditions just to save a few cents on their shopping. As a 'foreign' company outcompeting established Finnish chains, this allegation was potentially serious for the trading position of the German-based retailer. Meanwhile, in the US, the giant retailer Walmart raised its lowest pay in 2016 to $9 for untrained employees and $10 for trained staff, well above the federal minimum wage of $7.25. Walmart was once notorious for its low wages, as noted earlier. In 2014, the average supermarket cashier in the US earned $9.93 an hour; Walmart at that time paid $8.62. The average 2014 hourly remuneration for a US salesperson was $12.83; Walmart paid $8.53 (The Economist, 2016). In fact, Walmart's wages weren't especially low for the food retail sector; what distinguished them was that larger employers generally pay higher wages across any given sector. Walmart was paying corner-shop wages but reaping supermarket-sized profits. Other businesses paying minimum wage rates were reportedly concerned about the effects of Walmart's move on their own wage bills.

However, some supermarkets have tried to lessen the impact of any increases in the living wage. Morrison and Waitrose cut extra pay for Sundays and reduced paid breaks. Previously, a double rate was paid for Sunday and bank holiday hours. In 2016, the Belgian coffee chain Le Pain Quotidien ended paid breaks for its UK branch staff when the UK introduced a 'living wage'; the café was also accused of failing to pass on customer tips to staff. Other restaurant chains, including Zizi and Café Nero, have cut free food for staff or reduced the choice of free meals available to staff. Other chains have raised the targets for bonuses, in one case cutting the take-home pay of workers by £90 a month. It has been suggested that the recent (2018) merger between the two large British chains Asda and Sainsbury will result in backdoor cuts to staff remuneration, including the shortening of nightshift 'premium' hours, scrapping of Sunday overtime rates and cuts to shop-floor staff bonuses. Some supermarket workers may end up as much as £3,000 a year worse off. Sainsbury has publicized its rise in basic pay from £8.00 to £9.20 per hour, making it "the highest paying retailer in the country" (Wilson, 2018), a 30% rise over four years, but one in ten of Sainsbury's workers may end up worse off.

Low wages and poverty impose many negative externalities on society, including excess morbidity and mortality; it is well-known that life expectancies in deprived districts of cities can be an entire decade less than those in the most affluent areas, even when these districts are just a few kilometres apart. Obesity, with its many associated morbidities, is also strongly associated with poverty. If the retailer also sells unhealthy food, then society suffers a double burden, and the government is effectively subsidizing the supply of obesogenic food. It is also promoting consumption of obesogenic food, as those on low wages will eat more cheap food. Consumers may be aware that supermarkets exploit their staff, either on pay or conditions, but the supermarket can create a 'waterbed effect' by prominent positioning of other CSR initiatives reminders, such as local charity donations or environmental initiatives. The customer then feels good about shopping there again, enjoys the bargains from the supermarket that low wages partly facilitate and forgets any social shortcomings (Demmerling, 2014: 51). As the next two chapters show, it is even easier to forget about the pay and conditions of the invisible workers who produce and process the food we buy on the supermarket shelves, and to forget what is happening to the environment that food is produced in.

Notes

1. In 2018, the Waitrose café offer was considerably modified with the 'free coffee' element now removed. Instead, there are discounts on café food. It has yet to be seen whether High Street coffee shops benefited from the 2018 *My Waitrose* change.
2. Lower rates apply to workers aged under 25.

4 Food Retailing and the Environment

4.1 Energy Use in the Food Chain

The food industry is a major user of energy and therefore a large contributor to greenhouse gas (GHG) emissions. UK supermarkets are estimated to account for 1% of all GHGs directly and as much as 10% indirectly (Gouldson et al, 2013). Growing, transportation and retailing of food uses energy; we must include all stages of the food chain here, including the 'last mile' to the consumer and possibly also transport of food-related waste, such as packaging to a recycling or landfill site. Within the typical supermarket, energy is consumed by temperature control, lighting, refrigeration, ICT systems and staff travel. Meanwhile, agriculture accounts for 10%–12% of GHG emissions, or as much as 17%–32% if agriculturally induced land changes are included (Sodano & Hingley, 2013: 76). At the consumption end, food accounts for 30% of the total environmental impacts caused by household consumption (Tukker & Jansen, 2008). The construction or conversion of retail facilities also uses energy—a topic that has very little presence on supermarket CSR sites extolling how they are saving energy in everyday uses, such as lorry transport and refrigeration. On the positive side, some supermarkets have been quite imaginative, thinking outside the box when it comes to reducing energy use. The Swiss chain Migros has liaised with Mifa, a homecare products producer, to promote household detergents that can be used at lower temperatures (Roberts, 2017). Cumulative small measures such as these can add up significantly; perhaps the Earth won't be saved with a bang but a whimper.

In the 1990s, supermarket energy reduction initiatives were rather limited in scope, short-term and single-target focussed. However, by 2007, supermarkets had become more sophisticated and were adopting longer-term goals, and widening their energy-use reduction targets to include other stages of the food supply chain (Gouldson et al, 2013). Climate change, CO_2 emissions and the threat of rising temperatures and sea level rise have risen up the public agenda since 2000. Supermarkets have succeeded in reducing their energy intensity by 2%–3% per annum over the past decade, but these achievements are also classifiable as 'business savings', something the supermarkets would have wanted to do anyway, but can now trumpet as a CSR initiative. For example, Lidl's CSR website states,

> [Lidl has] reduced the leakage rate of its freezers to less than 1%. . . . making them more environmentally friendly, efficient and cost-effective than ever before. Each chiller cabinet also functions independently so that if one chiller fails due to external power loss, the other chillers will continue to operate. Over time this will significantly reduce write-offs and operation costs.

In other words, Lidl has found a way to save on electricity and food wastage, which is good for the planet and good for their bottom line. For this they won the accolade "National Retailer of the Year for Green Credentials" (PR Newswire, 2013). Supermarkets' initiatives on environment tend to focus on 'efficiency' rather than 'sustainability'. Supermarkets also care more about pressures (such as CSR praise or opprobrium) that impact on costs, rather than about those impacting "on-financial aspects such as brand and reputation" (Gouldson et al, 2013).

One commonly used term in CSR reports is 'CO_2 intensity'; this simplifies the energy impact of supermarket operations down to a single figure. If we could be sure that this figure has been calculated in a consistent way across different years, we might have a useful means of monitoring progress, in this area anyway, towards or away from sustainability. Total sustainability might mean zero net CO_2 emissions, setting off energy used against trees planted elsewhere, although as we saw in Chapter 1 that too can have negative implications. But what does this single figure of CO_2 intensity actually mean? Is it per employee, per store square metre sales area, per value of sales, per volume of sales, per food mile, or some other metric? As a highly derived measure, it may be massaged to produce the most favourable figure wanted. Tesco has made significant investments in 2002 with the aim of reducing its CO_2 emissions by 35% per square foot by 2006, but the company had to admit that greatly increased sales during 2003/4 meant it missed this target by over 50% (Jones et al, 2005). Companies doing well with growing market share will look bad environmentally, and, conversely, those losing market share may be rewarded with 'good' environmental credentials. We could also measure CO_2 per tonne of food, but should this be per gross tonne, or per calories or per nutrients? Per gross tonne would favour locally produced foods, but this might not always be the most environmentally friendly means of production (see "Food Miles", Section 4.2). Measuring per nutrients or per calories might favour obesogenic calorie-rich foods over calorie-sparse but healthy food, such as celery and cucumber. As always, the challenge is to find a metric that is simple to understand and comparable over time but not so simple that it misleads and actually favours unsustainable food chain practices (see Section 5.8 for carbon labelling issues).

UK consumers are generally environmentally aware, but their main priority regarding food shopping is price and then convenience. They are unlikely to permanently boycott a local cheap supermarket because it is poor on environmental impact. This probably accounts for the reluctance of European supermarkets in Sweden, Denmark, Germany, France and the UK to communicate information regarding the climate GHG effects of food consumption, probably because neither party was interested very much (Ekelund et al, 2014). Overall, a strong driver towards greater CSR in reduction of energy use is profitability, because CO_2 emissions not only impose a cost on the environment but also the energy use that generated them impacts on costs. However, for public relations purposes, a supermarket must not be seen to be cynically claiming environmental success when in reality it is reducing costs, even if that really is the case.

4.2 Food Miles

The concept of food miles, like CO_2 intensity, is another 'one figure captures all' metric that attempts to highlight how globalized and remote our food sourcing has become. For example, the report "Eating Oil—Food in a Changing Climate" (Sustain, 2001), describes how the average UK Christmas dinner contains 24,000 food miles, with the turkey coming from Thailand, the runner beans from Zambia, the carrots from Spain and the potatoes from Italy. British consumers may query why these foods originate from three foreign countries when all of them can be produced within the UK. However, it may be more energy efficient to grow tomatoes in Spain and then fly them to the UK than to grow them in continuously heated greenhouses in the UK. Cost is a consideration, for consumer health as well as supermarket profits. Vegetables sold in UK supermarkets can be sourced more cheaply from Zimbabwe because, although airfreight costs are 60% of the price, labour is very cheap in Zimbabwe. If the price of fresh fruit and vegetables rose because they were produced within the UK, poorer consumers might eat less fresh produce, with subsequent health costs to the UK economy. Shoppers also want produce 12 months a year, not seasonally, so food has to come from remote locations abroad so that consumers can purchase strawberries in Britain in January. But should the environmentalists say that we cannot have such fresh produce for several months of the year when dieticians would like to see us eat more fresh fruit and vegetables?

Supermarket food chain consolidation has also lengthened food miles. Supermarkets have achieved a fine balance as regards supplier size; the term 'supplier' here including farmers, food processors and abattoirs. These suppliers should be not too small and not too big. Too big and they might start to have some commercial power over the supermarkets.

Too small is also undesirable because it creates complex administration for the supermarkets, and a (fairly) large supplier that has invested in technology and has committed most of its sales to the single supermarket as customer may be more tied in, more vulnerable to the supermarkets dictates, than a small enterprise that can readily find another market for its entire output at some independent local shop. Consolidation has lengthened food miles because food has to travel from the farm gate to fewer, more remote, processors. In 1971, the UK had 1,890 abattoirs, but this is down to 249 in 2018. The example of the beef farm on Scotland's Orkney Islands, detailed next, is a typical example of consolidation producing sometimes absurdly long food miles, only for produce to end up very close to where it first originated.

In January 2018, one more abattoir was lost with the closure of the only such facility in the Orkney Islands, at Kirkwall. From this date, cows slaughtered on the Orkney Islands must be taken live by ship 150 miles to Aberdeen docks, a 10-hour voyage, where they then endure a long lorry journey a further 116 miles to the abattoir at Dingwall, near Inverness. The beef may now be taken 101 miles north up the A9 to Scrabster, where it is shipped across to the Orkney butcher, in Kirkwall. Overall, the beef has travelled 450 miles, mostly in a live condition, to end up in a shop less than a mile from where it was originally auctioned. If the cow is deemed underweight when sold, she may have an even longer journey, as she will spend a few months on a mainland farm to fatten up. This is an extreme example, but Mr Young, organic beef farmer from Worcestershire, reports that he has had to change abattoirs seven times since he opened his farm shop in 1984; each time the journey has lengthened, from 5 miles in 1984 to 40 today. Overall, food miles within the UK have grown by 50% between 1978 and 2005 (Starkey, 2018).

Lengthening food miles also raises animal welfare issues because it is more convenient to transport live animals than meat. Animals keep fresh; meat has to be refrigerated. Both lorry transport and marine transport, possibly in stormy conditions, is stressful to animals. Smaller local abattoirs like that on the Orkneys could boast that they knew the animals, with their different personalities, and could slaughter them more humanely; the Orkney abattoir slaughtered an average of 50 cattle a month. However, increasing regulation has made small local isolated abattoirs less economic; the Orkney abattoir had to send its by-products for incineration to Dumfries, and a vet from the mainland had to fly out to supervise each slaughter. The 450-mile final round trip of Orkney's cows also threatens a key food geographical origin brand because they can no longer be called 'Orkney beef'; to qualify as such, the cows must be born, reared and slaughtered on the islands.

The transport itself can be made more environmentally friendly; in 2007, McDonald's announced that it would turn its waste cooking oil into biodiesel to power its fleet of 155 lorries. Similarly, in 2017,

Waitrose said it would become the first company in Europe to use lorries entirely run on biomethane gas generated from food waste (Hipwell, 2017b). However, this raises questions as to whether this is a socially or environmentally friendly way to use food. Socially, it seems repugnant to use food for energy to fuel lorries when people are going hungry, and if one accounts for the energy that went into producing that food in the first place, lorries running on food waste may be rather inefficient in energy and CO_2 terms.

Perhaps the lowest food miles of all may be achieved with the help of a German company, Infarm, which sells cabinets for supermarkets where salads can be grown right in the store in front of customers. Infarm also claims its growing trays do not need pesticides, and the need for food packaging (Section 4.7) is also reduced. The issue of reducing food waste is further discussed in Section 4.9. Counterintuitively, the transport of food in large lorries may be more efficient than in multiple small vans and creates less congestion, although road wear and tear increases by the fourth power of the vehicle weight, so road maintenance (and congestion from road works) may increase from that. Evidently, the balance between sustainability, consumer health and diet and supermarket efficiency is very complex and trade-offs must be made, no optimum solution exists that will please everyone concerned.

Even farm shops and farmer's markets may not be as 'green' as some would like to believe they are. Farmer's markets are supposed to sell local food. The Farmers Market Certification Scheme, run by the Farmers Retail and Markets Association, stipulated in 2007 that farmer's markets produce must originate within a 30-mile radius, or 50 for coastal and urban markets. However, customers may drive greater distances to a farmer's market, or a farm shop, than to a supermarket. Some farm shops are part retailer and part tourist destination, with entertainment for the children; boutique niche products, such as speciality cheeses and ice creams; and a restaurant or café. Others are simply a replacement grocery shop for a nearby village; there are many small rural settlements across England where the only village shop has closed, but the residents can access everyday foods from a farm shop 'close by'. Yet 'close by' can mean a mile or two out of the village, meaning few will walk there, as they might have done to the village shop, so car usage is increased. Farm shops like to point out that their produce is not intensively cleaned as supermarket produce may be, but then consumers may use energy and hot water washing the vegetables. Farmer's markets may also be a source of food waste if the weather is rainy, warm and damp, because attendance drops and the produce begins to go bad, and there is little or no refrigeration. People may have false concepts of which firms are 'green' based on what the company produces as much as how it actually produces things (Aldhous & McKenna, 2010). Consumers may rate firms in sectors like food production and food retail, and even media companies producing nature documentaries like the Discovery Channel, as greener than companies like Google, Nike and Viacom, although the latter are rated by Trucost as more sustainable.

4.3 Water Usage

Reducing 'visible' water usage frequently features prominently on supermarket CSR websites. This water consumption includes that used in the toilets and cafés; the installation of waterless urinals and lower volume flush toilets, along with collection of rainwater for uses like cleaning, is a priority; again, this also saves the supermarket money on its water bills. Less obvious to the customer is the 'hidden water' contained, or sometimes not contained, in the food we buy from the supermarket. Oranges from hot, dry locales such as California, South Africa, Spain or Israel comprise around 90% water; Israeli citrus fruit exports amount to just over 150,000 metric tonnes per year (Verdonk & Shakel, 2016), implying an annual export of 140,000 cubic metres of water from that region. Less well known are the water issues in the Petorca region of central Chile, also an arid area, where avocados are grown. For a period in 2017 in the UK, there was a 27% rise in demand for avocados, which had been touted in the media as a 'superfood'. Avocado cultivation requires 100 cubic metres of water per hectare, and agribusiness is ensuring it gets the water before local people do. With 67% of UK avocados sourced from the Petorca region, this is a major source of concern for British supermarket chains such as Lidl.

The consumer does not see the water consumed in the production of beef or grain, but absent from the final product when bought in the shop (NFU, 2014). A tonne of wheat may take 1,300 cubic metres of water to produce in terms of irrigation; in prairie areas, such as the US Midwest, this water may have come from non-replenished underground aquifers. This water is transpired by the plant or runs off into rivers, so it is unsustainable in the long run. The supermarket company may argue that sustainable water sourcing for the food products they import is beyond their remit, and it is the responsibility of the farmer and the government of the country of origin, but supermarkets may force unsustainable irrigation practices on producers by the retailer exerting relentless downwards pressure on the wholesale price. Supermarket customers quite like lower prices—until the product is no longer present on the shelf.

Bottled water sales comprise another possibly socially irresponsible use of water by supermarkets. The plastic bottle itself is an environmental menace (see Section 4.7), and why do we transport cubic metres of water around on lorries, with each cubic metre weighing one tonne? It is not a product most people need, when tap water is generally perfectly adequate, yet this product somehow sells for a higher price per litre than milk (see Section 5.2). Demand for this product has largely been artificially created by marketing, and the need for water on the go can be satisfied by drinking fountains and refills of reusable containers. This issue is discussed further under "Plastics Pollution", Section 4.7.

4.4 Sustainability of the Food Chain

There is a certain idyllic image of the English countryside that seems unchanged for centuries, and never will change: thatched country cottages, fields with thriving crops and hedgerows and birds and woods, as well as little lanes leading to ancient timbered farmhouses. One doesn't need to go to the actual countryside to see this; it is another image frequently found on supermarket CSR websites. Some might say this is the only place one will see such an image in the future; in 2014, it was claimed that UK farmland was so damaged by unsustainable practices that there might only be about 100 harvests left and that urban soil could be of a better quality, with more nutrients, than farmland soil (Edmondson et al, 2014).

Even if the soil has not yet noticeably declined in fruitfulness (its productivity propped up by continual chemical inputs of fertilizers and weed killers), what is produced from it has declined in range and quality. There are scores of varieties of plums and over a thousand varieties of apples, but how many does one see in a large supermarket, a few yards away from the hundreds of brands and flavours of yoghurts, chocolates and desserts? Often the fruit varieties that are available in a large grocery store are not the ones shoppers might want; they would choose on flavour and texture, but supermarkets choose from their suppliers based on durability and resistance to damage in transit. This favours the harder, less tasty variants, although, as said earlier, if sweetness is what you want, go to the puddings and ice cream section. Strawberries are frequently the Elsanta type, a Dutch variety bred in the 1950s that is hard and robust and resists bruising. The more fragrant English varieties, such as Cambridge Favourite or Hapil, have disappeared because they don't stand transport well. But Elsanta keeps looking glossy even out of cold store. However, it is crunchy and less fragrant. In 2002, Elsanta accounted for 80% of the strawberries grown in the UK. Likewise, most mangoes are the Tommy Atkin variety, whether they are grown in Brazil, Israel, Venezuela, Egypt, Jamaica, Ecuador or elsewhere. The Tommy Atkin was developed in Florida in the 1920s, especially for export, because it can be picked green and unripe ('backwards') and stored for up to three weeks at 13 C. It has pretty green and rose shading, and doesn't have brown flecks. But other mango varieties are less fibrous and more silky texture, but may be yellow-green and look unfamiliar to shoppers. Other mango varieties favoured by the supermarkets are the Kent and Keitt, also of superior robustness but inferior taste. Firm black Angelino plums dominate that fruit sector, whilst varieties like Victoria, Marjorie seedling and Greengage have all but vanished.

There has also been a loss of human skills diversity from the country-side. Rural work has to an extent deskilled, just as jobs within the super-market have (Section 3.9). Whilst managing a farm has become much more technical and scientific, traditional skills such as hedging, thatch-ing and dry stone walling have become largely relegated to 'preserva-tion pursuits', like driving a steam train or maintaining canal lock gates. Rather than scenic rolling fields and hills and woods, a truer picture of our future countryside can be seen in the Fens, a vast flat almost treeless prairie-like area of England north of Cambridge. Not all British farmland is so monotonously flat, but much of it is becoming as devoid of trees and hedges, and traditional farm buildings and cottages, as fields are amalga-mated into huge animal free croplands (the animals are usually indoors in barns). Not traditional barns but big artificially lit metal sheds where much of the food is unnatural to the animals therein, which is not so dis-similar in some ways to the huge metal sheds their meat will eventually be sold in. The tragedy is that a traditional farm as depicted on a super-market website would probably be unable to supply produce in enough bulk at a cheap enough price to be a supermarket supplier.

4.5 Sustainability of Fishing

For many years, consumers have been told to increase their fish con-sumption, eat more oily fish, substitute fish for meat, but have also been aware that large areas of the oceans are overfished and unsustainably exploited. However, whilst economics students may be taught that over-fishing can be self-perpetuating, because the rising price of scarcer fish makes smaller catches with more effort worthwhile, the economic and ecological nuances of fish endangerment and conservation are less salient in many shopper's minds. The ocean is a vast blank space, too big to be overfished, surely ('there's plenty more fish in the sea'—until of course there aren't)—an unknown place where boats vanish over the horizon and come back, hopefully, laden with fish. It took the TV programme *Blue Planet II* to alert the public to the damage plastic pollution was doing; negative images of no fish have far less impact. Shoppers may see graphic maps of sea areas overfished from time to time in the media, but few will retain such images whilst thinking about tonight's meal in the supermarket aisles. Statistics, even alarming ones such as "90% of the world's predatory fish are gone", or "only 3% of the world's fish stocks are underexploited" (Aguirre, 2005: 4), may have even less impact. Like-wise, the damage done by fish farms, from seabed fish excreta pollu-tion to sea lice proliferation and genetic pollution of wild fish stocks, is unseen, literally hidden below the surface. The images such pollution creates, black murk on the seabed and microscopic sea lice, is either invis-ible (e.g. genetic dilution of wild salmon by escaped farmed salmon) or not nearly as photogenic as say cuddly seals or dolphins struggling with plastic debris. Still less are consumers likely to be aware of the sustainability differences between yellowfin tuna and the closely related bigeye tuna or tuna-like euthynnus fish, which are endangered or of uncertain sustainability, and which Greenpeace found in Lidl's Nixe brand tinned tuna in 2010 (Moses, 2010).

The secondary and tertiary impacts of unsustainable fishing and fish farming, such as impacts on indigenous fishing communities and other sea life species, are even less salient. In this respect, Kaufland, a German supermarket chain which operates over 1,600 hypermarkets in Germany, Czech Republic, Slovakia, Poland, Croatia, Romania and Bulgaria, should be credited with its CSR initiative of donating, in 2013, 100,000 Euros to help the traditional artisanal Gambian fishing industry modernize and become more sustainable (Marine Stewardship Council, 2013). Fishing practices are also often inextricably linked with political disputes, with patriotic sentiments such as "this is our sea, we have a right to exploit it but those foreign boats are doing the over-fishing"— a feeling generated by European boats off Britain, or British boats off Iceland. However, food celebrities, such as TV celebrity chefs (a media phenomenon that can be traced back to Fanny Cradock in the 1960s, but which has gathered momentum since the 1990s) can dramatically raise the public profile of unsustainable fishing practices. In 2010, TV chef Hugh Fearnley-Whittingstall organized a campaign against the wasteful practice of fishing boats discarding fish at sea once they had exceeded EU quotas for certain species. His media campaign not only raised consumer awareness of this practice but also actually managed to effect a change in EU fishery practices (Hall, 2016: 138). There are fish certification schemes whose effectiveness one has to take on trust, but these require a careful examination of the fish tin to check and may be absent altogether from the supermarket fresh fish counter, where prices and choice are the main things a supermarket wants shoppers to see. Shoppers may develop a loyalty to a particular retailer because of its promises on the sustainability of the fish it sells, with less appreciation as to what this sustainability pledge means or how and if it is really being fulfilled (Aguirre, 2005: 7).

Environmental certification schemes, for fish and for agricultural production, might also harm the livelihoods of small family-based fishing enterprises and farms, according to World Growth (2011), which reports that the large Australian supermarket chains Coles and Woolworths are refusing to buy produce originating with these enterprises because they do not comply with the same standards that much larger fishing and agricultural corporations adhere to. World Growth accuses these supermarkets, and larger organizations, such as Greenpeace and the World Wildlife Fund, of 'social irresponsibility' because the environmental harm done by such small producers is minimal, 'compared' (if such a comparison can be made) with the economic harm of such market exclusion. However, from a scale perspective, this argument may need further analysis. In its support, this insistence by the supermarkets on a 'level playing field'—that is, anything but level for the smaller players—mirrors the problems faced by small shops in developed countries. There, governments often insist that small shops comply with the same regulations, in terms of paperwork, accountability and the environment, as Tesco does, when Tesco has far more resources to direct towards compliance than a small family-run grocery shop does. As noted next, supermarkets have an interest in dealing with fewer, larger suppliers (who are then less nimble and more reliant on the supermarket as a monopsonist) than in having many small suppliers. Against the World Growth argument is the possibility that thousands of small fishing boats or small rainforest clearances can collectively do a lot of environmental damage in a way that is less open to regulation than if one large company were doing this. A collective body of environmental damage is being compared to the economic loss to individual families. Overall, much economic hardship may result, but what of forming co-operatives or selling in other markets locally? The jury is probably still out on this assertion by World Growth.

There are different technical methods of fish catch, with different impacts on marine ecology. Tuna can be caught using the so-called pole and line method or by FADs, Fish Aggregation Devices; the former minimizes the by-catch of other species, whereas the latter method traps dolphins, sharks, turtles and other endangered marine life that is simply thrown back in the sea dead. FADs may consist of a bait net containing seaweed and molluscs, which attracts the tuna (and other fish), and the bait net is then surrounded by a large purse seine net trapping any fish that have come to the bait net. Most of UK's main supermarkets (Marks & Spencer, Morrison, Sainsbury, Tesco, Waitrose) do sell only pole and line caught tuna in their own brand tuna products. However, these stores also sell John West tuna, often devoting more shelf space to this brand than their own brands. Meanwhile, John West has reneged on a promise, made in 2011, to catch at least half of British tuna by the pole and line method. Despite John West's commitment that by 2017 all of its tuna would be sustainably caught, in 2015, Greenpeace reported that just 2% of its tuna was harvested this way. John West, now owned by a large Thai seafood company, promised in 2017 to reduce destructive fishing practices after several supermarkets threatened to delist its products. In 2016, Tesco and Waitrose began delisting some 20% of its John West lines in order to gain environmental credibility with consumers. Meanwhile, Waitrose, in 2017, claimed that 100% of its tuna is responsibly sourced, caught pole and line from the Maldives. As so often happens, the consumer must take many of these claims on trust and is little inclined to check anyway.

4.6 Sustainability of the Rainforest

Deforestation, the destruction of large swathes of the world's tropical rainforests for commercial purposes, is an environmental threat that has been in the public arena for many years. Specific ecological losses from such deforestation include species extinction, soil erosion and CO_2 emissions, also loss of human culture as the indigenous inhabitants of the forest are displaced or worse. Tropical deforestation has been blamed for 20% the rise in of atmospheric carbon dioxide. The cultivation of palm oil, a key ingredient in many processed foods sold in developed-country supermarkets, is a significant cause of rainforest clearance, particularly in Indonesia, where this clearance endangers the orangutan monkey population, which has declined by 100,000, or 50%, between 1999 and 2015. From around 2000 onwards, supermarkets have been moving towards 'sustainable' palm oil, starting with the Swiss retail chain Migros, which in 2002 committed itself not to source palm oil from plantations that had been established at the expense of virgin rainforest. Migros won a UN award for this policy, and, significantly, it became an influencer on other supermarket companies as it gained considerable public praise for its initiative (Hebuch, 2010: 498). In the UK, the small supermarket chain Iceland has promised to remove palm oil from all own-label meals by the end of 2018, eliminating the ingredient from 130 product lines and reducing use of palm oil by 500 tonnes per year. The oil is being replaced with sunflower and rapeseed oil, and butter. Other supermarkets, such as Tesco and Sainsbury, have committed to 'sustainable' or 'zero net deforestation' palm oil, meaning oil from plantations not on 'recently cleared' forest lands; however, this strategy perpetuates the forest clearance already done.

In 2003, the Roundtable on Sustainable Palm Oil was set up: a trade and producers body aiming to promote sustainable production from plantations not set up on former rainforest land (RSPO, 2018). This sustainably produced palm oil is more expensive than that produced from new clearances carved out of virgin south-east Asian forests. Sustainable products sold by the supermarkets normally command a higher price, but this doesn't always apply when the supermarket is the purchaser. Supermarkets can squeeze upstream suppliers to deliver better 'quality' (sustainability, health, welfare) at the same price, effectively a price cut to the producer just as the squeeze on farm-gate milk price was, but you can't always squeeze nature the same way. So sustainably produced palm oil has had a hard time gaining market share (Pearce, 2009), with even Waitrose slow to shift towards sustainable sources. If palm oil were a recognizable good on the supermarket shelves, it could easily be labelled 'sustainably produced' and command a premium price, and the supermarkets would no doubt rush to sell it, probably ensuring that the percentage mark-up they paid for it over and above the planet-damaging variety was less than the percentage mark-up the customer was charged. But palm oil isn't like mahogany or bananas; it's a hydrogenated fat 'nasty': a saturated oil beloved by the processed food industry because its hydrogen-saturated bonds stabilize food and give it a nice soft mouthfeel

(Shaw, 2014: 19). It's not the sort of ingredient you can boast about and appeal to upmarket health-conscious consumers. In fact, palm oil is blamed for creating fatty deposits in human arteries. So there's no mileage in promoting premium 'sustainable' palm oil to the sort of consumers who would pay more for environmentally friendly food.

The Iceland initiative is disturbing to a range of commercial and political interests, from the palm oil producers to the Indonesian and Malaysian governments, as well as to developed-world supermarkets and their processed food suppliers. In 2018, the palm oil industry launched a counter-attack via social media on Richard Walker, managing director of Iceland, the line of attack has been fiercely personal, accusing Mr Walker as a "Bentley-driving trust funder who inherited his supermarket from daddy", who "takes a polluting jet to Asia to lecture Malaysians about the environment". The attackers, the so-called Human Faces of Palm Oil Development, are anonymous behind a website, and they purport to defend the interests of poor smallholding palm oil growers in south-east Asia. In fact, they are backed by interests closely allied to the Malaysian government, including the Malaysian Palm Oil Council and the Malaysian Federal Land Development Authority (FELDA) (Moore, 2018).

The whole question of whether usage of palm oil from the tropics should be curbed in the Global North has been shifted, especially by the proponents of small-scale palm oil production, from the purely environmental into the political and economic. The EU has been accused of 'crop apartheid', because it allows the use of (European) rapeseed for similar uses to palm oil. However, substitution of rapeseed for palm oil would then improve Europe's balance of payments and support European farming, which are perfectly legitimate aims of European governance, even though that may disadvantage the Malaysian economy. Malaysia has threatened to start a trade war with Europe, cancelling large defence contracts, and argues that the EU policy will hurt small farmers, who were given ten acres of land each by the Malaysian FELDA to provide them with an independent livelihood. Where did this land come from, and was it a rainforest before FELDA allocated it? Perhaps the real solution is to promote a return to healthier diets, away from processed foods, and to find alternative economies for the producers of palm oil; however, this would involve an expensive attack on too many vested interests at present.

4.7 Plastics Pollution

The world's first plastic, Bakelite, was produced in 1909, about the time the first supermarket opened, the Piggly Wiggly store in Memphis, USA, 1916, around the time Tesco began (1919) and Waitrose opened its first store (1904). Polythene came next, first synthesized in 1933. It then took around a century for the world to realize that the very properties of plastic that made it such an attractive material for manufacturers, retailers and consumers; its non-biodegradability, its resistance to water, its capability to be formed into almost any shape in any colour, including transparent (which looks to sea creatures like jellyfish and to birds like colourful food), would make the wonder material of the 20th century into the problem material of the 21st century.

Global plastic production remained negligible by today's standards until the 1950s. In 1950, annual global production of plastic resin and fibre was 2 million tonnes, and barely 20 million tonnes was created in 1960. The food retail industry in 1960 used very little plastic; shoppers bought food loose or in sturdy brown paper bags. Materials packaging and transporting was in metal tins, cardboard packets or on wooden pallets to be sold loose, and the huge range of household cleaning and beauty products we have today that come in plastic bottles had yet to materialize. By the late 1980, the world was producing 100 million tonnes of plastic a year—a figure that passed the 200 million tonne mark in 1998. In 2015, world plastic output was around 400 million tonnes (Geyer et al, 2017). Housewives of the 1950s and 1960s shopped locally, little and often, and carried their purchases home in wooden baskets or string bags.

A combination of factors has driven up the amount of plastics used by consumers. The convenience of the car-borne weekly supermarket shop depended on an easy means of transporting large amounts of shopping from till to trolley to car boot to home; multiple disposable single-use plastic bags capable of carrying several kilograms of shopping each were the answer. The first supermarket trolley itself was produced in 1937 as an answer to how customers could easily move bulk grocery purchases, and the size of such trolleys grew steadily larger to both tempt and to facilitate larger total purchases by customers. Consumers also demanded more 'sanitized' and 'lazier' foodstuffs. They wanted meat in slabs in polystyrene trays, topped by clear plastic, rather than meat from the butcher they had to physically touch and cut. Cheese now came, not in a huge block from the cheesemonger that you periodically scraped the surface mould from, but in ready-cut slices in a plastic container, ready shaped to fit the pre-sliced loaf that also had to come in a plastic bag because, pre-sliced, it would not hold together like a traditional loaf would. Shoppers wanted pre-sliced onions and shrink-wrapped cauliflowers, rather than the earthy ones from greengrocers you had to wash and check for bugs. These 'lazy' foods could also be sold at a premium; ready-peeled onions, which need plastic coating because the natural protection, the outer skin, has been removed, can be sold for twice as much per kilogram as the unpeeled sort. For the same reason, added value, the supermarkets liked the shift towards another form of lazy food, pre-prepared microwave meals, which also came in plastic trays (you can't microwave food in a tinfoil tray). Black was a visually appealing colour to market the food in; the food was generally pale coloured, so the black heightened the appearance of the food. Unfortunately, the black colour defeats plastic recycling machines so these trays tended to end up in the environment as landfill. Food processors came up with a whole range of desserts never found in nature, from yoghurts to mousses to ice creams, more colourful, sweeter and with more intense (artificial, sugary) tastes than the traditional fruit once eaten as pudding. These novel products, soft and squishy to add mouthfeel appeal, also had to come in plastic packaging. Convenience lazy food also meant 'food on the go', food you could eat at a desk or whilst travelling. People became busier, put in more hours at work, started lunching at their work desk or even 'deskfasting', or leaving home without having eaten breakfast, maybe to commute to work whilst eating it to save time. Higher house prices, forcing commuters further out into longer work journeys, did not help here. This meant sandwiches in plastic wrappers, drinks you consumed out of cans using a straw, disposable plastic cups you took away from the café or shop where they were bought and drank in the street. For safety reasons, some pubs switched from glass to plastic beer glasses, reducing injuries and losses from breakages, especially where drinking tended to spill onto the street. Artificial plastic fibres also gave us brighter cheaper clothes with varied fabric textures; their cheapness meant we didn't mind that they lasted less long than the old, stiff, harder, rougher cotton garments; we never thought about where all the microfibers eventually went to that fell off these garments every time they were washed. Then we had the ever widening range of household cleaners, shampoos and conditioners, moisturizing agents, cosmetic products, hair dye, to mention but a few such product types that also generally required plastic containers. Some would come in metal cans, such as aerosols, but plastic has become cheaper than metal; toothpaste, for example, once came in squeezable tin tubes, but now comes in plastic tubes. The supermarkets enthusiastically embraced all these product lines on their shelves as they increasingly became the one-stop shop that sold everything you wanted. With a plastic credit card and plastic loyalty card, of course. At the production end, plastic has also been widely embraced, from plastic fishing nets to shrink-wrap for warehouse palleted goods. Even the factory works sign is now likely to be bright plastic, not painted wood. We never thought much about what would eventually happen to all that plastic we were making, making it precisely because it was so long lasting, even for single-use products like bags and straws. In 2015 alone, the world manufactured 407 million tonnes of plastic and simultaneously discarded 302 million tonnes of it; the cumulative total of plastic waste since the 1950s is now 6,300 million tonnes (Quartz, 2017), of which just 9% has been recycled. Within the UK, which has just under 1% of the world's population, households alone produce some 1.5 million tonnes of plastic waste a year, of which over 0.8 million tonnes originated with supermarket purchases (The Guardian, 2018).

We used to think the plastic waste problem was largely one of huge land-fills and polluting incineration; however, just 12% of that 6,300 million tonnes has ever been incinerated. That leaves almost 5,000 million tonnes sitting in landfills, or somewhere worse. That 'worse' has turned out to be ugly plastic-strewn beaches, even in remote parts of the globe where the modern 'pornucopia' of plastic goods is still largely unknown. Or huge floating archipelagos of the stuff in the middle of oceans. The galvanizing event that raised public awareness of this was the David Attenborough programme *Blue Planet II*, shown on British TV in October 2017 and in the USA in January 2018, showing the effects of plastic pollution on the oceans and marine life. More distressing images have emerged of wildlife, birds and marine animals dead after having choked on plastic, or seriously injured after being entangled in it. Then we discovered that plastic microbeads and microfibers have penetrated every corner of the planet, land sea and air, and most worryingly the animals we eat, so this pollution has penetrated our bodies too. A supermarket disposable plastic bag takes 500 to 1,000 years to break down. Plastics contain predominantly carbon-hydrogen bonds, whereas bacteria and other living organisms like to break down the carbon-oxygen, carbon-nitrogen and nitrogen-oxygen bonds found in more complex organic molecules. Without a living system to break such plastic polymer bonds, plastics endure in the environment until light (generally, ultraviolet) or oxygen break them down abiologically. This is a very slow process, especially in the oceans or in landfills, where these two breakdown agents are scarce. What does happen is that plastic waste breaks down mechanically into smaller and smaller pieces (which are still plastic polymers). This can ultimately render the plastic invisible as waste and means it no longer entangles larger animals; however, these microscopic pieces can enter the food chain, especially in the sea. Eaten by fish, they will end up inside human bodies, with as yet unknown health consequences. Are they simply excreted again, or do the tiny polymer shreds embed themselves in all our cells and begin disrupting biological processes? Many plastics also contain endocrine disruptors, meaning they mimic and confuse the body's hormone systems. These chemicals known as bisphenols (Bisphenol-A is the most potent but other bisphenols also exist with similar bio-effects) and have been used since the 1960s to harden plastics. They are also present in plasticized paper products such as disposable paper cups that are superficially waterproofed to contain the coffee. When they disrupt the body's endocrine systems, they can result in low sperm counts, male infertility, breast and prostate cancer, as well as changing the gender entirely of some marine life. They can also cause heart disease, learning disabilities and even contribute to type-2 diabetes. Nowadays, they are estimated to be present in 90% to 100% of people and certainly in younger people and teenagers. Suddenly, the plastics issue has assumed a lot more salience than localized smoke pollution, overflowing bins and some dog waste bags dangling from trees.

The media now were filled with pictures of plastic-strewn beaches, rivers choked by plastic waste, even huge 'islands' of plastic in the planet's ocean gyres. More distressing were pictures of sea life entangled in plastic that would never decay; turtles trapped in plastic fishing nets, a huge floating net discarded in the ocean and containing many trapped and dead or dying fish, another turtle that had swum into a ring pull from some beer cans and become deformed as it grew with the plastic ring around it and larger fish with deep wounds where plastic had similarly entrapped them and cut in as they grew. Filter-feeding whales faced a large risk, as they were filter-fed on plastic particles too. Land animals were not immune; birds had straws trapped in their beaks or nostrils, other birds starved because they had fed, or fed their chicks, on colourful bits of plastic. On land, there was the rather ghoulish image of cows eating plastic bags, chocking or starving as their stomachs were blocked, dying and the plastic bag drifting away intact from the cows' skeleton to be re-eaten by another cow. Less dramatically, discarded plastic bags can maintain tiny pools of water where mosquitoes can breed, propagating malaria or dengue fever.

British supermarkets frequently keep their 'plastic footprint' secret due to confidentiality agreements they sign with agencies involved in the British recycling compliance scheme. British supermarkets pay much lower costs for plastic disposal and recycling than in France or Germany, with the UK taxpayer picking up much of the cost. Supermarkets are reluctant to give full details of plastic use and recycling in case this reveals details of private sales data. However, the Co-op did state that its use of plastic dropped by 44% from 78,492 tonnes in 2006 to 43,495 tonnes in 2016 (Laville, 2018). Meanwhile, Aldi's use of plastic packaging rose from 37,261 tonnes in 2013 to 64,000 tonnes in 2016; of these 64,000 tonnes, just 3,400 tonnes was recycled. Aldi attributed the rise to its rapid UK expansion over this period from 516 to 700 stores. The supermarkets are much keener to publicize, without specific quantities, the CSR initiatives and monetary contributions (with the financial amounts stated here) that they are making towards solving the plastics pollution crisis. Waitrose, for example, promised £0.5 million to the Commonwealth Marine Plastics Research and Innovation Challenge Fund, which was set up to prevent plastic ending up in the oceans and to promote low-carbon alternatives to plastic, also £0.5 million to the Marine Conservation Society's Beach and River Clean Up. Waitrose has also turned the ecological concerns over plastic pollution of rivers and seas into a CSR initiative to clean up major British rivers, in conjunction with the environmental charity Thames21 and the Marine Conservation Society. Waitrose further pledged, in September 2016, to stop selling cotton buds (which have plastic stems) and not to stock items containing plastic microbeads. This was ahead of UK legislation that banned the manufacture of products containing microbeads altogether from January 2018 and the sale of such products from July 2018. The major use of these beads was to provide texture and roughness for face cleansers and similar products. Substitutes exist, for example, shell fragments, salt and sugar (at least there is one non-obesogenic use for that semi-poisonous substance), but these substitutes may be more expensive.

4.8 Binning the Plastic

One of the highest profile campaigns against plastic was to ditch the single-use plastic shopping bag. In Britain, a coalition of charities, conservation groups and the media succeeded in having a compulsory 5p retail charge instituted for the previously free bags. It was now illegal for any large retailer to give them out free, and many smaller retailers also began to charge. Supermarkets were expected to donate the 5p, minus VAT and administration costs, to charity, resulting in a net donation of 4p per bag. The plastic bag charge was brought in to Wales in October 2011, to Northern Ireland in April 2013, to October 2014 and to England in October 2015. Across the UK, the charge has resulted in an 83% drop in the demand for these bags, a total of nine billion fewer such bags used in the three years to 2018. There was some initial protest by people who used disposable supermarket plastic bags as bin liners, making them two-use, not single-use, but they were still then discarded into the environment. However, accusations that this was simply a ruse to promote sales of plastic bin liners were drowned out by concerns for the environment; bin liners tend to be lighter-weight plastic, as they don't have to be 'load-carrying' to the same degree as supermarket bags; they can be made more easily out of biodegradable weaker plastics. The plastic bag charge is soon to be extended to all UK retailers; originally, those employing under 250 staff were exempt, although some of these charged the 5p anyway. In Britain, the supermarket Tesco, in 2017, dropped the 5p disposable bag altogether (Webster, 2018a). The supermarket will now only be selling 10p reusable bags. Tesco has promised it will still donate to charity 4p for every reusable bag sold, with 4p going towards the cost of the bag and the rest being taken by VAT (1.67p at 20% VAT) and administration. Greenpeace welcomed the move.

Many other countries have also taken steps to outlaw single-use plastic bags. In Europe, in 2016, some 100 billion single-use plastic bags were given out in 2016, equating to 200 per person per year. Ireland was one of the first countries to introduce a compulsory charge; from 2002, disposable bags came with a 15 cent levy. In 2017, Lidl became the first Danish supermarket to ditch disposable plastic bags altogether, substituting maize-based reusable bags or Fairtrade cotton ones. The UK chains Morrison and Iceland have even returned to the old-fashioned, heavy-duty brown paper bag, familiar to shoppers in the 1970s, to sell loose fresh produce in. However, it is Africa where the most draconian measures have been taken against disposable plastic bags. In Kenya, a penalty of up to four years in prison and a fine of £31,000 was introduced in 2017 for selling, or even using such a bag. These bags were not only damaging the environment and wildlife, but were a public hygiene problem due to the problem of 'flying toilets'; the practice of using the bag as a toilet and then throwing it away. Since the plastic bag ban began, more people in the deprived Mathare district of Nairobi have been using the public toilet block, which charges 5 Kenyan Shillings (4p), or 100 Shillings for a monthly pass. In the shops of Nairobi, sisal bags are available as an alternative to plastic but are expensive because sisal has been displaced by cash crops. (Watts, 2018). The Kenyan supermarket chains, Carrefour and Nakumatt, are offering customers reusable plastic bags. Other African countries where strict bans are in place include Cameroon, Ethiopia, Guinea-Bissau, Malawi, Mali, Mauretania, Tanzania and Uganda. Meanwhile, in Malaysia, many retailers now charge 20 cents per bag (Mohezar et al, 2016), with a message printed on the bag itself prompting shoppers to reuse, not discard.

The environmental benefits of replacing disposable plastic bags with reusable ones can be used to generate 'multiplier effects' by funding further CSR initiatives. Asda is ploughing the 5p bag charge back into projects that help the environment, or the local economy. In Japan, local artists can exhibit their work on reusable supermarket bags. Lidl Cyprus has gone one stage beyond this and integrated environmentalism, promotion of local artists and a cancer charity initiative with its 'Lidl—Buy the Bag, Carry the Cause' promotion. The supermarket chain is selling upmarket hessian bags printed with designs from local artists Demos Nadar and Andreas Georgiou, and has pledged that 5 Euros from every bag sale will be donated to the Arodaphnousa Nutrition Department, which provides special diets for cancer patients, as well as promoting early diagnosis and public knowledge of the disease.

Supermarkets have been considerable users of plastic in other areas besides single-use bags. Much of their food is sold already contained in some form of plastic container. Plastic, as discussed further next, has several attractions as a material for packaging food. It makes a robust and rigid but lightweight container for the many processed foods sold in supermarkets, from ice cream to ready meals. Plastic comes in many colours and is a good foundation for printing consumer information, from sell-by dates and country of origin to list of ingredients and cooking instructions. If we are going to continue consuming soft processed foods that lack the self-contained structure of a piece of fruit, some firm structured containment is necessary; cardboard may work for frozen foods but not for sloppy ambient or even chilled foods. More controversially, firm structured, non-sloppy fruit and vegetables may be contained within clear plastic bags. This has several advantages for the supermarket. Vegetables can be sold in set quantities, already bar-coded, the customer cannot pick and choose the best-looking produce, and the contents can be sealed in a modified atmosphere, prolonging their shelf life. Plastic bags are also useful for preserving food in transit from processor or grower to the supermarket. For example, loose spinach is contained within a bag with microscopic holes in it, to admit a limited amount of oxygen only. Without this method of preservation, loose spinach could not be easily sold at supermarkets. Potatoes are preserved in transit in opaque plastic bags, which keeps light away from them and stops them going green. A cucumber shrink wrapped in plastic lasts ten days, as against three for an unwrapped one. Therefore, food packaging can have a positive social and environmental impact by reducing loss through decay. Plastic seals off the food from bacteria and oxygen. Effective food packaging has great potential to reduce food waste in less-developed countries, where most of the food waste occurs due to poor transport conditions, before the food reaches the retailer. Ironically, Tesco was praised in by Defra (2006: 41) for introducing

> reusable plastic crates, known as green trays, into its distribution chain as an effective and environmentally friendly method of delivering products from suppliers into stores and using them for displaying products in store. The hard-wearing crates, which last an average of 10 years, are continually reused to take the place of secondary product packaging in distribution. In one year alone these trays saved 69,000 tonnes of cardboard packaging, [reducing] transportation costs.

Alternatives such as glass are heavier, so delivery lorries use more fuel—a cost that might be passed on to poorer shoppers.

Consumer health might even be adversely impacted by the shift from plastic bags. The hessian or cotton substitutes being promoted can, because the material is absorbent and is being reused, become contaminated with food residue and bacteria. In San Francisco, an estimated ten extra fatalities a year through food poisoning due to food touching a dirty reusable bag. Tesco UK urges customers to use separate reusable bags for raw meat, poultry, fish and fruit and vegetables, but how many shoppers will do this all the time? The hessian bags may also have a negative environmental impact through energy use and water consumption as they require regular washing. If the demand for cotton or bamboo or other biological materials rises, these crops could displace food crops— a version of the biofuels dilemma where growing crops to fuel engines resulted in less food crops being planted. Cotton is also a very water-intensive crop, and its extensive cultivation has been blamed for the environmental disaster of the Aral Sea, which has all but vanished as its main rivers, the Syr Darya and Amu Darya, have been diverted to irrigate central Asian cotton fields. It has been estimated that a cotton shopping bag must be used 131 times before its environmental impact falls below that of a plastic disposable bag, and similarly, a steel reusable water container must be used 500 times before it becomes preferable, environmentally, to a plastic polyethylene bottle. However, environmental impact may not account for wildlife suffering, which is what excites public opinion more than arcane data on CO_2 emissions (New Scientist, 2018). Clearly, the war on plastic is a good start, but we will have to tread carefully to avoid stumbling from one environmental catastrophe straight into another one.

Iceland supermarket has pledged to stop using black plastic ready meal trays and will substitute with wood pulp trays already in manufacture, for its own brand food. It will encourage the large food brand manufacturers to do the same. Waitrose has also said it will stop using these black trays for all fresh produce, meat or fish by the end of 2018 and for ready meals, chilled or frozen, and desserts by the end of 2019. Waitrose and Asda have also committed to substituting clear plastic bottle tops for black ones to aid recycling. In Norway, the government has gone one stage further and specified that only certain types of plastic, recyclable, can be used for plastic drinks bottles. Additionally, in February 2018, Asda promised to stop using plastic packaging for its own-label frozen foods and to substitute polystyrene pizza bases with cardboard ones, saving 178 tonnes of plastic annually. Asda will also make its own brand plastics drinks bottles out of clear plastic, so as to make them easier to recycle, a further saving of 500 tonnes of plastic a year. Meanwhile, Waitrose has also committed to replacing plastic trays for fragile vegetables, such as tomatoes with biodegradable punnets made from the stems and leaves of the tomato plants themselves, utilizing a resource that was previously discarded. Asda has made a wider commitment to reduce plastic use on all own-label products by 10% in 2018, with further reductions to come.

Iceland has launched 'plastic-free aisles' where all the plastic packaging has been substituted by biodegradable wood pulp etc. A similar approach has been taken by the Dutch supermarket Ekoplaza in Amsterdam, where the plastic-free aisle looks suspiciously 'plasticy' but in fact the food wrappings are made of plant materials and will completely biodegrade once the food inside has been removed, and the crinkly flexible cellophane lookalike material is buried in a warm moist compost bin. Waitrose also has tomato punnets where the punnet is made from the stems and leaves of the same tomato plant. There is currently a sort of 'race to the top' between Asda and Iceland to be the first to eliminate the use of plastic packaging in frozen food altogether.

A further target in the 'war on plastic' is, perhaps surprisingly, disposable paper coffee cups; they have a thin plastic lining that cannot be recycled. When they are discarded, the plastic lining will probably not create distressing images of struggling wildlife, but it will contribute to the tide of plastic micro particles that most animal life on Earth has by now ingested. In Britain alone, 2.5 billion such cups are discarded every year. Waitrose in 2018, a heavy 'emitter' of such cups because of its free coffee machine offer for any customer making a purchase, however small, announced it would ditch these at its coffee machines, customers would have to use a reusable cup instead. From a financial viewpoint, Waitrose used to give out these cups at the till when customers made a purchase (some less scrupulous visitors would buy just one grape as any purchase, however small, gave entitlement to the free coffee). Now, however, Waitrose may have a problem in ensuring that coffee drinkers have actually spent anything on groceries, rather than simply walking in and refilling. Asda has also committed to ditching single-use plastic cups and even plastic cutlery from its restaurants. Customers are to be given a zero-profit reusable coffee cup instead.

Asda and Iceland will also change the 2.4 million plastic straws a year it uses to paper. Plastic straws can become trapped in the breathing holes of marine animals. Plastic straws are also being phased out by a wide range of other organizations, from the Buckingham Palace catering organization (Ampersand) to the Scotch Whisky Organisation (at its hospitality events), and by the fast food chains Wagamama and Pizza Express. Other ecological, plastic-free innovative packaging being trialled in 2018 includes beer bottles made of compressed grass and shampoo bottles made from algae. The co-operative chain is to stop using plastic in tea bag seals, saving 9 tonnes of plastic a year; if all tea bag manufacturers do the same, 150 tonnes of plastic a year could be saved. Meanwhile, France has introduced a 'bonus/malus' scheme where supermarkets are taxed more on use of non-recyclable materials and taxed less when they use recyclables. We could also design plastics not just for their immediate purpose but so they can be recycled too; one of the main appeals of plastic as a material was the almost infinite range of physical properties it could have.

A further plastic reduction scheme is to encourage the reuse of plastic drinks bottles. In 2018, the Co-op and Iceland supermarket chains broke ranks with the other large UK supermarkets by declaring support for a deposit scheme to encourage the return of empty plastic drinks bottles (Webster, 2017a). Reverse vending machines would take the old bottles and give money back, perhaps 10p or 20p, or a coupon that can be used in the participating store. Compared to the UK, with no bottle deposit scheme and a bottle return rate of 57% for plastic bottles, countries with a deposit scheme achieve bottle return rates of over 90%—e.g., Finland 92%, Lithuania 93% (0.1 Euro deposit), the Netherlands 95%, Norway 96% and Germany 98%. There may be increased littering if poor or homeless people rummage through bins to recover bottles, so-called bin-mining. One suggestion is to add clips to the outside of bins for people who can't be bothered to return the bottle themselves. However, the British Retail Consortium said the machines could cost hundreds of millions of pounds and undermine household recycling. From 2018, the UK major coffee shop chains are to offer free tap water refills so as to reduce plastic waste from water bottles. However, 70% of people feel uncomfortable asking for free tap water without making a purchase, so participating shops are to have a recognized 'free refills available here' blue sign to encourage people to use the scheme.

Some shoppers are taking 'direct action', by removing plastic wrapping from products they pick up in supermarkets before they put them through the till. Some motivation for this may be from less frequent bin collections as much as from an environmental imperative. A well-publicized event of this sort took place at the Tesco supermarket in Keynsham, a suburban town between Bristol and Bath, in March 2018. The store manager was good-natured about the heaps of plastic left in the store; the whole exercise constituted free publicity for the company and was a boost to its environmental CSR credentials. Meanwhile, the UK government is also examining other ways to tackle the plastic waste problem, with suggestions that it should be buried for future 'mining' as a fuel resource, once we have solved the problem of the pollution it emits when incinerated. A process already exists to turn plastic into fuel oil by pyrolysis, but the process is currently inefficient and not financially viable.

As noted earlier, plastic has been of great utility to supermarkets and to shoppers. The campaign to reduce or even eliminate it (there is a niche 'zero-waste' organic whole foods store in Totnes, Devon, that uses no plastic at all) will not be problem-free. An early issue was people stealing the wire baskets or even trolleys to take their purchases home, back in 2012, when people were accustomed to the use of free disposable plastic bags. In Wales, where the 5p bag charge came in earliest, the Morrison store in Aberystwyth lost half its wire baskets within a month of the new bag charge, whilst the Tesco in Denbigh was left with just 150 of its original 500 baskets. Supermarkets had to resort to security-tagging the baskets to stop them from being taken out of the store to the car park, as if they were valuable alcoholic drinks; the cost was £1 to £4 per tag, but a new basket would cost the store £5 to £15. Supermarkets hate waste, when it is costing them money. However, there is one form of waste the supermarkets have been very much guilty of, and surprisingly, it does not cost them very much at all, which is food waste. Food waste does not cost the supermarkets much because, as we shall see in Section 4.9, the costs of unsold food can be passed straight back to the producer. However, whilst food waste might not be an immediate problem for the large retail chains, it is a considerable issue for society and even the environment.

4.9 Food Waste

Morally, it is indefensible that any food is wasted when people are starving in the Global South, and there is hunger and malnutrition even in the cities of the developed world. Environmentally, food takes energy, also resources, water, land, fertilizers, to produce and these resources should not be squandered. It is even more iniquitous that food waste occurs largely for political or economic reasons. In the Global South, food waste occurs largely at the production and distribution stage. Wars, civil conflict, damaged infrastructure and poor storage conditions cause much food to be lost. Global-South consumers, however, tend to be thrifty with food, as poverty dictates. In the Global North, it is the opposite; production and storage is generally efficient, although political issues can cause losses within the distribution side of the food chain there too. The *Times* reported (Paton, 2015) that every month £2 billion of fresh produce bound for the UK was written off because migrants at Calais were breaking into lorries. However, retailers and consumers waste much food because they can afford to (Shaw, 2014: 162–3). Misshapen or 'ugly' produce is rejected by retailers, because consumers often won't buy it. Consumers are also tempted to overbuy with Buy-One-Get-One-Free offers and then discard the food because it has gone bad. Sometimes, the food actually is still edible but is simply past its sell-by date. Consumers routinely throw out food that is past its 'sell-by' date that was perfectly edible; this form of waste means that in developed countries some 40%– 60% of food waste is generated by households (Griggin et al, 2009).

Globally, huge amounts of food produced for human consumption are wasted; overall, around 40% of all human food that leaves the farm gate is never eaten by people (Fox, 2013). Paradoxically, that represents an opportunity to feed the growing global population of the 21st century and beyond, which may rise to 10 or even 12 billion, from its current 7.6 billion, by 2100 (Garbero & Sanderson, 2014: 669). If humanity is just about feeding itself now, on 60% of the food we grow for human consumption, then by reducing food waste from 40% to say 10% we effectively raise food availability by half, from 60% of what we grow to 90%. Then with no other changes and assuming water and fertilizer remain available as now and the climate does not deteriorate and curb food production, we can feed not 7.6 billion but half as many again, 11.4 billion people.

Much food waste by households due to ignorance about when food becomes unsafe. As noted earlier, supermarkets and their sanitized plastic-wrapped food has promoted a disconnect between the consumer and the food we eat so that shoppers rely mechanistically on a use by or sell-by date, at which point overnight the food suddenly changes from consumable to poison. Our grandparents knew by the look and smell of food whether it was edible or not. UK households throw away 500 million pints of milk a year of which 100 million pints were still drinkable but past its use-by date (Webster, 2017b). Milk is one of the easiest foods to check if it is still drinkable, because it develops an odour and changes texture long before it becomes undrinkable; in fact, sour milk is the basis for many dairy foods we do consume, such as yoghurt and cheese. Our forebears knew how to salvage stale food, toasting old hard bread, for example, or making bread and butter pudding. Shoppers want unblemished perfect-looking produce, even though the misshapen stuff is just as tasty and nutritious, and the original shape is gone when chopped and cooked. Households don't want bits like the broccoli stalk or the darker green 'flags' on leeks, although these bits contain the most nutrients such as iron. They can also make tasty soups, but few shoppers have the culinary skills or time to make soup anymore.

We may no longer learn cooking skills from our grandmother, but there is always the Internet. In fact, Friends of the Earth has 40 tips online for using stale bread (Friends of the Earth, 2017), yet many households just discard such foods and go out and buy more, which suits the supermarkets very well. British households discard 25 million slices of bread a day perceived to be 'stale' that could have been toasted and eaten. This is just a part of the 7.3 million tonnes of food, £13 billion worth, that was needlessly binned in the UK in 2015. This food, if it had been eaten, "would have had an environmental benefit equivalent to taking one in four cars off the road" (The Guardian, 2018: 59). Meanwhile, in Australia, with a population less than half the UK's, 44 million tonnes of food is wasted annually, almost 2 tonnes per person per year (Edwards & Mercer, 2012). Australia has an even more concentrated retail grocery market share than the UK, with the top-three supermarkets having 82.0% of the market; in 2016, Woolworths took 36.3% share, Coles took 33.2% and Aldi, fast growing, took a 12.5% share (Roy, 2016). This concentration gives the two top players enormous power over growers to reject 'inferior', misshapen produce. This commercial power may partly account for why Australian food waste per capita is so high. Our caveman hoarding attitude to food doesn't help either. If a supermarket, or restaurant, runs out of food, we think it's a failure; we don't concern ourselves about the surplus food left over if it doesn't run out.

Supermarkets waste even more food before the consumer ever sees it. Some of this isn't even because the food 'looks ugly' or is misshapen; it is for purely mechanical reasons. Long potatoes that don't fit the oval, nearly round, ideal shape may be rejected, as they don't roll well in the mechanical harvester. Supermarkets prefer standard-sized, straight cucumbers because 40 of these fit well in a standard box. Supermarket economics also waste food. It was once said of Centre Point, a large office block in central London, that it was better for the owner not to rent it out because the annual growth in its capital value was higher than the rental income per year if it had been let out, which would have then 'frozen' the actual income the building was generating (Childs, 2015). In a similar manner, it may pay supermarkets not to discount food near its sell-by date, but to throw it away after closing time because nobody has bought it at full price, when it has nearly expired. The retailer doesn't want to set a new lower price point expectation amongst canny shoppers who may time their shopping trip for near the end of the day when such discounts may be made. The wasted food can go to biofuel, which is better than dumping it in a landfill where it produces methane and carbon dioxide. Nevertheless, this is a very inefficient use of the food, the resources and energy that went into its production and transport. Unfortunately, government fiscal incentives, developed for the useful purpose of promoting renewable energy and reducing greenhouse emissions, create a perverse incentive to send food for biofuel rather than donate it to charities for the poor. Anaerobic digesters are paid a subsidy of £60–70 for every tonne of food they receive, whereas the charity FareShare has to charge retailers £60–80 for every tonne of food received to cover storage and distribution costs. In the year to March 2013, Britain's anaerobic digesters received a £29 million subsidy, and the UK has 82 plants that consumed 1.6 million tonnes food, and a further 213 plants already have planning permission. They will consume an additional 3.3 million tonnes of 'surplus' food annually, yet, of course, there is no such thing as a 'surplus' food, only food discarded by supermarkets, unwanted by shoppers, but which could have gone to feed someone, somewhere. It is possible to make improvements in the destination of unwanted food, in terms of it always being more efficient to feed it to people than animals and more efficient to feed it to animals than to use it as biofuel. In the UK, Adnams Brewery has arranged with the supermarket chain M&S to utilize the leftover bread crusts from M&S sandwich supplier Greencore to make beer. Beer is made with grains, such as barley, wheat and rye; the same materials used to make bread. The surplus bread would otherwise go to animal feed, and this process reduces the CO_2 emissions from the brewing process. Bread is a major contributor to food waste in Britain, with households throwing away 24 million slices a day—44% of the total they buy. M&S sells 93 million sandwiches a year, none of which utilizes the bread crust end (Smithers, 2018).

France, which in 2015 discarded 7.1 million tonnes of food a year, 67% by consumers, 15% by restaurants and 11% by shops, has actually made it a criminal offence for supermarkets of size over 400 square metres to throw away unsold food. Some French supermarkets had been pouring bleach on discarded food to deter 'freegans'. Freegans comprise a loose and heterogeneous group of the ecologically concerned, those protesting against the inequity of global capitalism and those simply wanting to live cheaper. A huge amount of perfectly edible food can be salvaged from supermarket bins after closing time, but there are downsides for the supermarket, for society and for the freegans themselves (Tibbett, 2013). Freegans are trespassing (a small crime perhaps compared to discarding food, on a moral as opposed to a strict blackletter legal conception of the law anyway) and some freegans may scatter rubbish as they salvage. If they injure themselves, the supermarket may be liable, and freegan food is not without its health risks, including cuts in sharp objects, falls and contamination by chemicals, bacteria, rodents and faecal matter. This may impose costs on the health services. Also, supermarkets may be concerned that whilst they suffer no direct loss from people recovering their discarded food; they may suffer an indirect loss as less food is then sold through the regular food retail system. Discarded surplus supermarket food in France must be donated to charity, and the supermarket must prepare in advance a 'donation contract' specifying where unsold food will go. If food is thrown away, the supermarket manager could be fined up to Euro 75,000 or even face up to two years prison. The supermarket must not simply dump all surplus food, wholesome and rotten, on the charity but must present the edible food in a 'ready to use' form. Food banks now can donate fresh food to the poor, whereas previously, it had been mainly tinned and dry goods; this improves the nutritional health of the poor, who can now consume more fresh fruit and vegetables.

Supermarkets have begun to tackle the issue of discarded food, as they realize the potential for good publicity that can be gained through CSR initiatives in this area. The major food retailers can gain a double benefit from CSR initiatives that divert unwanted foods from the bin, or the biofuel processor, to deprived households, both efficient use of such food and helping the disadvantaged. Tesco, in 2016, threw away 1% of all its stock because it is out of date or damaged, a total of 55,400 tonnes of food, of which 30,000 tonnes, or 70 million meal equivalents, could have been eaten. The company has now linked with the charity Fare-Share in a programme called Community Food Connection to donate food to charity for human consumption. Tesco uploads details of unsold food to the food cloud app, which charities can then come and collect. Food collected goes to homeless shelters, domestic violence refuge hostels and after-school clubs. Similarly, Waitrose has developed a mobile app, FairShare Go, which enables store managers to tell charities what surplus food they have to donate. Managers input food details and charities then receive a text message. Trials of FairShare Go began in 2017 at 25 Waitrose supermarkets. Asda also organizes leftover food distribution to charities through its website, In Kind Direct, which supports over 8,000 smaller UK charities by organizing distribution to them of non-food and ambient food surpluses from supermarkets. It is easy to overlook the non-food needs of charities dedicated to feeding the homeless and destitute; charities themselves need stationery, bathroom and kitchen supplies, and other non-food items, and the charity beneficiaries will need not just food but clothing, medical items, cooking utensils and much else from the wide range of goods the large supermarket corporations sell. Tesco, from 2018, will allow employees to take unsold food on its sell-by date for free. Lidl also donates fridges and freezers to charities distributing food to the poor and homeless. An issue with such charities was lack of facilities for preserving fresh food with a short shelf life, meaning that they could only distribute less-healthy tinned or dry foods.

A parallel system of food donations from supermarkets to the not-quite-so-poor exists, called 'social supermarkets'. The first social supermarket opened in Barnsley, Yorkshire (UK), in December 2013. Food is donated free by M&S, Morrison and Ocado. The food is then sold cheaply to members, who are limited in the number of times they can visit to get the reduced price items. Members have to provide proof of low wealth when they sign up, as with food banks (which also restrict 'withdrawals'), a reference from the Benefits Office, for example. The social supermarket may locate for free in a vacant industrial unit on the edge of town, donated by the landlord, who would rather see the premises occupied and looked after than empty and prone to decay and vandalism. Tesco donates much stock here, including food with wrong weight printed, which can't be legally sold in a Tesco store, or mislabelled items, such as chocolate mousse with a lemon mousse lid on top. In an echo of the moralistic philanthropy of the Quakers, no alcohol or cigarettes are sold. In Copenhagen, Denmark, there is the WeFood social supermarket where proceeds from food sales of food donated by the large supermarkets are used for aid in developing countries. This initiative required a change in Danish law (which WeFood successfully lobbied for) because previously all food sold in Denmark was subject to a sales tax.

It should be noted, however, that these very worthwhile schemes are nevertheless by no means a panacea for poverty, for several reasons. Society may feel that the problems of inequality and poverty have been 'solved' by having the supermarkets as food suppliers of last resort to the poor; it might be better to go back and ask why, even within wealthy countries, destitution and food poverty exist. This point was made by Les Gars' pilleurs, a food action group based in Lyons, France, which has retrieved discarded yet edible food from supermarket bins to give to charity, was not totally happy. They asserted that the legal measures by France to outlaw supermarkets throwing food in the bins referred to earlier could make people complacent, that the supermarkets have solved the issue of food waste, whilst the issues of overproduction and waste in the entire food industry go unaddressed. Also, supermarket-donated food is often non-essential items shoppers don't want, such as unusual flavours of yoghurt (e.g. lemon and coconut) that were trialled but nobody wanted to buy. Meanwhile, Oxfam has reported that recipients of food bank aid have had to return rice, spaghetti and soup since they have no electricity to cook the food. The very poorest may live in hostels or bed and breakfast accommodation where they have no access to a kitchen and may be forced to leave between morning and evening. They may lack storage and refrigeration space for food, and even sleep in an environment where nothing can be stored securely. Food donations to the poor via charities should be seen in a wider socio-economic context, or perhaps this is incorrect politics; as Archbishop Helder Camara of Brazil said, "*When I give food to the poor, they call me a saint. When I ask why they have no food, they call me a Communist*".

In terms of helping households to reduce the amount of supermarket-purchased food they waste, there are also some technological solutions, but these may need some refinement before they can be universally adopted. In 2016, Sainsbury's launched its 'Waste Less Save More' campaign, a £10 million, five-year campaign to get households to waste less food—food that households were going to discard is first weighed on scales connected to an iPad with an app called Winnow. This tells the user what the retail price of the food item is; a nudge factor to tell them how much money they are wasting. In Sainsbury's £1 million Waste Less Save More Campaign, participants also kept food diaries and worked with chefs and food nutritionists to go 'back to basics' in how they bought, stored, prepared, cooked and ate food, Sainsbury gave out free fridge thermometers to help set fridges at optimum temperature. In this campaign to reduce food waste, Swadlincote, a town in Derbyshire, UK, population 35,000, was chosen as it already had a recycling rate above the national average. Households were also given pasta portion measures, so people didn't cook too much. However, surplus cooked pasta can easily be utilized later with, for example, melted cheese on top, or served in home-made salads. Other solutions included weekly meal planners, with magnets to stick on the fridge, and encouraging the use of shopping lists. Nutritionists accompanied shoppers to the supermarket to advise on easy but healthy recipes, advising, for example, on how to make banana bread out of over-ripe bananas. The local council also provides a booklet with simple recipes and tips to avoid food waste.

Trials suggested households could reduce food waste by 68% within a month, saving them £258 a year, but after a one-year trial the target of reducing food waste by 50% was dropped after it proved hard to change consumer behaviour. The greatest savings were made by families who were already educated, ecologically minded and familiar with technology, whereas it was the less food-knowledgeable households who could benefit most from reducing the costs of food waste. Perhaps the target should have been, not to avoid 'food waste' at the initial use stage, as people are imperfect and not always ideal at planning meals. Rather, the aim could have been to show how to avoid throwing away 'surplus' food, such as excess pasta, storing it safely and then re-incorporating it into later meals. Regarding food wasted by households, the Australian supermarket chain Woolworths has a programme called Food Savers, encouraging Australian households to use, not throw away, leftover food, with innovative recipes for such foodstuffs.

There have been several initiatives in the area of 'ugly' or misshapen food to ensure that such food gets accepted by consumers rather than being thrown away. In France, the Intermarche supermarket chain, in

July 2014, began a sales initiative called 'vegetables moche', which translates as 'inglorious vegetables'. They sold, at a 30% discount over normal-looking fruit and vegetables, the misshapen ones that shoppers used to reject and supermarkets throw out, or refuse to buy in the first place from growers (Intermarche, 2014). Growers benefitted from sales of previously unsaleable produce and shoppers got cheaper produce. Intermarche itself realized a direct commercial return, as it saw a 24% rise in footfall. To convince shoppers that misshapen vegetables taste exactly the same as their more photogenic brethren, the store also market fruit juices and vegetable smoothies made from these same misshapes, all in a special aisle branded 'moche', with a major advertising campaign to back up the new produce line. In 2017, the UK supermarket chain Asda adopted a similar scheme, selling 'wonky veg boxes' at £3.50, a 30% discount compared to normal-looking produce, and in 2018, Morrison began selling 'wonky chillies' at a 39% discount. They have the same taste as 'normal' chillies, but may have 'extreme curvature' or missing stalks. Across the Pyrenees in Spain a Barcelona-based group, Espigoladors, takes poor people out to farmers' fields where unsightly produce has been rejected by supermarkets at the farm harvest stage. The poor can then take this produce free to feed themselves and their families. Importantly, this avoids the stigma of using a food bank or church handout. Spain 2015 discards some 7.7 million tonnes of edible food a year, 163 kg per person. Espigoladors estimates it has recovered some 70 tonnes of this food; they aim to recover more and create employment too by having some of this rejected food turned into soups, jams and juices for sale. These would be sold under Espigolador's brand name, 'Es Im-perfect', meaning 'It's Imperfect'. Espigoladors tries to separate the idea of aesthetics from food by showing schoolchildren pictures of misshapen produce, heart-shaped potatoes or three-headed lemons; the children find this hilarious, having only ever seen standard-shaped produce in supermarkets and want the items for themselves. Across the entire EU, some 90 million tonnes is wasted because it is 'ugly' or damaged (a dented tin, for example) or too close to its sell-by date. Espigoladors currently only operates around Barcelona but aims to spread across Catalonia and to other regions of Spain.

Environmentalists have also alleged that supermarket food marketing practices increase food waste, especially the BOGOF, or Buy One Get One Free offer. Such 'multibuy' offers may encourage households to buy too much, which then goes off before it can be eaten, or BOGOFs encourage over-eating and promote obesity. Most BOGOF food is unhealthy, and 40% of supermarket food is bought on such deals in 2018 (Smyth, 2018a), 'most of it unhealthy'. Tesco has suggested modifying BOGOF into deferred deals, "buy one now get one free later". In 2016, Sainsbury's scrapped multibuy deals, saying customers 'found them confusing' as well as increasing household food waste. However, there was also a motivation to match the standard unit prices of the discount supermarkets

Aldi and Lidl, who are rapidly gaining market share at the expense of the larger UK supermarket chains. Scrapping such deals might appear to be a 'middle-class' response to food waste, as they can afford to pay the full price more than poorer households can. Perhaps part of a common CSR standard for supermarkets might be, how much healthy fresh produce they offer on BOGOFs, rather than unhealthy sugary food, along with some educational initiatives on how to 'rescue' vegetables slightly past their best but still edible, for example, make them into soup.

Overall, 'the environment' can be quite a slippery term when it enters the realm of supermarket CSR and is all too often used for profit or to gain green credit rather than make a genuine improvement to the ecosystems of our planet. However, at least the environment has a range of activists campaigning for it. This is an advantage that the hidden army of people, farmers, farm staff, food processing workers do not have. This may leave them open to exploitative conditions imposed on them so as to keep supermarket shelf prices low. The effect of supermarkets on this 'hidden army' is the subject of Chapter 5 of this book.

5 Food Retailing and Supermarket Suppliers

5.1 Supermarket Monopsonies and Farm Prices

The size of the supermarkets, their buying power, is a crucial factor in how far down they can force food supplier prices. As we saw in Chapter 1, in most developed counters, a few supermarkets impose considerable monopsonistic power. Moreover, the supermarkets are usually international in scope; the farmers and food processors who supply them are often small and national, with a few exceptions, such as the US fruit conglomerates. Fox and Vorley (2004: 8) illustrated that a retailer with 5% market share would be paying 100% average supplier price, and smaller retailers with around 1% market share were paying 101% to 105% average supplier price. However, retailers with 10% to 15% market share were paying 98% average supplier price, and the retailer with 25% market share (unnamed, but would likely be Tesco) was paying 96% average supplier price. Most developed countries have one or several supermarkets with 20% or more of the market share each. In 2004, Blythman (2004: 137) wrote of how British farmers lived in fear of upsetting the supermarkets, because "fall out with one [supermarket] and you get blacklisted (delisted) by the lot of them because they all talk to one another". As another farmer put it back then, "As soon as you [complain] that's a nail in your coffin". The supermarket buyers, who moved in to actually negotiate contracts after the supermarket CEOs had idealistically expressed their wish to support and work with the farmers, were young and ruthless. There was some suggestion that these buyers were deliberately moved around sectors, kept inexperienced, to prevent any long-term personal supportive relationships being built up between buyer and producer. The buyers may be as hard pressed to get results as the farmers are to produce, monitored by supermarket head office on their profit generation, and not in the same post long enough to care about general food chain sustainability.

Both farmers and supermarkets operate in a business environment that can sometimes change radically, in a matter of hours. For the farmer, a pest infestation, adverse weather, floods or even sudden shifts in input prices, such as oil or fertilizer can suddenly reduce the size of the harvest, or its expected financial return. Yet farming is by nature a long-returns business; inputs take weeks or months, sometimes years, to mature into saleable goods. Ideally, therefore, a farmer would want a long-term contract from their customer whilst at the same time having the flexibility to vary what they deliver on that contract with no commercial repercussions. On the other side of the negotiations desk, supermarkets face the same issues. Demand for their goods can vary up or down within hours; a product scare, or a cookery TV programme calling for some ingredient, can send demand plummeting or soaring. In fact, celebrities such as TV chefs are supposed to notify supermarkets if they intend to broadcast a recipe which calls for some item that will rarely be available in bulk in the average supermarket. Occasionally, this system breaks down, as when Delia Smith, in 1990, described a recipe for truffle torte using liquid glucose. The supermarkets had not been warned in advance, and the shelves were soon cleared of liquid glucose across Britain. This results in both disgruntled customers and TV viewers complaining to the broadcaster (Bonner, 2011: 232). Supermarkets need dependable supplies, yet with the freedom to change order amounts at short notice, just as the farmers do, substituting 'supply' for 'order'.

5.2 The Price of Milk

The issue of milk prices illustrates issues of supermarket prices to wholesalers.

Supermarkets, because they are very few in number compared to the multiplicity of food suppliers, are by far the most powerful players in the food chain and can effectively hold upstream suppliers, including farmers, to ransom over prices, retrospectively enforcing price cuts or delaying payment until long after the food has been delivered. Alternatively, the supermarkets can behave ethically and play a role in supporting an often beleaguered sector that enjoys much sympathy with the public. Consumers, perhaps cash-strapped themselves, may exhibit inconsistent purchasing habits, simultaneously seeking the lowest priced produce whilst blaming the supermarkets for impoverishing farmers. This double attitude applies both to UK and overseas producers; the same consumers who seek low grocery prices may then buy Fairtrade and feel good about this ethical purchase. Farmers facing cost pressures from downstream may then pass these cuts on to their employees in the form of reduced pay and conditions, and this can occur in the UK as well as overseas, leading to political issues, such as the employment of migrant labour on illegal sub-Minimum wages, undercutting indigenous farm labour.

The price of milk, how it gets from cow to consumer, and the collateral damage from the 'milk price war' that supermarkets have waged on suppliers presents a whole microcosm of the deleterious effects of supermarket commercial power on the farming industry and wider rural society.

Milk is frequently priced artificially low, because it is a Known Value Item (KVI), meaning the consumer has a good idea of what milk usually costs in the shop. With thousands of product lines in the average supermarket, and numerous variations in brand, size, flavour and quality, most consumers have little or no idea of what most of these lines 'should' cost; they are price-takers for most of these items. UK supermarkets, competing on price with each other and, since the 1990s with the hard discounters Lidl and Aldi, are keen to offer KVIs at as low a price as possible, whilst maintaining wider profit margins on non-essential items. These non-essentials are bought less regularly, and consumers can be persuaded to put them in the trolley by a whole panoply of marketing techniques, even at higher prices, whilst milk may even be sold as a loss leader, a line sold at below cost to lure customers in. Milk is a relatively price-inelastic good, meaning that lower prices do not generally raise the quantity consumers demand. Supermarkets will appreciate this, because they don't want to sell too much of a good that is low in price—rather, they want consumers to buy increased amounts of the more profitable lines, along with the milk purchase. However, this means that low milk prices cannot be credited with increasing consumption of beneficial nutrients, such as calcium, and the dairy farm industry sees no benefit of increased demand either. Nevertheless, this doesn't stop Walmart from claiming 'low prices on healthy food' as a CSR tagline.

Unfortunately for dairy farmers, the supermarkets have determined that the 'loss' in loss leaders should be borne by the dairies and behind them the farmers, not the retailers. Table 5.1 illustrates the decline in the farm-gate price paid to farmers, even as the retail price rose between 1995 and 2005. The retail price of milk spiked in 2009 with the boom in commodity, oil and energy prices associated with the Credit Crunch, but some supermarkets also used the general price rise as an excuse to widen their profit margins in milk, getting a profit of up to 26p per litre. At this time, the farm-gate price was 25p to 30p, so just below the breakeven

Table 5.1 UK Price of Milk, Per Litre

Year	Farm gate*	Breakeven farm price	Retail (cheapest, non-organic)**
1995	25p		45p
2005	20p		55p
2009	25p–30p	30p	65p
2014	31.6p	30p	40p
2015	24p	31p	38p
2016	26–28p	30p	38p
2018	26.5p		43p

*   Price paid by dairies to farmers.
** This price was derived from a search of the websites of the UK cheapest grocery retailers, e.g., Aldi and Lidl, and was for larger packs of 4 or 6 pints.

farm price of 30p. The farmer was getting zero (or even negative) profit for producing the milk; the dairy was getting a few pennies per litre for collecting, bottling and pasteurizing the milk, yet the supermarket was getting the lion's share of the profit for simply driving the milk to super-market branches, putting it on shelves and selling it (and the customer was doing most of the 'selling' work, if they bought at an automatic till). Retail milk prices fell back even further after 2010 due to keener com-petition from the expanding deep discount chains Aldi and Lidl, coupled with the general economic recession of the Credit Crunch. Again, this price squeeze was passed back to the farmer, with farm-gate prices falling as low as 24p per litre in 2015, when the farm breakeven price was still 30p. In 2014, Morrison, for example, was selling 4 pints (2.3 litres) of milk at 51.3p per litre in 2014, and in some supermarkets, the same 4 pints could be bought for as little as 38.7p per litre. Tesco in March 2014 cut the price of their 4-pint packs from £1.39 to just £1.00 (from 60p per litre down to 44p) and then even the upmarket and socially responsible Waitrose chain price-matched this for MyWaitrose cardholders, a price point already attained by Aldi, Asda and Lidl. By early 2016, the retail price of milk had drifted even lower still, with Waitrose selling 6 pints at 43.4p per litre, whilst the same quantity retailed at Aldi for 37.9p per litre. Waitrose Duchy organic milk, meanwhile, was priced at around 85p per litre. The local north-western UK chain of grocers, Booths, did guarantee a farm-gate price of 35.5p (2014) with its supplier, Wiseman. Chris Dee, CEO of Booths, commented, "a lot of our stores are in rural areas and dairy farmers are our customers" (Doward, 2014). As are the people who depend on the rural dairy economy, from farm workers and mechanics to accountants and architects.

In 2018, with the issue of farmers getting below-cost prices for their milk having faded somewhat from the public arena, dairies were again squeezing the farm-gate price back down below 27p per litre. Mean-while, the supermarkets continued to retail this milk at between 43p and 60p a litre.

Events 2,000 miles to the east of the UK also depressed the milk price as President Putin of Russia, in revenge for Western sanctions imposed over the Ukraine, ordered a boycott of European food products in 2014, resulting in a milk surplus in Europe. British farm-gate milk prices have also been dragged down by cheaper prices prevailing in the rest of the EU, where land and labour may be cheaper. Long run, global warming may also be raising grass growth and milk yields, lowering the global milk price (as noted earlier, milk is price-inelastic; more supply will just mean a lower price). In 2015, the average EU price per litre was 22.7p, 1.3p below the UK level; European prices ranged from 41.3p in Cyprus down to 16p in Lithuania. However, the breakeven price for many UK dairy farms was 30–32p a litre in 2014, and for Cotswold farmers, the water the cows drank to produce the milk could be more profitably sold, as bottled spring water, for 80p a litre (Lawrence, 2008: 77). In Tesco (2017), milk was retailing for 45p per pint (79.2p per litre); at the same time, Highland Spring water was on sale for 50p for 500ml, or £1.00 per litre. Similarly, in Australia, in 2011, Coles was retailing milk at 1 AU$ (ca. 50p) a litre, again leaving little or no surplus for the farmer.

In Australia, Coles supermarket cut the price of milk to 1 AU$ per litre "to ease the cost of living pressure on Australian families, and was accused by its main rival Woolworths of dropping prices so quickly that farmers and processors had no time to adjust" (Wilson, 2011). The individual consumer, buying a couple of litres a week, may see little connection between their few pennies or cents price saving and hardship for the farmer, but one should remember that with an average dairy farm producing 1 million litres of milk a year, from 130 cows, a 1p fall in the price equates to a cut in farm income of £10,000.

In summary, UK consumers in 2014/5 were paying around 45p a litre for milk, with the price even lower in 2016, and the farmers were receiving 25p for this milk, even though the farm-gate breakeven price was at least 30p. It wasn't the processors, the dairy giants like Arla, Dairy Crest and Wisemans, who were making the most profit out of this price differential; the processor gate price of milk was around 36.5p in 2014, and the processors had to collect the milk from the farms and package it. The milk processors have indeed squeezed the farmers, and suffered farmers protests against that, but the supermarkets have been the biggest winners in the milk price war.

The squeeze on the farm-gate milk price has forced farms to copy the supermarkets and merge to attain greater economies of scale. Smaller milk producers have been forced out of the market, with the number of herds of 1,000 of more cows in the UK almost doubling between 2012 and 2014, from 23 to 44 whilst over the same period more than 1,000 small dairy farms, with fewer than 100 cows each, closed. The number of dairy farms in the UK has fallen from 35,000 in 1995 to just 13,000 in 2014, whilst the number of UK dairy cows has risen by 100,000 since 2011 to 1.9 million. Whereas once a dairy farm had less than 10 cows, the average number per farm is now around 150. Such a huge herd requires considerable capital investment to operate efficiently, with farms installing computerized milking parlours that might cost £250,000, for example. This investment in capital which could neither be put to any other use nor re-sold raised significant exit barriers to dairy farmers and put them even more under the control of the supermarkets. Effectively, the normal supply price curve has been inverted. Instead of sloping up, meaning a reduced price elicits less quantity supplied, the lower price of milk has prompted farms to invest in technology that increases the milk produced, and the more milk is produced, the more the price is likely to fall. The milk supply price curve now effectively slopes downwards. There is also a 'hog cycle' effect with rising dairy farm investment in

2013, when the farm-gate price peaked, and then rapid disinvestment is not possible when the farm-gate price falls again. The heavy investment in technology and equipment by farmers effectively traps them into producing commodities (and not only milk) even when the farm profits sink into negative territory.

The milk processors have sought their own economies of scale, angering farmers in the process. Arla, Dairy Crest, Muller and Wiseman have bought out local dairies and created regional monopolies; farmers now have no choice over which dairy they send their milk to, leaving them even more vulnerable to price cuts, and lengthening food miles in the process. The processors also cut the price they paid farmers for milk from 35p per litre in May 2014 to just 27p per litre in November 2014, resulting in protests by Farmers for Action outside Wiseman Dairy in Shropshire in 2015. Small farmers were suffering the most because some dairies pay a 'volume bonus' of 2p extra per litre to farms producing at least 23,000 litres a day, which is only attainable if the herd is at least 1,100 strong. This is because it is cheaper for dairies to collect at fewer larger farms than to visit many smaller ones. Because of this regional monopoly, when Muller proposed to cut the price it paid for milk from 23.15p to 22.35p per litre in September 2015, farmers could not go and sell it elsewhere. Dairy farmers have also mounted protests against supermarkets, ranging from taking the milk to the checkout and leaving it there, to pouring it away on the supermarket floor, to buying all the milk in a supermarket and giving it away to charity, to taking cattle into the supermarket itself. This last incident occurred in Stafford, where a farmer uploaded footage on YouTube, saying, "A litre of milk should not be cheaper than a litre of water"; social media enabled the protest to reach a global audience. Farmers have also protested outside supermarket regional distribution centres, blocking the movement of lorries in and out.

Organizations such as the Free Range Dairy have attempted to revitalize and segment the milk market so that 'premium' can generate a better return for small dairy farmers. They would like to de-homogenize the milk market, saying that the pooling of milk by large dairies means milk has lost its 'terroir', or regional flavour, an interesting parallel with the French wine market here. The annual milk yield per cow in the UK rose steadily from 5,500 litres in the 1990s to 6,900 litres in 2005 and to 7,800 by 2015, raising issues of animal welfare as cows suffered mastitis and infections. In turn, the risk of infection compels the overuse of antibiotics, which spreads the risk of antibiotic resistant bacteria causing hard to treat human ailments. Concern over the large usage of antibiotics in farming led M&S, in 2017, to become the first UK supermarket to publish details of the use of antibiotics in its farm supply chain (Harvey, 2017). More antibiotics are now used in farming than on humans. There are concerns that, for example, the increasing prevalence of drug-resistant bacteria such as methicillin-resistant *Staphylococcus aureus* (more commonly known as MRSA) may make routine hip operations difficult or even impossible in the near future.

Cows are kept in sheds permanently and never graze outside because it is easier to milk them three times a day, although this is an energy-intensive process, so not good for the environment either. Holstein cows can produce 30 litres a day compared to just 23 litres from shorthorns, which raises an issue of potential breed loss amongst cows. Farmers would commit to outside grazing for their cows, reassuring to consumers who would like 'cruelty-free' milk; farmers can take their herds indoors during winter or in periods of exceptional weather such as summertime floods and storms. The Free Range Dairy points out that milk from outside grazed cows contains higher levels of Omega-3 and other dietary essentials. However, the problem is that such considerations will only be noted by a small section of wealthier consumers; for most people, milk is just "the same homogenous white stuff", to be purchased as cheaply as possible.

5.3 Other Supermarket Food Prices

Milk is not the only item that supermarkets sell cheaply to create a halo of 'low price' about the whole store. Bananas, like milk, are a KVI; they are also a popular fruit, sweet and easy to peel, children like them, and they are deemed to be healthy. As they are a KVI, once one supermarket lowers the price all others have to follow suit, and the price reduction is passed back up the chain to producers. Like milk, the actual workers who pick them, equivalent to the farmers who actually milk the cows, may get disproportionately little of the final retail price the UK consumer pays in the supermarket. The wholesale banana market is largely controlled by giants like Fyffes and Chiquita, who have merged and control 14% of the wholesale banana market, also Del Monte and Dole Foods. However, once again, it is the large supermarkets who have the real power, even over these food processing giants.

As with milk, supermarket competition has driven British banana prices down, from £1.00 per kilogram in 1994 to just 90p in 2010. In 2010, banana plantation workers got 4% of the UK retail price, the growers got 20%, the transporters who took the bananas from the plantations to the EU got 23%, an EU tariff accounted for a further 12% of the retail price, the companies who ripened and then distributed the bananas within the UK took 12%, and the supermarket retailer (who as with milk merely shelves and sells the fruit) took the largest share at 29% (Nicholson & Young, 2012: 18). In the UK, once Walmart took over Asda, it negotiated a lower banana price with Del Monte, reducing the wholesale price of the fruit from £1.08 per kilo to £0.85 in 2003 (Prieto-Carron, 2006: 101). By 2012, supermarket competition had driven the retail price of bananas down even further to 85p and then 79p a kilogram, plunging to 68p a kilogram in some shops. At 81p and below it was not economically possible for a Costa Rican plantation to pay its workers the legal minimum wage. British shoppers may be aware of farmers being squeezed, and they cherish the British countryside; they know very little of the plight of Costa Rican banana workers and may have no concept of the Costa Rican countryside or its social problems. Mostly, all the shopper sees is huge bright aisles full of 'cheap' food; to paraphrase China Mieville's book, *The City and the City*, "when in Supermarket, see Supermarket"[1] (Digital Spy, 2018). It is no accident that Tesco feels able to give free bananas away in its store aisles, a move aimed at children, but anyone can take them unmonitored, and the whole move comes across as a health-oriented CSR measure. Bananas are healthy, but the health of the UK consumer has been stolen from the well-being of the Costa Ricans. The economy of the Caribbean Islands itself is damaged, and the race to the bottom imperils the better wages of these workers compared to those in mainland South America, where hazardous work includes 10–12 hour days and exposure to harmful chemicals. Ultimately, the burden of the cost reduction for that bunch of bananas in UK shopping baskets will be borne by workers in all banana plantations.

A wide range of other food items are also sold in supermarkets at a price where the retailer takes most of the money and leaves very little for the farmers, processors, transporters and others. In 2010, the supermarket retail price of Costa Rican pineapples was split, 4% to the plantation workers (the same as for bananas retailed in the UK), 17% to the plantation owners, 38% to the international traders who brought the pineapple from Costa Rica to the supermarket and 41% to the supermarket retailer (Nicholson & Young, 2012: 9). The actual workers get paid so little that their wages could be raised by 50% with very low impact on the retail price in Britain. Meanwhile, prawns from Thailand and tomatoes from Florida are regularly produced by slave, or at best highly exploited labour. Concerning British beef and vegetables, the farmer often gets just a quarter of the price the consumer pays at the supermarket till, with many farmers earning below the statutory minimum wage, once the long hours they put in are taken into account (Oram et al, 2003). Meanwhile, Woolworths Australia makes a positive point out of the fact that according to its website (Woolworths, 2014: 10) a kilogram of bacon cost the Australian shopper 4% of their average weekly wage in the 1950s, but only 1% of the average weekly wage in the 2010s. Evidently, intended for customers not suppliers, this statistic implies that either pig farmers' revenue has declined by 75% or that pig farming has become 400% more efficient—at what cost to animal welfare, rural employment and the environment?

A range of international organizations, including the International Chamber of Commerce (ICC), the United Nations (UN), the ILO and the Organisation for Economic Co-operation and Development (OECD) have issued guidelines for multinational companies' CSR policies regarding 'host nations' (overseas countries where supplies are imported from). The big supermarkets appear to be, at least indirectly, breaching a number of these guidelines, listed in Table 5.2.

Some improvement was achieved in November 2015 when Asda became the first UK supermarket to commit to sourcing Rainforest Alliance certified bananas for 93% of its supply, with the other 7% from Fairtrade. In early 2016, Lidl followed suit with a promise to source 100% of its bananas sustainably by the end of the year (Smithers, 2016). This move comes against an economic background of Fairtrade sales falling in the UK, in 2015, for the first time since the scheme was founded 20 years ago, as British consumer spending tightened in the face of stagnant real wages that had persisted for several years since the 2007 Credit Crunch. Lidl, which entered the UK in 1994 as a deep discounter but which has more recently begun stocking more upmarket foods also, may

Table 5.2 Internationally Recognized Good CSR Conduct and UK Supermarket Compliance (Rec = policy recommended)

CSR recommendation	From ICC	From UN	From ILO	From OECD	UK supermarket compliance
Do not interfere in host-nation politics		Rec		Rec	Indirect economic squeeze
Consult with government, employees, employers, on appropriate development	Rec	Rec	Rec	Rec	No
Reinvest some profits in host country	Rec				No
Respect host nation's control over its natural resources		Rec			No
Do not bribe public servants		Rec		Rec	Yes
Develop and adapt technologies to host country needs	Rec		Rec	Rec	No, poor plantation conditions
Respect host country conservation laws		Rec		Rec	Exploitative conditions encouraged
Preserve consumer health and safety through adequate information		Rec			Consumers OK but ill informed
Respect host-nation worker collective bargaining			Rec	Rec	Worker wages squeezed
Respect host-nation human rights, fundamental freedoms		Rec			Exploitative conditions encouraged

Source: Adapted from Peng, 2009: 357

see the move into Fairtrade bananas as a marketing strategy to capture more of the middle-class spend who are seeking lower grocery bills overall. However, as the earlier table shows, there is some considerable way to go yet before the supermarket food system can be deemed socially responsible, either within the UK or internationally.

5.4 Supermarket Clothing Prices

Supermarkets do not just sell food, but have diversified into a wide range of other goods, including clothing. Here too, the garments are frequently made by low-paid workers in Bangladesh, on around £33 per month (2010). In Bangladesh at this time, the minimum wage in 2010 was £30 to £35 per month (graded by job function), but a living wage "for a [Bangladeshi] worker to feed, clothe and educate their family, would be around £100 per month" (ActionAid, 2011: 2). The economic implication is that cheap child labour is very likely to be utilized in Bangladesh, which will be damaging to education, reduce the qualifications of the next generation and perpetuate the very poverty that engenders low wages and families committing their offspring to child labour. Yet, as with some food items, labour costs are so low they comprise just 1% of the total retail cost of a garment so that raising wages to the 'living' level would add just 7.5p to the payment to the supplier for each article of clothing. Excessively long hours worked, often compulsorily, often because they need the extra income, by female employees may also damage the childhood of their offspring. Even the family diet may deteriorate, in similar fashion to the nutrient-poor junk food diet of many poor in Europe, because women avoid "buying and cooking vegetables as it takes too long on the shared stove. With the problems with blackouts and sharing a kitchen I want things which are quick to cook" (ActionAid, 2011: 5). Medicines, in a country that cannot afford a comprehensive free, at-point-of use healthcare system may also be unaffordable for these textiles workers, let alone school books and other learning aids.

Supermarkets such as Asda could also share their expertise on efficiency with the Bangladeshi clothing factories. One factor that keeps Bangladeshi textiles workers' wages low is extreme inefficiency, where production is at "as little as 30% [of potential] productivity, suppliers and retailers face problems of low-quality product, high levels of waste and unreliable delivery times" (ActionAid, 2011: 7). As with child labour perpetuating poverty into each succeeding generation, so such inefficiency perpetuates low wages, which in turn keeps workers on long hours, tired and producing waste and more inefficiency. Global-North supermarket corporations are very lean efficient organizations, and whilst there is considerable emphasis in many of their CSR statements on ensuring their suppliers meet 'minimum standards' in various areas, there is much less evidence of sharing management techniques that might facilitate suppliers in meeting these standards.

In China, too, Walmart, who own Asda UK, have been accused of promoting a relentless squeeze on workers. Walmart demands, each year on the previous, either a cut in price or an improvement in quality, from its suppliers (GMB, 2005). Walmart squeezes its suppliers, often in remote and poor areas of Global-South countries, in regions where its customers would be very unlikely ever to visit; in turn, these suppliers relentlessly squeeze their workers. Chinese workers making goods for Walmart have been forced to work 130 hour weeks, sometimes staying at work well into the night until 4.30 am the next day, often without overtime payments. Anyone who dares even question factory conditions (let alone form a trades union, something Walmart deems impermissible even in the USA) is sacked immediately. Any factory inspection is only carried out with 20 days' notice, giving plenty of time for clean ups and time-card falsifications. In Lesotho, workers making goods for Walmart were required to come in on Sundays, but were not allowed to clock in because this would provide evidence of violation of a Code of Conduct. No doubt this Code of Conduct can be found somewhere on Walmart's CSR website, written of course in English, but not in Sesotho, Zulu, or any other language generally spoken in Lesotho. Even in the US, factories are given 15 days' notice of inspections, making it hard to detect violations of laws such as those on child labour (GMB, 2005). In this manner, Global-South governments collude with the Walmart squeeze. The incentive for the Chinese government, and other countries hosting such exploitative sweatshops, is a massive trade surplus with the US. In practice, this surplus goes to building up Chinese government sovereign funds and to the wealthy elite who own the factories, with very little going to the workers who actually make the products. Nobody has both an incentive to change the system and the power to do so; the nearest we have to such an agency is the US consumer, so long as they can be bothered to a) find out what is going on across the Pacific and b) have the conscience (and the financial capability; many US consumers are squeezed too, albeit to a far lesser extent) to boycott such artificially cheap goods until the price is raised, just a little, enough to pay decent wages back in China, Lesotho, Bangladesh and elsewhere.

5.5 Supermarket Payments to Suppliers

Not only do many supermarkets ruthlessly squeeze down the contractual standard wholesale price they pay to agencies further back up the supply chain, they also make further efforts to cut back on the cost of those payments by delaying them or finding reasons for reducing them yet further or even demanding payments from the producers. Pre-2007, when global interest rates were higher than in 2018, supermarkets would hold back payments for a month or more, which would bring in considerable amounts of interest for the retailer. In 2005, Asda generally paid between 33 and 58 days after delivery—an average delay of 40 days. Sainsbury pays 30 to 60 days after, an average late payment of 45 days. If interest rates were at 5%, that would bring in 0.5% of turnover as extra profit, or some £200 million on Tesco's 2005 turnover. Supermarkets may also unilaterally switch from monthly to three monthly payments, in arrears of course. So a farmer that got £10,000 a month now has to wait three months to get £30,000, which will likely cause them considerable cash flow issues. If the farmer needs to make up this £10,000 a month that is being delayed for one or two months, they will likely have to take a bank loan, charged at 1% per month, so costing the farmer a total of £300 per quarter in this instance. This also imposes a delay of average 1.5 months on two-thirds of the payment, equivalent to a delay of 1 month on all payments.

Supermarkets have also instituted a whole range of what might be termed 'supplementary' charges back onto their suppliers, fees and 'penalties', often rather dubious in ethical terms.

These payments include the following:

Slotting fees are charges for allocating optimal positions on shop shelves, also known in the US as 'pay to stay' fees. The best place for sales on a supermarket shelf is about 1.5 metres off the ground, just below shopper's eye level as most people look slightly down when purchasing. The supermarkets justify slotting fees on the grounds that some 80% to 90% of new products fail, so without them, the risk to the store of introducing any new lines would be considerable. However, slotting fees raises barriers to new supermarket entrants. By effectively forcing the supplier to subsidize lower retail prices at the incumbent supermarket, attempts by new retailers to win trade via low prices are blocked; slotting fees have been illegal in Poland since 1993 and are also banned in China, and the US has outlawed them on alcoholic drinks from 1995. Not all supermarket chains demand slotting fees; Walmart does not, although it can negotiate much lower wholesale prices instead due to its size.

On the positive side, for the producer, slotting fees help fend off competition from rival goods, but this arguably reduces choice for the shopper. Slotting fees are one reason why smaller brands are disappearing, whilst large sections of shelves are dedicated to many similar sub-brand variants of the dominant brands. Moreover, the dominant brands are seldom the healthiest ones, leading to less consumption of fresh produce. However, shoppers may then be encouraged to shift to the deep discounters Aldi and Lidl, where numerous tertiary brands can be found at low prices, and increasingly, these discounters are stocking lines not always found in the big supermarkets; the 'centre aisle' of an Aldi frequently has a range of non-food goods seldom seen in a Tesco, and this selection changes weekly, encouraging shoppers to return in case they miss a bargain they never even thought of buying before.

Marketing or distribution fees are a variant of slotting fees and are charged by the supermarket for running a marketing campaign to promote a product: a taster session or cut-price deal, for example. In the case of a BOGOF, the supplier may have to pay for the second item. In one case, a supermarket told a Brussels sprout supplier, at short notice, that it was running a cut-price promotion for four weeks, and this price reduction was being passed back to the supplier. In one case, the price reduction was because the product was being delisted by the supermarket, but failure to pay would have been commercial suicide.

Refunds and discounts include any refunds the supermarket pays to customers or discounts because a product has failed to sell well and is nearing its sell-by date and are routinely charged back to suppliers.

Solus agreements are when the supermarkets demand that the producer does not sell to any other retailer. The supermarket then has huge commercial power to demand other terms and conditions—for, example continued slotting fees. The supermarket is relying on the producer not being able to find a market for all its produce elsewhere. With solus agreements, stringent conditions can be set; for example, Oxfam has alleged (Wilshaw, 2016) that in one case, a shipment of fruit was rejected "on spurious grounds, actually coinciding with a period of over-supply in the market".

Third-party kickbacks. Supermarkets have insisted that growers use a certain haulier or type of packaging, which is not the cheapest; the supermarket has been paid by the packaging manufacturer or haulier to enforce this condition (Seth & Randall, 1999: 284).

These fees started to appear in the 1970s, but were rarely used until the 1990s. However, they have been increased since the Credit Crunch began and supermarket margins began to be squeezed as never before. US retailers are said to take in US$ 18 billion from such fees in 2015, up from US$ 1 billion in 1990 (Economist, 2015: 66). In the UK, such fees may be higher than the operating profits of the supermarkets, and in Australia, they have boosted average supermarket profit margins by 2.5% average, up to 5.7% between 2010 and 2015. Farmers and other producers are afraid to protest, as they may be delisted without notice.

A stage beyond squeezing existing producer brand suppliers with fees and charges is for the supermarkets to establish their own brands. A brand can be copyrighted like any other original idea, and quite often the supermarkets have been accused of imitating or ripping off established brands with copycat own-label versions, selling their own very similar versions of these products. Sainsbury closely copied the 'Comfort' fabric freshener, and were forced by Coca Cola to stop selling a very similar version of their beverage. Meanwhile, Asda were ordered to stop selling 'Puffin' biscuits, a close copy of Penguin chocolate biscuits (Seth & Randall, 1999: 281). However, the original brand owner can often only hope to win against such parasitic plagiarism when they too are large; smaller producers cannot afford to alienate the supermarkets by being too litigious. However, the Hotel Chocolat company did succeed in forcing Waitrose supermarket to back down when the UK supermarket chain began selling bars very similar in appearance to Hotel Chocolat's, at half the price. The taste, however, was rather different, with Hotel Chocolate starting a strategic initiative to undermine Waitrose's copycat version by offering to exchange a partly eaten Waitrose bar for its own. In May 2018, Waitrose agreed to stop making them, but were allowed to sell those already manufactured. Hotel Chocolat was aiming at consumers who "will have bought [the bar] thinking they're buying Hotel Chocolate quality, taken a couple of mouthfuls and realised they're actually stuffed full of sugar" (R Davies, 2018). In this instance, Hotel Chocolat had the advantage that Waitrose is an upmarket chain that would very likely suffer bad publicity for ripping off a boutique chocolate manufacturer. In the short term, this free-riding on other companies' commercial research and investment may widen consumer choice and save them money, as the supermarkets like to point out; in the longer run, it will likely reduce consumer choice and leave them vulnerable to monopolistic (or at least oligopolistic) pricing by the supermarkets, when the original product is no longer viable to produce. There is nothing wrong with own-label brands as such; they must, however, be sufficiently distinguishable in appearance from competitor primary brands so the consumer knows just what they are buying.

The complexities of disentangling, legally and morally (not always coincident), what is a legitimate 'ask' from the supermarket for better terms from the supplier, from a coercive 'demand' based on bullying commercial clout, are not easy, as illustrated in the 2016 case of the ACCC (Australian Competition and Consumer Commission) against Woolworths; ACCC v Woolworths Limited. Judgement in the Federal Court was handed down on 16 December 2016, and the ACCC lost against Woolworths, although it won in a similar case against Coles in 2015 ((Temby, 2016). The ACCC's allegations are reproduced here as they broadly summarize the concerns of UK and other supermarket suppliers regarding the major supermarkets:

- There was no legitimate basis for Woolworths to seek payments under the Scheme in asking for payment from suppliers. Woolworths was taking advantage of its stronger bargaining position.
- Woolworths conduct was inconsistent with prevailing norms in both the supermarket industry.
- The scheme could not properly be considered 'business as usual' and was a last-minute 'grab for cash'.
- The profit gap that Woolworths was trying to fill was not the fault of the suppliers.
- Woolworths had no contractual entitlement to the money sought from the suppliers.

- Whilst couched as requests for payment (known in the industry as 'asks'), they were in truth *demands* for payment.
- The financial calculations relied on by Woolworths to justify the payments were arbitrary and no attempt was made by Woolworths to check if the calculations were rational.
- Woolworths made no allowance for its own responsibility for poor performance or the shortfall in profitability.

Woolworths winning defence was that

- The ACCC did not truly understand the market and the ACCC's case relied on a "simplified and mistaken characterization of the commerce in question".
- Woolworths regularly and routinely engages in ongoing and ad hoc discussions with suppliers about different levels of support that the suppliers can provide to Woolworths. This support can take many forms: being promotional support, pricing discounts, rebates and, in some cases, direct payments to Woolworths—all of which ultimately impact of the cost of goods to Woolworths. The scheme should be understood as being no more than a continuation of this conduct, which was common throughout the supermarket sector.
- The fact that only a small number of the 821 suppliers deemed to be underperforming were contacted under the scheme meant that the requests made under the scheme were measured and justified. The requests were made after some analysis and weren't simply an attempted 'cash grab' from its suppliers.
- Responsibility for the subjective assessment of the position and performance of different suppliers was placed in the hands of those that knew the suppliers, and their circumstances, best—namely, buyers and category managers. In making requests, the buyers and category managers were given scripts that required them to at all times be 'polite and courteous' and not make unreasonable demands or threaten suppliers.
- The evidence led by Woolworths did not support a finding that they held a superior bargaining position or that the suppliers were in a vulnerable position in their negotiations with Woolworths.

This again illustrates the opacity and tangled nature of supermarket-supplier relations, and the near-impossibility of deciding what is fair, and what is legal, and what societal norms and ethics say 'should' happen in such complex relationships. The ACCC was given until mid-January 2017 to lodge an appeal, but decided not to contest the judgement.

A Supermarket Code of Practice was introduced in the UK in 2002 to redress the imbalance of power between supermarkets and suppliers. However, the paucity of complaints under this code has led some to suggest that fear of delisting was preventing many suppliers from using the Code to seek redress (Blythman, 2004: 186). In April 2010, the Grocery Supply Code of Practice, came into effect. This arbitrates on payment disputes between supermarkets and suppliers, and in 2013, the Grocery Code of Adjudication was established; this was redrafted in 2017 to provide further protection against supermarket coercion. However, this only applies to major supermarkets dealing directly with farmers and not with smaller retailers or where an intermediary, such as a food processor is involved. The new Grocery Code of Adjudication applies to One Stop, as a subsidiary of Tesco, and now that Tesco has taken over the Bookers buying group, it will take effect there too. In the last few years, the supermarkets have begun to improve some of their payment terms and procedures to small suppliers, for fear of bad publicity. In October 2015, Tesco announced it would (from June 2016) pay all small suppliers (those supplying Tesco with under £100,000 goods a year) within 14 days, and it would pay medium-sized suppliers 5 days faster than large suppliers. In January 2016, Waitrose also began to speed up payments to small suppliers after it was revealed that the store, which positions itself as a champion of British producers, was in fact taking considerably longer than Tesco to pay some of its small suppliers.

5.6 The Pressures on Rural Society

Supermarket payments and conditions are not just an arcane matter of small rural farm finances or small town food processor viability. The supermarkets, indirectly, are responsible for the vitality, or otherwise, of large swathes of rural society, in the UK and beyond. An example of the sudden and drastic effect a supermarket boardroom decision can have was what happened to the Romney Marsh Potato Company, founded in 1950. Soon after 2000, Tesco demanded an 'overrider', a fee which was a percentage of the company's turnover, which rose from 2% to 3.75%; effectively, a rebate for Tesco on the wholesale price it paid for its potatoes. Then in spring 2004, this company, which had supplied all its produce to Tesco for 47 years, was suddenly ditched by the supermarket giant with no reason and no notice given. Tesco never actually had a formal contract with the potato grower. Annual sales plummeted from £12 million to £1 million, and in February 2005, 81 of the 120 staff were made redundant. The Romney Marsh Potato Company closed down in 2007; the nearest town, New Romney, has a population of just 7,000 and is relatively isolated with no rail link, so finding new jobs for these 100 or more employees, as the Credit Crunch got underway, would not be easy.

Across the UK, between 1980 and 1994, the number of farms fell by 11% and the number employed on those farms fell by 34%. Those made redundant would probably have to find work on industrial estates on the edge of towns, either facing a long commute on low wages or moving.

This in turn erodes village life as village homes become occupied by commuters who spend most of their waking hours outside the local community, so the village shop, the pub and the school close down. In Australia, a decline of 56% in number of independent fruit and vegetable retailers, from 3,670 to 1,611, between 1992 and 1999, had been blamed on 'aggressive activity' by the big two supermarket chains, Coles and Woolworths, which in 2000 controlled 65%–70% of the take-home fresh food market. The Australian supermarket duopsony has been blamed for "reducing the viability of small fruit and vegetable growers, forcing farmers to 'get bigger or get out', as complex accreditation, quality assurance schemes, and contracts can make providing directly to supermarkets unfeasible for smaller producers" (Keith, 2012: 61).

Those farmers who still have contracts with the big supermarkets are only a little better off. Many dairy farmers are working very long hours, perhaps 80 to 90 hours a week, a factor in the rising farmer suicide rate in both developing and developed countries (Fox & Vorley, 2006). Farm worker conditions are also squeezed; low wages may be invisible, but one sign of this deterioration is the multiple caravans that have appeared on the edges of farm complexes in recent years. Most car drivers and even walkers passing by will not see these temporary-permanent homes for low-paid rural workers, but they are very visible from the Google Street View camera, mounted some 3 metres off the ground and seeing over the hedges. Occasionally, a major tragedy hits the headlines, such as the drowning of the Morecambe Bay cockle pickers on 21 February 2004 who were working in the UK illegally, employed by gangmasters at below the National Minimum Wage. This tragedy precipitated the passing of the Gangmaster Bill into UK law, as discussed next, but for the most part, people who go out to enjoy the rural scenery and then go home and shop, forgetting where their food ultimately came from and who harvested it. They give even less thought whilst in the supermarket as to who is squeezing the farms and why farm employment is so poor; they almost certainly give no thought whilst in the fish aisle as to what employment might be like on the boats that brought in that fish. Just so long as the food price is low, everything is all right. It is no coincidence that, across the UK economy, slavery is most prevalent in economic sectors where the workforce is the most atomized, working for the smallest employers, is least unionized, on the most precarious contracts, with long but uncertain hours (which leave no time or energy for worker organization). Sectors such as building, cleaning, distribution and security are notorious for these poor employment conditions. As regards agricultural workers, one can add to the factors just noted earlier, extreme physical isolation, as one can witness by taking a drive along the remoter lanes of the English Fens and passing countless anonymous farms and food processing plants lost in the vast horizons of emptiness. No doubt some are responsible employers; many are not. The landscape may be flat and bleak, but many of the unseen workers labouring unseen out here in the parody of rurality offered by the north Cambridgeshire and south Lincolnshire landscape face even flatter and bleaker work prospects. Yet these lanes are barely an hour's drive from the expensive lanes and bijou expensive shops and cafés of historic Cambridge itself. Add in further isolation from being in a foreign country and not speaking the indigenous language, let alone being aware of the indigenous employment rights, and exploitation or even slavery is almost inevitable.

Occasionally, the huge submerged continent of invisible underpaid exploited labour that exists to provide our cheap groceries several stages back upstream along the food chain develops a peak that comes rather close to the visible surface where we conduct our supermarket transactions. Quasi-slavery sometimes occurs not just in remote farms but on the supermarket premises itself. In 2014, the Australian supermarkets Coles, Costco and Woolworths came under investigation regarding the employment practices relating to trolley collectors on their retailing sites. Areas of concern to the Fair Work Ombudsman included low wages; lack of payslips; general lack of transparency in the remuneration system, also of the workers' rights relating to holiday and other leave; and a general usage of 'vulnerable' people (Australian Government, 2016). The report noted, on pp. 7–8,

> According to the 2011 census, of 1 500 trolley collectors across Australia, almost 50% are under 25 years of age and 40% do not have education beyond Year 10. We consider this number of trolley collectors an under-estimate, with Coles alone reporting it has oversight of 2000 trolley collectors. Vulnerable workers are often unaware of their rights in the workplace and can also be reluctant to report their working conditions.

In an echo of the gangmaster system operating in the Fens, the Australian supermarkets had contracted out their trolley collection services, so direct legal responsibility for their remuneration was one stage removed from the retailer; however, moral responsibility is not so easily shunted away.

One effect of the Morecambe Bay tragedy was to accelerate the passing in the UK Parliament of the Gangmaster Bill, introduced on 7 January 2004 as a private members' bill by Jim Sheridan, a Labour MP from Scotland. Most private member's bills fail due to lack of support from other MPs, but the death of the cockle pickers galvanized public opinion, and the influential Labour MP David Blunkett lent his support. The Gangmaster Bill received Royal Assent on 8 July 2004, and the Gangmaster Licencing Act came into force on 1 December 2006. Anyone supplying workers to the agricultural or food processing industries must be licenced or face a prison sentence of up to 10 years. However, there were swift moves by the government to limit the bill's scope; DEFRA suggested that the bill should not cover secondary food processing, meaning that 200,000 workers in the processing and packaging industries would not be protected (Pollard, 2006: 126). DEFRA is the UK government Department for the Environment, Food and Rural Affairs. Interestingly, the UK government was more concerned about the maintenance of cheap food, which kept down inflation and interest rates, rather than the welfare of the workers who get that food to the table, and all this was not under a Conservative government but the Labour administration of Tony Blair (1997–2007).

UK farm workers may be migrants from Eastern Europe of further afield, with a poor command of English and little knowledge of their rights, and no means of enforcing those rights anyway. Wages may not even meet the legal minimum wage, and there are frequent unfair and excessive deductions, such as for transport to work (poor) accommodation, or tax that is never actually paid by the gangmaster (even if tax was payable anyway on such low wages). Deductions of dubious legality for arbitrary and unexplained reasons from 'administration expenses' to interest and charges for minibus transport to the fields and passport confiscation are common and may take net wages to below 20% of UK minimum wage. Furthermore, reports of child labour and assaults on workers, regularly appear in the media in locales from Grimsby to Greece (Pollard, 2006). Employment is also insecure, with no set hours. This may mean too few hours work; a zero-hours contract, with no paid employment actually guaranteed. Or it may mean too many hours, hours being worked but not paid. Workers are frequently employed 'indirectly' by agencies, so they can be paid for less hours or days than they actually worked. Necessary breaks are either not allowed, or are an excuse for further pay deductions. Low farm wages may also drive down pay rates at nearby non-farm workplaces, just as Walmart can depress neighbourhood wages. The conditions of fishing crews, even less visible to the affluent end consumer of food, frequently originating from outside the EU to work EU waters, are on call to work 24 hours a day whilst at sea and are paid just £1,060 a month on average, barely over £30 a day (Moulds, 2017). Oddly, middle-class consumers sometimes seem more concerned about the sustainability of the fish stocks being harvested than they do about the welfare of the people doing the fishing.

Issues of low pay, poor conditions and even worse, child labour, labour exploitation and slavery may well occur 'out of sight, out of mind' of affluent Global-North consumers in Global-South countries where tropical products, such as chocolate originate. Plantations where unethical labour practices prevail are also likely to be environmentally damaging; it is unlikely that the owners of these enterprises care about the environment if they care so little about worker welfare. A further peril such exploited workers may face is exposure to harmful chemicals, such as organophosphates, which can cause convulsions, cancers and death. As pesticides, these chemicals are designed to kill and prolonged exposure can do just the same damage to humans also. They are often not dissimilar, in molecular structure and function, to chemical weapons agents, such as Novichok. These chemicals may be taken home on workers' clothes, or drift into communities and school playgrounds, imperilling children who because they are small face even greater danger from exposure to low level but continuous doses of these pesticides. Reduced IQ is another side effect of exposure to these chemicals, which may mean the workers' children leave school with lower qualifications and can only find work in the low-paid agricultural sector, and then in turn expose their children to these same harmful chemicals.

Inadequate work training also causes employment injuries and even fatalities. In the UK, chicken processing industry alone, between 2010 and 2017, there 1,173 injuries to employees reported to the Health and Safety Executive; of these, 153 were classed as 'major', with one death (Fitzpatrick & Young, 2017: 46). The pressure for cheap chicken from supermarkets has played a significant role in causing these accidents. The health hazards of cheap food processing may extend beyond the farm or factory, right to the consumer's table. Migrant workers in fields in Spain and the UK may labour without any toilet facilities to produce salads and vegetables at a cheap price for UK supermarkets; for toilets they go in the bushes, with no hand-wash facilities. The need for the big UK supermarkets to remain competitive in price with the deep discounters Aldi and Lidl has intensified downwards pressure on workers' wages and conditions. Similarly, in food processing plants, food (especially chicken and other meat products) may become contaminated and dirty, which may impact back upon the health of the very consumers who like their food bills kept as low as possible.

Cacao, the raw material of chocolate, is mostly produced in Brazil, tropical west Africa, India and South-East Asia. The finished product is a luxury hedonistic item which may have reached the consumer by a complex food chain; the supermarket is the last link before that a chocolate company, such as Lindt, or maybe a lesser-known brand such as Moser Roth (from Aldi), and before that a range of shipping and plantation enterprises. Consuming 'feel-good' chocolate, one may have concern for the environment, for the shop workers at the supermarket where it was purchased and the CSR statements from Aldi and Lindt will concentrate on reassuring images of energy saving, green environment, good supermarket and factory staff practices, sponsorship of local charities, maybe even of Ghanaian artists and entrepreneurs. However, it will be a long and arduous chain of research to trace that bar back to the specific Ghanaian plantation the original cocoa beans came from and to check on all the CSR statements of every company involved, assuming the smaller players further back along the chain even actually publish such statements. Taste the nice creamy smooth Lindt; are you really going to undermine that nice feeling by intensive hard research into exploitative and destructive production practices many stages back and thousands of miles away? Highly processed products of remote origin, such as chocolate, illustrate that good CSR on the surface may cover a multitude of sins in the darker remoter recesses of the global food chain.

5.7 Animal Welfare

If consumers push the welfare of farm workers on remote corners of the UK, or in even more distant parts of the Global South, out of mind, they may think even less of the welfare of animals on those farms. Even out in the countryside, we may not notice something that is not there any longer. Over the past few decades, a quintessential element of the British countryside has indeed slowly faded from sight: farm animals. Sheep may still be seen in the higher grassland pastures, but cows, chickens and pigs are not seen as frequently as before. What may be seen more often is large metal sheds, and it may well be here that the farm animals have vanished to. Keeping animals indoors has several attractions for farmers; the animal uses less energy than if it were roaming outside, so the farmer gets more weight of carcass for his feed. What the animal eats can be tightly controlled, and it is less exposed to diseases which might reduce its growth rate. Farmers may be less enamoured with the concerns of animal welfare campaigners, who argue that cows, chickens and pigs are natural foraging animals whose instinct is to roam around for food, and dislike, as humans would, being effectively sentenced to life imprisonment in cramped unnatural conditions where even the normal diurnal rhythm, of day and night can be disrupted or modified by artificial lighting. On a longer timescale (actually not that long, farm animals have greatly shortened lifespans compared to their wild ancestors) the growth schedule of the animal can also be disrupted, modified so as to speed up the 'production line'. However, when less-valuable parts of the animal, such as its legs fail to keep pace with rapidly increasing bodyweight, then suffering is likely. Animals, say organizations such as the Royal Society for Prevention of Cruelty to Animals (RSPCA) and Compassion in World Farming (CIWF), are not simply mindless machines for turning feed into meat and milk for humans. The financial imperatives for ever greater efficiency and cost reductions imposed on farmers by the supermarkets, however, suggests otherwise.

Supermarkets are highly dependent on a mass supply of cheap outputs from chicken farmers, both eggs and chicken meat. Eggs are used as binders, clarification agents, stabilizers and emulsifiers in a wide variety of products, not as just boxes of half a dozen eggs, but in a range of supermarket products, including bread, chocolates, cosmetics, frozen dairy products, ice cream and other desserts, mayonnaise, medical products, microwave meals, sauces, wine, yoghurts and even in biodegradable food packaging (BEPA, 2009; Government of Canada, 2017). Many of these uses are invisible to consumers, who are then shopping without thought for the welfare of the chickens that produced those eggs. Chicken meat is also used in ready meals and sandwiches, again less visibly; one place where chickens are intended to be prominent in supermarkets is the roast chicken spit, because the aroma of roast chicken, along with that of baked bread and coffee, is a known appetite arouser. Shoppers are very prone to purchase more food when they are hungry.

The categories of chicken husbandry may be as opaque to many supermarket customers as is the uses the eggs are put to. They may be aware that 'battery' cages are bad and have in fact been illegal within the EU since 2012, but this does not by any means imply that all chickens can now wander outside in the sunshine. On fact, only 5% to 10% of the 900 million chickens slaughtered each year in the UK have enjoyed outdoor access, and most are in sheds at 17 chickens per square metre, grow too fast and therefore suffer lethargy, with a third enduring painful lameness. There are so-called enriched cages, also known as 'colony cages' or 'furnished cages', but they are still cages; the birds have less than 0.1 square metres each and cannot go outside. The RSPCA sets standards for chicken housing, and chicken products sold from birds kept at that standard can be labelled 'Freedom Food'. In 2010, Sainsbury's supermarket applied for the 'good chicken' award from the CIWF, which the CIWF understood was being awarded on the basis that all Sainsbury's chicken would meet the Freedom Food standard. Sainsbury's had a different understanding that by 2015 it would be "the biggest retailer of Freedom Food" but not across its entire chicken products range. By 2018, Sainsbury's said it was "returning the CIWF award because it disagreed with the CIWF's approach to animal welfare", whereas the CIWF said it was "publically withdrawing the award because Sainsbury had failed to uphold promises on chicken welfare" (Butler, 2018). About as confusing as the average shopper is about furnished, enriched and colony cages. Co-op, M&S, Sainsbury and Waitrose do not sell eggs from hens kept in cages. In 2016, Iceland promised to end egg sales from caged hens by 2025 at the latest, reasoning that customer antipathy to animal cruelty outweighed any greater profit from the cheaper egg raising methods. Tesco, Morrison and Asda also intend to go 'cage free' by 2025.

Pigs may also suffer welfare issues. Two-fifths of farm pigs are born outdoors, but 90% are confined indoors after being weaned. Kept in barren pens, with no opportunity to forage, they start mutilating each other out of boredom. The consumer may want to buy ethically, humanely raised pork and be willing to pay more for that, with almost half of consumers saying they buy free range whenever they can. However, as with chickens and cage standards, they are likely to be confused by a multiplicity of labelling systems, such as organic, Finest, free range, outdoor bred, outdoor reared, Red Tractor assured and more. 'Outdoor reared' means the pig spends the first half of its (20-week) life outside, whereas 'outdoor bred' means it spends the first four weeks outside, until weaned, and then 16 weeks indoors. The Red Tractor logo simply means the pork complies with certain trade-set standards, and organic means it is antibiotic-free. To add further complexity, there are both environmental and animal-welfare drawbacks to raising pigs fully outdoors; they may suffer from the cold in tin sheds in fields, and their natural rooting behaviour may promote soil erosion, meaning they can only be raised outdoors in certain soil areas. Furthermore, restrictions on sow stalls in the UK, where pigs are confined in narrow crates, has pushed consumers seeking cheaper pork to buy from European countries where sow stall conditions are even worse. Perhaps not as bad, though, as the conditions exposed in 2018 at the idyllically named Fir Tree Farm, owned by Elsham Linc in North-East Lincolnshire. Elsham is a pretty village, with a picturesque hall close by where tourists can have tea and enjoy the sight of local peacocks roaming around. It is a million miles from Fir Tree Farm, out on the remote bleak windswept Humber bank flats 20 minutes' drive away where an anonymous lane leads to a large complex of low concrete farm buildings, oddly protected by a chain-link fence to deter intruders. Here, where Tesco sourced some of its pork from, terrible mistreatment of pigs was uncovered by Animal Equality (Webster, 2018b). The farm had Red Tractor certification, which was withdrawn after the exposure, along with the Tesco contract, but what is worrying is what other cases of animal abuse may be going on as yet unseen at the head of our supermarket food chains. Perhaps the concept of eating 'ethical' or 'humane' meat is too much of a paradox, and those who care about such things should really just try and reduce or even eliminate meat from their diet.

5.8 Food Labelling

Food labelling is meant to advise the customer, but as noted earlier in the case of chicken welfare and pork standards, it often obfuscates more than it informs. Food from outside the UK, or from industrial production, may be given nice 'rural farm names'. For example, Tesco, in 2016, used names such as 'Redmere Farms' and 'Boswell Farms'. The actual produce may be British, or come from as far afield as Africa or South America, and wherever its nation of origin, it probably didn't come from a premise, looking like the mental image that 'Boswell Farms' might conjure up. Idyllic farm names, with the accompanying pictures of rural thatched cottages and free roaming animals may constitute a kind of greenwash to distract from "wider concerns about sustainability and the impact of industrial animal agriculture" (Lever & Evans, 2017). The National Farmers Union also objects to these labels as they blur the distinction between supermarket food and organic farm produce, perhaps sold at a farm shop. Richard Baugh, proprietor of the Woodside

Farm Shop, Nottinghamshire, has faced confusion with shoppers to his premises, or his website, because Tesco uses the same name for some of its food brands. However, supermarkets have justified the use of rural scenes on food products that come from animals who spend all or almost all their time indoors as depicting "the rolling hills of Ireland [where the recipe for this product originally came from]", or "an illustration, in cartoon form, of Witchingham Hall [where the corporate head office is located]" (Webster, 2018a). Nobody has asked the consumers yet if they are happy with this connection, or they think it might be a little bit stretched.

UK consumers may like to think they are buying British food, a phenomenon known as 'food patriotism', but here too the labelling can be misleading. A food product's 'country of origin' is where it was last processed, so Tesco can sell beef from Irish cows processed into sausages in Cumberland and call it Cumberland sausage. Similarly, sheep can be sent to a Welsh farm for the last six weeks of their lives, and then their meat can be branded, at a premium, as 'Welsh lamb'. Occasionally, the supermarkets have to backed down and amended their branding; in 2017, Waitrose had to change the name of its 'British' range of lamb dishes to 'Classic' after it emerged the packs contained meat from New Zealand (Humphries, 2017). Waitrose responded to the charge of misleading labelling by saying that the label 'British' was meant to refer to the origin of the recipe. However, country of origin of the food is not the only way that food labels can mislead. Food labels may encourage unnecessary binning of food that is still perfectly edible, just past its sell-by date. Besides sell-by dates that encourage BOGOFs and overbuying, there are other labelling issues that have been levelled at the supermarkets. These generally involve attributing the food product with some environmental or social quality, which adds value in the consumer's mind; the question is, how genuine are these 'added attributes'?

Fairtrade is a label familiar to many shoppers. The first Fairtrade label was applied in 1988, by Max Havelaar, to Mexican coffee sold in Dutch supermarkets. Fairtrade encourages consumers to buy 'sustainable' products, but perhaps necessarily oversimplifies some aspects of the whole supply chain. For example, the Fairtrade minimum price for coffee, US$1,600 per tonne, was not reviewed between 1993 and 2010, despite complaints from producers (Vark, 2016). Yet purchasers of Fairtrade coffee might take it for granted that the producer was getting a 'fair' price, whatever that really means. Also, if a producer buys 20% of their raw materials Fairtrade, they can label 20% of their chocolate bars as Fairtrade (so-called mass balancing), but the consumer cannot know if an individual bar was produced under Fairtrade. The Fairtrade label will create a halo of fairness that may make shoppers feel good about the entire shopping purchase, but the main beneficiary here may well be the retail chain, not the original producer.

Carbon labelling is intended to help consumers choose products with less impact on the environment but, like Fairtrade, is necessarily very much a simplification of the entire picture. The idea is to have a version of the traffic light system, with Australia, for example, having three 'footprint' symbols, green for least carbon emissions, yellow and then black for the highest. But what does this actually tell us? Foods brought in by ship, in bulk, may have a lower per item carbon footprint from a supermarket near the coast than those produced in the same country and driven to the supermarket over several hundred kilometres by lorry. However, if the same product were bought in a store inland near a domestic producer, the situation would be reversed. In what terms should carbon intensity be communicated or measured; do we say "this item resulted in the emission of 3kg of CO_2", or "this item resulted in the same emissions as driving a car 50 kilometre?" There is no such thing as an average car or an average drive, but stating the absolute amount in kilogrammes would be meaningless for many consumers. We might even create a perverse feeling of "I've arrived at the supermarket by a low-carbon travel mode, so I can buy high carbon intensity products and not feel guilty". Do we include just CO_2 or other emissions such as methane (from beef products, cows emit a lot of methane), and methane creates more global warming per kilogramme than CO_2 does, but has a shorter life in the atmosphere. Should carbon emissions be disaggregated by manufacture, packaging and transport, and should they include the emissions resulting from the final user of that product, their journey to the store and back home and their disposal of the product packaging? There will be logistical issues of product overload on the packaging, and problems with legibility if the writing is too small for many to read; other important information such as nutritional data or storage instructions may be obscured. Carbon labelling might favour home produced foods over those shipped long distances, but this could favour foods produced by high carbon methods at home over less carbon intensive production from abroad, so the overall carbon per food globally might rise, if much of the product is sold not domestically but abroad (whilst the satisfied domestic consumer thinks they are helping to avert climate change). It is no surprise that Tesco dropped carbon labelling from its products in 2012, blaming the cost and complexity of accurately classifying all its 70,000 products and the fact that its competitors had largely not followed its lead. Overall, if averting climate change is the main goal, there may be better ways to achieve this such as reducing beef consumption and promoting home produced food and less unnecessary consumption of non-food items, rather than relying on one labelling system.

Overall, there is considerable scope for misleading consumers over environmental CSR claims, a practice termed greenwashing. This would include showing factory farm produce meat with labels featuring idyllic rural scenes, open countryside, squirrels, birds, grass and tractors, when in fact the meat is from 'zero-grazing' cows, cows that never go outside the barn they are kept in. The issue of animal welfare has been discussed in more detail in Section 5.7, but there are some terms in common usage in supermarkets now that sound good but in reality may mean nothing material at all (Demmerling, 2014: 43). Some of these terms are listed next.

Biodegradable

Everything degrades in the environment, eventually, even plastic. A crucial point is, what does it degrade down into, even more harmful chemicals maybe? An electronic device such as a computer contains substances that are harmless so long as the machine remains intact, but gather several thousand old computers and dump them in landfill, and gradually the heavy metals they contain will begin to contaminate the groundwater. Even genuinely biodegradable items like paper-based packaging may breakdown into GHGs, such as methane and CO_2, the problem being that consumers think they are helping the environment by using more of this packaging, when really they should be aiming to consume less, use less packaging altogether.

Non-toxic

As we saw in Chapter 1, the dose makes the poison; nothing is toxic in small enough amounts, and everything is toxic in sufficient quantities. Excess vitamin doses can kill. Also, toxic to what? Dark chocolate is toxic to dogs but not humans; tardigrades can withstand radiation that would kill a person. Furthermore, if something is biodegradable and non-toxic, what does it biodegrade down into? Something that is toxic to some organism, somewhere? But the phrase non-toxic sounds good on supermarket cleaning products, for example.

Recyclable

So it can be recycled, but will it be? Just about everything can be recycled, sometimes with considerable energy input, like melting down glass bottles to reuse. Plastic bags can be recycled, as bin liners, as padding for fragile goods, as draught excluders, but this is probably not what campaigners against plastic bags had in mind.

Recycled

A bit more positive than 'recyclable', at least this term has been legally defined by the US Federal Trade Commission, but even in the USA, checks to ensure 'it has been recycled' do not always happen. Also, there are several types of recycling, some more environmentally friendly than others. Post-consumer waste material, such as old newspapers or used bottles, can be returned to the production process and may constitute a genuine environmental saving on the number of trees cut down for paper, or the amount of sand mined for glass. However, the term 'recycled' may also include waste at the production stage, such as wood shavings from furniture manufacture reconstituted into chipboard. Although it could be argued that this too saves trees from being cut down, this sort of recycling simply constitutes more efficient frugal use of resources already taken from the environment; it is not quite recycling as some consumers think it is, a reuse of materials already consumed once.

Cruelty Free

This term has no legal definition and can essentially mean whatever you want it to mean. At the one extreme, it is 'cruel' to keep even free range animals from ranging free in their natural habitat, cows in marshlands, goats on mountain grasslands. At the other extreme, do factory-farmed animals even have a concept that they are being 'cruelly treated' if they have known nothing else all their (short) lives? But it sounds good on food packaging.

Free Range

This word has a little more meaning than 'cruelty free' but not much more. In the US, for example, free range legally means "chickens must have access to the outdoors for an undetermined period each day". So five minutes access would qualify their eggs as free range', whether they actually do go outdoors at all, often in a large flock in a huge shed, they do not get outside from the far end of the chicken shed at all.

The issue of relating supermarket CSR to what is going on further up the supply chain is complex; as we have seen, we should not let the supermarkets get away with saying, "It's not our company doing this", because of the great influence exerted by supermarkets upon their suppliers. Upstream product supply CSR ranges from global climate issues to worker and animal welfare in distant regions to tertiary effects on the wider communities these upstream companies operate in. A large supermarket also exerts a significant influence, for good and bad, upon the community it sells to and its local neighbourhood, and this is the subject of the next chapter of this book.

Note

1. The essence of the plot of *The City and the City* was two cities, Ul-Qoma and Beszel, somehow spatially adjacent, simultaneously superimposed and yet separate. Apart from a sort of secret police elite called Breach, citizens of one city, though they could cross the frontier into the other city, were not supposed to be aware of the alternative city to the one they were in at any one time. Although some awareness was possible, and dissidents were thus cognisant of 'the Other'.

6 Food Retailing, Community and Consumers

6.1 Assistance for Customers

Supermarkets have instituted a range of measures to cater for a wide range of customers of different abilities and attributes. A large supermarket car park will contain both wide disabled and mother and child spaces, with special toy-car trolleys for toddlers. Inside the supermarket, there are quick purchase facilities for the time-pressed, disabled toilets, baby-changing facilities, electric scooters for the disabled and a taxi call point for those with no car. There may even be facilities for dog owners to tie their dogs and give them water. They may also sell disabled-friendly household equipment, such as cutlery and tin openers designed for the arthritic. Less visible, but still crucial for some customers, many supermarkets have a web of free bus routes spanning out across town, hearing induction loops at checkouts, and staff trained to cope with disabled needs. On the surface, supermarkets represent a much more disabled-friendly shopping environment than many corner shops do, with their narrow doors, often a step up to enter (as they were once residential properties), aisles too narrow for a walking frame and lack of wide tills for wheelchairs. In Britain, the Disability Discrimination Act 1995 was supposed to make all shops, along with other public areas, accessible to the disabled by 2004 where practicable. However, many inner city 'corner' shops are former 19th-century terraced houses located in hilly suburban areas, with steep steps to the door. The work would simply be so expensive that the shop would close down, and it is exempted. The disabled access issues in these small shops are similar to those also faced by mothers with pushchairs. However, some small shopkeepers can cater to their regular disabled customers' needs in a less visible way, by establishing a personal relationship with them, but this is always going to be dependent on the same shopkeeper continuing in trade. A large supermarket is always going to have the resources to make special adaptations for a wide range of disabilities, and some retailers have gone even further and made special arrangements for certain customers with particular needs, as detailed next.

Autism

Coles supermarket, Australia, 2017, has started a 'quiet hour', or 'low sensory environment', to help customers on the autistic spectrum do their weekly shop. Every Tuesday, from 10.30–11.30 am, normally a quiet hour for shopping with less distracting crowds, the lights are dimmed by 50% and the store radio turned down to the lowest volume. The store has trained staff members on how to assist if any issues arise, such as stock being moved from its customary place in the aisles. Research suggested that autistic people, or their carers, tended to shop on Tuesday mornings, also that bright lights, music, cash registers beeping and queuing were difficult for autistic people. Similarly, Lidl, Northern Ireland, from October 2017, has trialled 'autism friendly' shopping hours from 6 till 8 pm on Tuesdays, again with dimmed lighting and no store announcements or music, and specially trained staff.

Elderly

The elderly, even the infirm elderly, have received less attention than the younger disabled. Perhaps this is because they often suffer not one major disability but a range of chronic disadvantages, physical, mental and social; poverty may also be a major role in their condition. Older people may be lonely and isolated; they may not drive, bus services may be cut, they may have no partner or no family or their families live a long way away. Physically, they are slower and prone to falls if their balance and agility is impaired. Mentally, they may be slower at everyday tasks, such as paying at the till and being unfamiliar and averse to newer technology, such as automatic tills. Depression may set in and can also be a symptom of early Alzheimer's disease; this exacerbates their isolation and mobility issues. This combination of factors makes it harder for them to both get to the shops and to cope with a possibly fast and crowded environment within the store. In extreme cases, pensioners have starved at home not because they couldn't afford food but because they couldn't get out to buy it. Social services, whilst they attend to falls and other medical issues, do not want to take on the further responsibility of ensuring that there is adequate food, or even any food at all, in the home.

Supermarkets have to cope with impatient customers; many people don't want to spend too long on buying food any more than they want to spend more time than necessary cooking it. They don't want to be held up even for a few seconds behind someone much slower than they are and certainly not behind someone slowly counting out change at the till as they queue behind. Supermarkets also face a 'litigious society' where if a pensioner falls over and breaks a leg (they may have osteoporosis and fragile bones), and then if the pensioner doesn't want to sue, the family, now greatly inconvenienced by extra visiting and suddenly greatly increased responsibilities, may well seek legal advice. This has resulted in some supermarkets banning pensioners who have fallen over in the store (this diverts scarce staff time too), exacerbating their problems of accessing food; the frail pensioner is probably not going to be ordering online. There are an estimated 1.3 million infirm pensioners who are malnourished at home, and this malnourishment may be what precipitates a hospital stay, which may be extended due to further lack of mobility whilst in a hospital bed. Such malnutrition is estimated to cost the NHS £12 billion a year.

In 2016, Katherine Vero of Newcastle on Tyne, UK, launched the idea of 'Slow Shopping' (rather like the idea of *citta lente*, slow cities, where life is supposed to be lived at a less frenetic pace for everyone). Local supermarkets such as Sainsbury Gosforth have 'slow shopping hours', akin to the 'quiet hours' for autistic customers noted earlier; on Tuesdays between 1 and 3 pm, the store puts chairs out (some elderly like to be able to rest a bit mid-shopping, and most supermarkets have nowhere for them to sit except the café, which is not convenient to get to in mid-shopping trip), also they have staff to assist the inform and even a stand with tea and cake put out. By encouraging the elderly to get out, this performs a valuable social function, avoiding isolation and helping them make new friends. Waitrose Bath has a similar initiative, between 10 and 12 on Tuesday mornings. The store also avoids loudspeaker announcements during that period (not good for those with poor hearing) and ensures that there are no crates left in the aisles, which could be a trip hazard and obstruct disabled-scooter users. Tuesday mid-morning or mid-afternoon is usually a quieter shopping period. Slow checkout lanes have also been proposed, similar to the quick 'ten items or less' checkouts, where pensioners and others can feel comfortable about paying by cash and even having a chat with the till operator. Like the provision of free supermarket buses, which improve access in some areas that are 'food deserts', there is both a CSR and a commercial profit aspect here.

The Lonely

If old age is a 'Cinderella condition' then loneliness is even more so. It's a failure to be lonely, even a bit 'odd'. Yet loneliness has been shown to be as physiologically as damaging as smoking, and as noted earlier, it is a significant part of the array of problems afflicting many pensioners. In the UK, the Waitrose chain has become well-known for its cafés and customer coffees, although other large supermarket branches frequently have cafés as well. Waitrose, in 2017, began a 'community table' initiative in all its cafés with more than 40 seats, allocating 20% of tables as 'community tables', with invites to sit together with a stranger and cards encouraging 'conversation starters'. Waitrose Newbury branch has linked up with Coffee Companions to provide café tables with 'chat mats', green side up for "come and have a talk with me", red side up for 'not today please'. This scheme is running across a range of locations in southern England, mainly independent coffee shops. However, supermarket cafés could also be a good venue to connect the isolated and encourage social interactions in a society that sometimes moves too fast to care for its slower members.

6.2 Local Charity Donations

The list of the world's largest companies is dominated by a few sectors: minerals, automobiles, utilities and electronics. These corporations have the resources to help the world's charitable causes, but, generally, they are very remote, in physical terms, from the actual points of need. The large supermarkets are in a unique position here because, although they are large (Walmart remains the world's largest company by revenue), they also have numerous local neighbourhood points of contact, by definition, their business model; supermarkets requires access by local residents. Supermarket managers may even have a better picture of local needs than central government does, and if not, they can, and do, ask their customers who live around the retail premises. Asda has adopted the 'Asda mile' or 'your square mile' as a means of focussing on local community issues. This is essentially an urban initiative in large cities, such as London or Birmingham, where each supermarket will serve an area of about one square mile. Not only will the supermarket staff, or their customers, have a good idea of what local causes could benefit from supermarket largesse but also the logistics of delivering such assistance will be easier from a local supermarket than from a corporate head office many kilometres away. Supermarkets can provide one of the most basic needs of the destitute and homeless: food; the donations of large retailers to food banks are discussed next. The supermarket may ask its customers directly what charities they would like supported. In 2008, Waitrose began the Community Matters scheme, which allowed customers to vote on what proportion of a total sum of a few thousand pounds every few weeks should go to each one of three charities. The charities were chosen by each store branch, every one or two months, and were local to it. Customers received a token at the till which they could deposit in one of three clear Perspex boxes, one for each good cause. Over time, each box would gain more or less tokens, the final supermarket donations being divided according to the number of tokens deposited in each box. This Waitrose scheme has now been copied by many other UK supermarkets, such as Tesco and Asda.

Customers can feel good about choosing their own good cause (at least from a set of three) and from seeing afterwards how large a donation their voting has resulted in. They may seldom consider the obverse side of this. Why are supermarkets donating to homeless charities, medical causes, animal charities and so on? Perhaps, according to *Feminist Ire*

(Lord, 2014), because the government has cut funding for such organizations whilst the global corporations have cut wages to the bare legal minimum? Writing from a feminist perspective, Stephanie Lord queries, "If women were paid a little bit better, they would have more options other than underfunded domestic violence shelters when leaving abusive relationships". There are two replies one could make to this argument. Firstly, Tesco is just one corporation, albeit a large one, and can scarcely be expected to change the entire neoliberal privatized global governance system on its own, and secondly, given this, at least it's better if Tesco or some other corporation donates than if nobody does. In fact, the danger of passing charitable support from the government on to private hands is that governments are accountable democracies; corporations are not. Not quite, anyway; customers do 'vote' with their money, by choosing Tesco over Sainsbury's, say, but the mix of charitable donations supported will be an infinitesimal part of this choice, lost amongst all the other considerations of price, location, choice, convenience and so on. However, a government in power can always be influenced by pressure groups, even outside of election time. As Lord (ibid) points out, "Which children's charity will criticize Tesco for making it cheaper to feed children rubbish high-sugar food when it could potentially one day be Tesco's charity of the year?" Charities may also face, or at least perceive, curbs on their activities if these are over-critical of governments that fund them, but it is more feasible for popular pressure to turn (or overturn) a government than to force a large corporation that people more or less have to patronize for their food to change direction. Ultimately, any social pressure arising from 'charity censorship' by the large retail companies is best directed, not at the company itself but at the government to step in and provide support. At best, these local initiatives provide funds for small causes that might otherwise never get off the ground and never afford the publicity they need to get going. At worst, they are a sort of local greenwash, ameliorating the (also local and often largely unnoticed) effects of supermarkets on local independent retailer economies. A small butcher closing is scarcely local news, let alone national, especially when such local shops frequently struggle on for a few years after the supermarket that is going to put them out of business has already opened and the fanfare of its arrival has died away. Hopefully, these independent shop owners will not be using the food banks, another popular donation point for CSR-conscious supermarkets.

6.3 Food Banks

In the past few years, many UK supermarkets have installed a food bank box, usually in the so-called dwell zone. This is the entrance area to the supermarket—a sort of transition zone where arriving consumers make the psychological transition into 'shoppers'. It is called the 'dwell zone', as the function of this zone is not to sell anything directly, but to increase the dwell time: the total time the shopper spends inside the store retail area itself. The dwell zone often contains information on special offers in-store, recipe cards and the customer information desk. This zone also contains the fast-visit sales area, the newspapers, tobacco, lottery and sandwiches sales area, where visitors who only want these convenience goods can purchase them without being delayed by long queues; this builds a favourable impression of the store in their minds for future major shopping trips. As an extension of this idea, pet food boxes have appeared where cat or dog food may be deposited for local animal charities. Food bank deposit boxes create a feel-good mood in charitable-minded shoppers, who can also dispose of food items they no longer want to consume in a socially responsible manner. Ocado, the online grocer, has adopted a version of this idea, where customers can make a credit card online donation to the food bank, and Ocado promises to match it with the equivalent sum in groceries. However, some of these charity deposit boxes have been removed because, at some Asda supermarkets, for example, people were taking food items from them; this deterred depositors, who could not then be sure their donation was going to charity.

The supermarkets may be criticized for some aspects of their charity donations, such as insufficient security, or for having some profit element also incorporated. However, some schemes may be unfairly castigated; the well-known Tesco Computers for Schools initiative may be one such programme.

6.4 Tesco Computers for Schools

In 2003, Tesco ran its Computers for Schools scheme, where shoppers got vouchers which when enough were collected could be exchanged for ICT and sports equipment for local schools. But the scheme was much derided because to get enough vouchers for an office scanner, which Tesco itself sold for £80, you had to spend £44,900 in Tesco. A set of three tennis balls that retailed for £1.25 required a Tesco spend of £1,140 and a trampoline required a spend of £1,000,000 (Blythman, 2004: 246; Simms, 2007: 291). Furthermore, Tesco was encouraging schools to design promotional material for this offer, effectively outsourcing its advertising campaigns for free. To be fair, however, supermarkets operate on very small percentage profit margins; this is the whole basis of their huge economies of scale, which enables such small margins to generate still-large returns. In 2003/4, Tesco's UK sales were £24,760 million, and its operating profit was £1,526 million, a margin of 6.16%. Now assume that 4% of profits could be given to charity, a reasonable ballpark figure for large retail corporations (Moneybox, 2013). We can now calculate in Table 6.1 for the two items where the retail cost and the contemporaneous required spend in Tesco to purchase the items are both known.

Table 6.1 Tesco Computers for Schools Scheme Evaluation

Item	Scanner	3 tennis balls
1) Required spend in Tesco	£44,900	£1,140
2) Retail cost of item	£80	£1.25
3) Percentage of profit on spend at Tesco (6.16%)	£2,765.84	£70.22
4) Four percent of profit for charity	£110.63	£2.81
5) Percentage of 'expected donation'—i.e. (2) as % of (4)	72.3%	44.5%

Thus table suggests that Tesco was being a little stingy, but not so much as the Blythman and Simms figures suggest. Remembering that Tesco is a low-margin company, it is giving around half to three-quarters of what the 'benchmark 4%' figure would suggest. Although one could argue that the wholesale price to Tesco of these items is well below the retail price (2), that retail price represents the opportunity cost to the company; in other words, what it could have sold those articles for. As an aside, Mullerat (2013: 7) quotes a much lower figure of 0.5% to 1.0% of pre-tax corporate profits given to charity, which would make Tesco's scheme rather generous indeed.

6.5 Other Supermarket Charitable Donations

In some cases, supermarkets may be forced into charitable CSR initiatives because of bad publicity about their corporate policies—a sort of flip side to the manner in which supermarkets like Iceland and Tesco have become trendsetters, forcing rival chains to follow suit in the area of reducing plastics pollution. In 2017, the Ilford (London) branch of M&S attracted negative publicity for deterring rough sleepers bedding down in its doorways by sounding an alarm at intervals. This came against a background of rising homelessness and rough sleeping in Britain, as stagnant wages, austerity and government services cutbacks coexisted with continued high housing prices. Other companies had resorted to installing sprinkler systems to deter doorway rough sleeping. Further concern about street sleeping in the UK was aroused by the protracted cold winter of 2017/8. In 2018, M&S has liaised with local councils to provide 'pop-up' hostels for the homeless, made from old shipping containers and sited on council land in Redbridge, East London. A range of other organizations, including the retail chains, Debenhams, Metro Bank and the charities Salvation Army and the Refugee and Migrant Forum of Essex are also involved in an initiative called Redbridge Together.

Besides their financial assets and their food, supermarkets can use other assets to assist in charitable causes. Mobile scanners for common cancers, such as lung and prostate, can be hosted in the supermarket car park, which is seldom completely full anyway. The NHS benefits from earlier diagnosis of such ailments, and people may be more willing to visit such facilities whilst out shopping, rather than the inconvenience of a special visit to a doctor. Men especially may be reluctant to visit a doctor until perhaps it is too late for effective treatment. The supermarket car park may also make a convenient location for a weekly Farmer's Market, which many towns now hold in their main High Street periodically. High Street–based street markets can cause inconvenience for local people and shoppers. Car parking becomes scarce, and stalls and crowds may block narrow pavements, forcing the disabled in wheelchairs into the road. Traders' vans which remain parked all day may also cause a nuisance, and the regular High Street shops may complain that they lose trade because people cannot access them or even see them behind the street stalls. All of these issues, crowding and parking, can be resolved by utilizing a far corner of the car park; the supermarket, of course, receives more visitors and may gain a 'halo effect' of association with healthy organic food as well.

Members of parliament and local councillors may also hold a different type of 'surgery' in the supermarket foyer. Waitrose Hull has a small police interview room just off the café area. This is a useful feature for people wishing to pass information to the police in a city where someone emerging from a real police station can be regarded with great suspicion and may be rather forcefully asked exactly what information they gave. Many supermarkets provide a free small personal adverts noticeboard and have a book exchange where people can bring surplus books, and others can pick them up and make a voluntary donation to charity. Supermarkets are then becoming community hubs, well beyond their original remit of selling food; in a similar manner to the Mediaeval church, which over time became a community meeting place, information exchange and even marketplace. Of course, just as religious purists lamented this secularization of a holy place of worship, some may see it as sinister rather than good that the supermarkets are adopting this overarching role within the community.

In other CSR initiatives, Woolworths Australia will provide barbeque equipment and a gazebo so people can run charity fundraising events. The actual barbeque food must be ordered from the store, so they make extra sales this way. Woolworths Australia also supports agricultural shows and scholarships to study agriculture and food production. Perhaps those students, when they have graduated and are making a career in the food and agriculture industry, will look more favourably on Woolworths when negotiating food contracts. In Greece, the Flora supermarket in Mykonos, a popular tourist area, hosts a short history of the island and a guide to the tourists sights on its website (Flora Supermarkets, 2018). Since few people will choose their holiday destination on the basis of a local supermarket website, and tourists tend not to buy supermarket food (unless going self-catering, of course), this cultural contribution to the island's heritage probably provides little material gain to the supermarket itself, other than good publicity.

Lidl intervened to assist in Romania when the state educational system pulled out of teaching children about road safety. Store car parks were converted into mini replicas of city streets, with buildings, road crossings and traffic signs. In the first eight months of 2014, 30 children died and a further 261 were seriously injured in a country with a total population of 20 million. This is the equivalent in the UK of 140 child traffic deaths and 1,200 serious child injuries every year, and even this was an improvement from 2013, the year Lidl Romania began its educational programme. The payoff for Lidl was huge publicity in the national media, and it was estimated that 10 million Romanians, half the population, had read about the initiative. Also, in Romania, Lidl pioneered the construction of stores with 'green' (vegetation-covered) roofs, which create a whole range of environmental benefits. Besides absorbing pollution and converting CO_2 into oxygen, the store is cooled in hot summers, reducing the need for air conditioning, and rainwater is absorbed, lessening the danger of urban flooding. The store roof also makes a space for insect wildlife and creates an attractive area, especially for apartment dwellers and office workers in tower blocks seeing it from above (Sempergreen, 2017).

In various guises, the supermarkets not only manage to sell virtually everything we need, including not just food but clothing and even housing too; they are becoming the protectors and benefactors of the homeless, the environment and even mediators of road safety. There is yet one more role they have adopted, a far less well-publicized one: custodians of our data, even our most confidential and private information.

6.6 Supermarket Customer Data

In return for our shopping, we hand over more than just money to the main supermarket chains. We also almost inevitably, unless we always pay with cash, never order online or never have a home delivery from them and hold no loyalty card, give them something even more valuable: information. Even then, there is a technology waiting in the wings that will prove to be a huge mine of data for these corporations: Radio Frequency Identification tags, or RFID for short. Meanwhile, for the majority of us who do pay by credit card and use loyalty cards, we may ask who else can buy, or illicitly access, this information. Supermarket data collection and its analysis for personalized marketing initiatives has become very sophisticated. Supermarkets track the weather forecast by the hour and by the town, because they need sophisticated models of consumer behaviour to track and facilitate their 'just-in-time' ordering system. An obvious example is that if the day is sunny, people buy more beer and ice cream, whereas if it is wet and cloudy, soup and pudding sales rise. It all becomes a little more sinister when such consumer behaviour is linked to the individual shopper through the abundant electronic trail that modern shopping leaves. Furthermore, what has not kept pace with this sophisticated 'collection' and 'analysis' is 'security', as the experience of Facebook in March 2018 mentioned next illustrates. Data about your shopping can give away details of your personal life that even the most dedicated user of social media might hesitate to post. The range of goods sold by supermarkets is now very large and all under one roof, so is the likelihood of doing a single one-stop shopping that sums up your entire life. Add in the data provided by usage of a loyalty card, and one is virtually making one's house, one's life and one's personal habits and illnesses a public space, as Table 6.2 illustrates.

Table 6.2 Information Potential of Supermarket Credit Card and Loyalty Card Data

Supermarket data on your shopping	Information about the shopper
Data generally supplied by the customer when registering for a loyalty card	Your name, address, email and phone contact; probable income level (from your postcode); perhaps family size; home tenure; and any other details asked for, either at time of application or in later questionnaires.
Time and place you shopped	What times you are often away from home (many households have a regular shopping routine). Where and when you went on day trips, commuting, holidays. Do you like rural holidays, city breaks and walking holidays, and in what locations and how often (related to income and personality)?
Foods you bought	Your probable income level, your general fitness and obesity level and your likelihood of contracting a range of illnesses, including diabetes, heart disease, osteoporosis, arthritis, liver disease (from alcohol purchases), lung cancer (do you buy cigarettes?). Any older people in your family? Presence of young children in the household. Probable number of people in your household.
Toys and books you bought	Presence of children in the household. Your personality preferences (cooking books, gardening, fiction, puzzle books). Might you fear Alzheimer's disease? Colouring books, for adults or children—are you an artistic dreamy sort of person?
Clothes and jewellery you bought	Age, personality, wealth, sexual orientation.

Supermarket data on your shopping	Information about the shopper
What periodicals you buy. What magazines you buy	Your political views (the *Guardian* or the *Daily Mail?*). Your hobbies. Your social class and income level (*Yachting* or *Real Ale* periodical, football, golf, dog-racing, darts or angling magazines? Car maintenance magazines; holiday magazines—in various destinations, safe or adventurous).
Do you buy microwave meals, other convenience foods, freezer food, fresh/ organic food, electronic goods, eco-friendly goods or cheaper goods?	Food as fuel or food gourmet fanatic, ecologically concerned or not. Cash rich, time poor or vice versa. Luddite or techie. Health concerned or hedonistic, future focussed or present oriented.
Petrol purchases	Your income level (car or no car), also indications as to your ecological views and fitness commitment (how far you live from the supermarket and do/don't drive there).
Health-related goods, vitamin pills, laxatives, headache pills, shampoo types, skin creams	What illnesses you have now, or fear you may have. What illnesses run in your family.
Condoms, pregnancy test kits, the 'morning-after-pill', Viagra (all available from UK supermarkets)	Your sexual activity and concerns.
Financial services	Your financial standing, credit rating and housing tenure.
Tesco office equipment and stationery	Do you run your own business (insecure income? Untaxed side income?)
Your response, or not, to advertising initiatives	Personality: gullible or obstinate? Greedy or simple life? What needs do you have, or perceive you have, and how do these change over time as you age, health changes, finances change, family changes?
Music and film CDs	What music and film tastes do you have. Country folk of heavy metal rock? Musical tastes may be linked to white supremacism, or sympathies with some ethnic minority conflicts worldwide.
Tesco Clubcard also asks for, or can potentially gather, (Tesco Clubcard, 2017) links to online data, which of necessity is made via a credit card; browsing information (Tesco and other sites); your personal contacts (if accessed via a mobile device). Charities you may donate to	Your income level (what sort of device you use). Ultimately, Total Information Awareness—a US intelligence term for linking all available electronic data about a person, from health records and facial recognition data to employment history and previous convictions. Your religious beliefs (any donations), also concerns about animal rights, poverty and other international issues.

Naturally, Tesco assures us that it would never dig so deeply or intrusively into your personal life. But can it guarantee the integrity of its data on you from third-party hackers, either criminals or state snoopers? On 19 March 2018, Facebook shares fell 7% in one day, wiping US$40 billion (UK£ 28.5 billion) from the company's value, because of breaking news that Cambridge Analytica, a consumer research company, might have gained access to and misused personal data from Facebook. In further fallout from this incident, Cambridge Analytica went insolvent in May 2018 as the episode left it with mounting legal fees and disappearing clients. One can only imagine the fall in value a major supermarket would suffer if they experienced the same data breach. It is also amazing what data we would never put on our social media page, but will divulge, directly or indirectly, for the sake of 1% off our shopping bill.

If the potential of supermarket loyalty card data gives one the uneasy feelings of ghostly creaking in the attic, then RFID is equivalent to full-blown supernatural possession. RFID technology has the potential to transform the supermarket retail system more comprehensively than out-of-town supermarkets have transformed the original High Street shopping routine. RFID essentially consists of a tiny printed circuit containing a 96-bit code, an antenna to pick up an external radio 'beacon' and software to garner energy from the radio beam and transmit back the code embedded in the circuit. RFID, therefore, can be read passively, with no input, knowledge or consent necessary from the owner of the article being 'read'. Ninety-six bits sounds small, but this gives a possible total of 2 power 96 different codes, or, approximately, one million, million, million, million, million (10 power 30) individual product codes. Given that our planet will almost certainly never have more than 0.1 million million (10 power 11) people, corporations, administrative agencies and NGOs, that is a lot of codes, or individually identified products, per person, agent or company.

RFID has been used by supermarket delivery systems to label entire trucks of goods and to track their progress from factory to supermarket delivery door. However, RFID is also already in use to identify individual objects. When you use an automatic book return at the library, RFID is how the machine knows what books are being returned—and who the borrower was. It can identify individual animals, with a link to their history, feeding, medical history and so on, or, presumably, individual people, a few of us who have already opted to have microchips implanted in our arms to speed up entry to clubs, for example. RFID is tiny, about the size and thickness of a full stop in normal type font. The radio signal that powers it and sends the return signal can penetrate brick walls, just as you can listen to a radio indoors. RFID chips could be invisibly and permanently implanted in almost anything: clothes, books, banknotes, credit cards, food packaging, automobiles and even your arm. The main reason it has not yet been widely adopted in your local supermarket is that bar codes are even cheaper, as are the wages for the bar code scanning operatives. In fact, such wages fall to zero when you scan your own shopping. However, if RFID was adopted, perhaps because the RFID chips became even cheaper, and the information they could provide became more valuable, or consumer resistance to self-scanning continued and shop till staff wages rose, what CSR issues would an RFID-based supermarket raise?

Shopping at such an RFID-enabled supermarket might be a rather eerie experience, especially if you visit at a slack time, because the shop floor could be virtually staff-less, apart from a couple of security guards maybe and someone at customer service for when the RFID has given you the wrong price because someone forgot to programme in that week's BOGOF, or the end of the offer date had been wrongly entered, assuming that you notice the missing offer discount, of course. Essentially, you would load up your trolley and exit through an airport security-style gate, within which would be embedded the RFID radio beacon and reader. There would be no checkout staff, just a gate which you could only open using your credit card (so the machine knows who to charge for the shopping). Or maybe you would wave your arm in front of it, with your personal RFID chip implanted just under the skin. The security guards are there to ensure nobody leaps the barrier, as they might do when arriving ticketless at a railway station. People are already accustomed to automatic payment, sometimes with prior insertion of a loyalty card, at supermarket petrol pumps, railway stations and a host of other retail outlets; biometric machine readable passports also promote this technology. The first CSR issue would then be massive job losses. Although checkout staff could be redeployed to shelf stacking or moving goods in the warehouse, experience suggests the opposite will happen; jobs will be lost here to automation, just as has happened at Amazon's warehouses. Shelf restacking by robots could take place at night, facilitated by the trend away from 24-hour opening in recent years, because customers might not interact too well with shelf restacking robots.

RFID would raise the same privacy issues as credit cards plus loyalty cards, initially, but the privacy concerns of RFID go a lot further. Essentially, one could be tracked wherever one went, without consent or even knowledge. Buy a pair of jeans or some shoes in a supermarket with a credit card, and assuming they are for your own wearing (most items of apparel, especially shoes, are bought by the intended wearer, or someone close to them), any RFID machine behind any brick wall could gather data on who goes where, when and even how fast or how long you loiter there, and this is without any facial recognition or gait analysis software, in the dark, with your face covered. You may be wearing a coat your aunt bought you, but the majority of RFID tags in your shoes, socks, underwear and shirt will have been paid for on one credit card account: your own. There's an app for sorting that RFID crisis out.

Finally, without straying too far from the realms of CSR into science fiction, RFID could have significant implications for personal privacy and freedom of choice. Once the supermarket food is at home in your fridge, an RFID reader embedded there would know if you have food that is nearing its sell-by date and should be eaten first, or if you haven't bought milk for a couple of days and might be running out. It would also know if you have too much sugary processed food in there and not enough vegetables; fresh produce might all be in environmentally friendly biodegradable packages by then, no loose items or perhaps the loose produce scales will have a capability to programme a blank RFID tag inbuilt within the price sticker the scales spit out. You are eating your way to diabetes, risking blindness and amputations? That's expensive for society, in medical care and lost work capability. Maybe you have too much alcohol in your home; a smart meter could scan for that as well as measure your power consumption. Now we have the 'Internet of Things' (Shaw & Shaw, 2015: 249), where you can tell your cooker to preheat the ready meal you left there this morning; why shouldn't your fridge tell the supermarket not to sell you any more chocolate? Try and that security gate barrier will fail to let you through until you have removed the calorifically offending items from your trolley. All for your own good, of course. The major supermarket chains would then have reached their ultimate destiny as not just commanders of our diet but overlords of our lifestyles, health and morals too. Perhaps this is the ultimate supermarket CSR. Perhaps the Luddites who hate using automated checkouts should start using them now to reduce the incentive of supermarkets to go down the full RFID route. It is possible for any such future privacy concerns to be allayed by removable tags, products where the location of the RFID chip is made obvious and can be removed after purchase. RFID chips can be programmed to self-kill after a set period of time; on food, this could coincide with the use-by date of the food, ensuring that it is unsaleable after that. A second or two inside a microwave oven will also disable current RFID tags. But such privacy issues, the demand for tags that self-kill or could be removed in the first place, would depend not on the corporations but on continued public vigilance. In a world where people are willing to chip their own arms to save a minute or so at a nightclub door, how strong might such vigilance be?

6.7 Effort Made by Supermarkets to Ensure the Food from Food Processors Is Healthier

No supermarket wants a reputation for selling obesogenic food, even if its customers, by their food choices, tend to go for the unhealthier options: ready meals and sugary desserts rather than the fresh produce. In a mirror image of the societal contradiction of fashion demanding slimness in a food world that promotes obesity (Shaw, 2014: 81), the supermarkets generally have their fresh fruit and vegetable selections towards the customer entrance, creating an impression of naturalness and wholesomeness, whilst the vast majority of aisles contain more sugary, fatty, salty fare. However, in certain specific food categories, those with a high public profile, the supermarket chains make an effort to appear 'responsible' and in touch with social and environmental concerns. Iceland, for example, whom we saw in Chapter 4 to be rather pioneering in the areas of palm oil and plastic pollution, has also been one of the first supermarket chains to remove genetically modified ingredients from its own brand foods back in 1998; again, this influenced other major supermarket chains to follow suit (Smith, 2004: 218). Most supermarkets have also been swift to cater for the ethnic minorities that have settled in their catchment areas, especially since 2000. In Britain, Polish, Halal and Chinese aisles are common, also Kosher sections in some areas, with Japanese and Hispanic food aisles similarly prevalent in US supermarkets. Other minority food consumers are similarly catered for, with vegetarian, vegan and gluten free food shelves in most large food superstores.

The presence of sweets at supermarket checkouts has been a particular irritant to parents. It is almost inevitable that a child, bored after half an hour or an hour's shopping, will exert 'pester power' on their stressed parent, who does not feel up to a fight to stop the child from just taking the sweet, which then has to be paid for, adding financial stress to the entire experience. In fact, it is not good for business to have the parent's last impression of a supermarket as angry and stressful. After a long campaign by UK parent's groups, "Chuck Sweets Off the Check-Out", supermarket chains began removing them, pioneered by Aldi in 2014 (Daneshku, 2014). In fact, impulse checkout buys may be quite rare. In an experiment in the Bronx, New York, USA, it was observed that just 4% of supermarket customers bought anything from the checkout (Adjoian et al, 2017), but for those who did, a checkout containing just healthy items caused those in it to purchase in future shopping trips healthy items twice as much and unhealthy ones 60% less than shoppers at standard checkouts.

6.8 Marketing to Children

Away from the checkout, supermarkets make efforts to ensure that they are attractive places for children. This starts before they even enter the building, with mother and child spaces, little trolleys and plastic 'cars' for toddlers, and continues inside with the larger hypermarkets always stocking a range of children's clothes, toys, colouring books and crayons, along with specific foods aimed at young children, from yoghurts to chocolate bars. Unfortunately, these 'children's foods' are often high in sugar, also brightly coloured and heavily oriented towards the 'dessert' range rather than the 'savoury' end. Babies are born with a very simple sense of taste, sweet versus sour, which was a crucial survival mechanism thousands of years ago. Toddlers will put anything, even dirt, in their mouths, which is how they train their immune system and pick up some of the beneficial bacteria which are vital for biological functioning of the adult body. In nature, poisonous things are bitter, whereas nothing sweet is hazardous, so this sweet/sour taste mechanism protects children from poisoning themselves in their early years (Shaw, 2014: 51). Children then develop more sophisticated taste preferences, being predisposed to like the foods they come across in their family settings, again a useful adaptation to ensure that they eat well and thrive on the foods most readily available to them.

Unfortunately, the prevalence of sugary sweetness in foods has crept up the age range, as sugar has become cheaper in real terms, and processed foods create more profit for supermarkets and food manufacturers than fresh vegetables do. Concerning healthier foods, supermarkets have historically tended to shift the burden of responsibility from themselves to parents (Colls & Evans, 2008). However, the increasing alarm at growing child obesity rates has forced the supermarkets to take a more proactive role here. From Autumn 2015, Tesco began giving free fruit to children, bananas, apples and oranges could be taken free from a box in the fruit and vegetable section; Woolworths Australia operates a similar scheme. Critics might question why the fresh produce initiative is fruit (sweet) based rather than savoury vegetables. The Tesco initiative was not only to appear to be combatting child obesity but also aimed at reversing a falling market share and rising customer complaints about poor service, tackling increasing price competition from Aldi and Lidl, and counteracting the bad publicity from an accounting scandal in which profits were overstated. Of course, if the free offer was pieces of carrot or broccoli, this would have to be cooked and then kept heated, with additional costs and health and safety implications, but this does not stop supermarkets from selling fresh chicken on the spit to flood the store with an appetite-stimulating aroma to make shoppers hungry and to buy more food.

In 2014, Tesco began its Eat Happy Project, aiming to invite all UK primary school children for an open day to a UK farm that supplies Tesco to reconnect children with where food comes from; one child on the accompanying video (Tesco, 2014) seemed to have previously believed that potatoes grew on trees. Children get to see cows, chickens and mushrooms being grown and much else. Tesco pays for everything, the staff to supervise the children, even the bus to transport them, and the trip will free up considerable staff time at participating schools for other tasks. A more cynical viewpoint on these trips was provided by the Food Assembly (Turns, 2017). This commentary emphasizes the huge marketing boost that Tesco gets out of these trips, which are almost irresistible to schools in the current climate of education funding constraints, with the children even wearing yellow tabards with the message "I'm Learning

Where My Food Comes From—Farm to Fork—Part of the Tesco Eat Happy Project". The 'free' aspect of the Tesco school trips attracts opprobrium, as it appears to be 'a cute marketing trick' to take more market share from small High Street butchers and from local farm shops, who have to charge for small-scale, one-off school trips. Urban farms, like the ones in Hackney, London, offer free entry to school parties, but the school must still pay for transport and teacher time; a similar situation applies to any Scottish school trips to the Royal Highland Education Trust (RHET), although they can arrange free visits to schools by farmers who volunteer to give their time for this. In England, LEAF (Linking Environment And Farming) and Farming and Countryside Education run the same initiatives.

Critics of the Tesco Eat Happy Project accuse Tesco of imprinting itself on young minds to convince them that Tesco is the only contact point between farmers and consumers. Of course, it is far too early to know if children who have been on these trips are more likely to use a Tesco supermarket when they grow up rather than a Sainsbury or Asda, or even if they will buy a lower percentage of their groceries from independent shops overall. Like most supermarket CSR schemes, Eat Happy will probably be replaced by something else, and if anyone tried to follow through on the cohort of children who have participated to check their food diaries as adults, there would be far too many confounding factors—income, place of residence, accessibility of supermarkets and independent retailers, use of a car, tastes, acquired cooking skills, preference of spouse—to arrive at any meaningful correlations. The Sustainable Food Trust, another online critic of Eat Happy (Miller, 2014), pointed out that Tesco failed to indicate that none of the fruit and vegetable or bakery items the children were enjoying seeing in the supermarket, and had been given samples of to take home, were locally produced. As for price, although Tesco's 'ordinary' produce was considerably cheaper than that of local organic farmers, Tesco's organic produce was of similar cost to the farm shop gate prices. Meanwhile, the local farmers were using much less chemical-intensive, more sustainable, farming practices compared to the huge agri-businesses that supply Tesco.

Should Tesco run its Eat Happy Project? Not running it could leave many children with less contact with the food chain, since not all schools are near a city farm or can afford the teacher time to visit a farm with RHET or LEAF. Tesco is a business, not a charity. Its huge size and massive profits, which mean it can fund a CSR initiative that in turn may increase its sales yet more, has undoubtedly come at the expense of others, from suppliers and the small shops sector to the environment and arguably the taxpayer, if one believes that large global corporations pay 'too little' tax. Therefore, the critics of Eat Happy are really saying that the government should tax Tesco more to pay for the negative externalities it causes and plough some of this extra tax back into funding schools to organize food and farming trips, such as Tesco does now. But that is akin to saying that a centralized government should have more control of our food system, not a private corporation. Who is right? Is a government, elected once every five years, more accountable than an oligopoly of a few large food retail companies, which most consumers are free to choose between 'voting for' with their purchases once a week or more (Shaw, 2007)? The answer to 'should Tesco run Eat Happy?' is then beyond simply CSR; it is a fundamental political question as to where society and the economy should place itself on the spectrum between a neo-liberal unfettered free market on the one hand and a statist centrally directed system on the other. What we have now is very much at the neo-liberal end of that choice, and without revolutionary changes, it may be best to encourage large corporations to give as much as possible back to society in CSR programmes, even if that CSR also creates some profit for the corporation too.

In early 2018, a specific sugar-related food retail issue hit the headlines with the news that young children were consuming energy drinks. These are drinks, such as Red Bull, that contain high concentrations of caffeine along with large amounts of sugar. The concept of 'energy drinks' as in drinks that perk you up can be traced right back to Lucozade, marketed as a recovery drink for the ill in the 1920s. By the 1980s, these drinks were being used by joggers and sportspeople for an extra boost. However, by the 1990s, this 'energy boost' was also being sought by people who were just too busy to have breakfast before rushing out to their sedentary jobs and wanted something to combat the morning tiredness resulting from going to work on an empty stomach; this was scarcely healthy, of course. Somehow, by the 1990s, we were becoming too busy to have a traditional breakfast before leaving for work or school. The Cardiffian reported (Clements, 2018) on one 16-year-old who said, "I usually pick up a bag of crisps and a drink like Red Bull or Lucozade. It keeps me going until break time", he said. When asked if he had eaten breakfast, he said, "I had a bit of toast before I left the house but I need something else and this gives me energy to concentrate".

In 2018, Waitrose became the first UK supermarket to ban sales of energy drinks, with over 150mg caffeine per litre, such as Red Bull, to people under 18, effectively treating these beverages as if they were alcoholic drinks (Musaddique, 2018). This was in response to concerns about children being hyperactive and teachers having to deal with the bad behaviour resulting from this in school, also the long-term health effects of drinking so much caffeine. This might include sleepless nights, raised heart rate and even seizures. A small energy drink can may contain as much caffeine as two cups of strong filter coffee, but any bitterness is overlaid by the sugar content, which can amount to as much as 20 teaspoons of sugar per can. By April 2018, all the main UK supermarket chains had a stated policy of not selling these drinks to those under 16.

However, there is some way to go here, as on 6 May 2018, the *Mail on Sunday* reported (Narain & Powell, 2018) on a 12-year-old girl who was sent to a branch of all the main supermarkets in the Brighton area and succeeded in buying, without question, a can of Red Bull at Aldi, Asda, Sainsbury's and Waitrose. She was refused at the Co-op, Iceland, Lidl, Morrison and Tesco. The 'guilty' supermarkets were rather non-committal when challenged afterwards, saying they were sorry; they would investigate, and we have reiterated our policy to all staff.

Energy drinks can be made to appeal to the cost-conscious consumer, and be normalized as part of an everyday diet, by their inclusion in meal deals. These meal deals, where various choices of food items, usually comprising one of several starters, main courses, drinks and desserts are bundled into a discount deal priced well below the separate cost of these items, seem a good value, unless as with most bundling one would not normally be buying some of the items. Frequently, less-healthy items are included, such as sandwiches, crisps and fizzy sugary drinks. Yet the phrase 'meal deal' makes it seem as a 'square', nutritionally balanced' meal is on offer.

6.9 Supermarket Food Labelling

One function of supermarket labelling is to enable shoppers to make healthier choices; whether this is true or not, and if so, which labelling system works best, is another topic (Shaw, 2014: 145–6). What would be of concern is if these labels were misleading; tests by *Which* magazine have found 4g fat in a Young's Fisherman Pie, where the label said 2.4g / 100g, and 6g of fat in a Vesta Chow Mein from Premier Foods, where the label stated 4g / 100g. (Devlin, 2014). The law allows for variation, because some foods are, for example, sprinkled with cheese topping by hand. EU rules allow a margin of error of 1.6g in products with under 10g fat / 100g and 20% margin if over 10g fat / 100g. However, the food packaging can be carefully and prominently worded to give a 'healthier' impression than the smaller nutrition label says. For example, Asda Premium beef mince has a stated (nutritional label) content of 9.2g fat / 100g, in which was found 12.8g, but the food package can be labelled as 'typically under 12% fat'. Another ploy is to label foods as 'low fat' or 'less than 1% fat' when they would never be high in fat anyway (e.g. sugary fruit-flavoured desserts), but they may be high in sugar. The term 'sugar' itself can be disguised by using its chemical names, dextrose, sucrose or fructose. Meanwhile, the salt content of children's meals can be made to appear lower by using a smaller bowl than a normal serving for calculation, or using adult salt guidelines on meals mostly eaten by, and targeted at, children. Conversely, yoghurt single-size pots, often aimed at the child consumer, tend to be high in sugar, and some are too large for a child single portion. Because the actual yoghurt inside is only a small proportion of the total cost of the pot, food marketers are tempted to raise the size of the portion to make it more attractive to adult consumers too.

Besides nutritional information that may make some food products seem 'healthier' (i.e. lower in fat, sugar or salt) than they really are, supermarkets have a range of other labelling and packaging techniques that make food products seem better value, sometimes whilst actually raising the price. Most products are accurately labelled and presented, but since UK shoppers spent (2015) £115 billion on groceries and toiletries, of which 40% was on promotions, even if 1% of those offers were misleading, that is a £20 loss per household per year. A common tactic since the rise in food inflation soon after 2000 was to reduce the product size without a price reduction, a practice known as shrinkflation. In fact, a size reduction may even be accompanied by a price rise, as when McVities dark chocolate digestive biscuits fell in size from 332g to 300g, but the price rose from £1.59 to £1.69 (Bennett, 2016). Customers often complain that they find the packaging is the same size they are used to, but the packet is now only half full. The weight may be accurately stated, and the customer can feel the weight as he or she picks the product off the shelf, but we overwhelmingly assess products by eye. Supermarkets know that people may judge visually by apparent size but are poor at judging by weight, so a lighter-weight packet does not generally alert people to shrinkflation. Deceptive packaging does not stop at half-filled bags. A common ploy is to have the product in a clear plastic sachet with a large central sleeve label, which typically covers the middle third of the packet. Then the product is presented in two halves, each pushed to the far ends of the container, but the section under the sleeve is largely an empty void. This tactic is frequently used with shrink-wrapped meat and fish slabs, where the close-fitting plastic ensures that the product stays at the ends. Rings of prawns may be packaged with a large central label, again covering a void; it is logical that the product is in a ring, but hurried shoppers have a psychological impression of a much bulkier product. A further deception is to have the product looking much more attractive on the packet than it ever is in reality. Pizza pictures with more cheese or salami than they ever have in the real product is a common occurrence. Of course, the shopper may eventually become aware of this and even start to boycott the product, but by then, the packaging or food range will have changed, leaving customers no wiser than before. Supermarkets may also utilize misleading price comparisons with other supermarkets, or use higher prices for a short time to give a false impression of price cuts. Other tactics include banners with "Two for £2" (when the product is on sale for £1 each), encouraging overbuying and possibly causing food waste (Nicholson & Young, 2012: 16). Food retailers may deploy a whole arsenal of confusing price changes, size changes, special offers, multipacks, larger packs at higher pence-per-weight price than smaller packs, along with a riot of bright garish colours, especially colours associated with 'bargains' (red, white, yellow combinations). Brands and package size ranges change frequently, along with product location within the store. The aim is to prevent time-pressed shoppers ever forming a comprehensive mental picture of what is in the store, where it is and at what price per kilogram. Even milk, a well-known KVI (see Chapter 5) can be obfuscated into a panoply of numerous sizes, types, brands and subvariants—for example, semi-skimmed, skimmed, full fat, organic, chocolate milk, almond milk, soya and so on. Retailers do not want consumers to have a reliable and dependable 'price anchor'. Supermarkets are generally safe in these methods because this area of product promotion and confusion straddles a grey area between social irresponsibility and accepted sales tactics, and it is something the average shopper has become inured to and usually just puts up with. With all retailers using similar tactics, they have little choice anyway.

We have seen how a large range of other agencies both impact on healthy eating and may affect the CSR policies of the major supermarkets. The next chapter reviews the role some of these agencies, including the media and hospitals, as well as other locales where the state serves food, such as schools, prisons and the military, can play in promoting healthy food. By having these other agencies promoting a better national diet, the supermarkets might also be nudged into a more meaningful and healthier range of CSR initiatives.

7 Other Food Suppliers and Food Promoters

7.1 Schools, Prisons and the Military

Schools are far more than a place where the 'hard' skills of mathematics, science and languages are taught; they should also instil the 'soft' skills of reading, studying, research, social interaction and responsibility. These soft—that is, untested—skills, are foundational to the hard learning and are even more vital for fulfilment in life. Sound dietary habits and cooking skills should also be included under this skill set. Naturally, it would be hoped that the parents would also play a major role in teaching these soft skills, but for various reasons, many do not; the advantage of school as a learning venue for these life skills is that at least a minimum standard for all children can be set, rather than the hit-and-miss system of relying on parental guidance alone. School should be an important nutritional gateway where children learn a basic standard of cooking, understand what comprises a balanced diet and why that is important, and comprehend what food is, how it reaches the plate and what environmental, economic and social factors are embedded in various food items. That way, we produce a generation of knowledgeable consumers who are able to understand and face head on the supermarkets and their marketing programmes, and who can demand the necessary set of CSR initiatives from them.

Food, cooking and nutrition, rather than being an extra burden on teaching schedules, can in fact contribute to and reinforce many areas of the traditional 'hard' curriculum subjects. The study of food, its origins and effects on the body can contribute to biology, chemistry and geography. Researching the costs of food, the food retail system and quantities of food produced and consumed can contribute to mathematics and economics lessons. Food items can even be used in language lessons while teaching about the geographical origins, the names, production and consumption cultures of food. Food could even be grown on the school premises, either outdoors or in greenhouses and in laboratories. The physical effort of growing food outside could make a useful contribution to physical exercise. Schools could also make efforts to buy British produce, supporting British farmers and reducing food miles; they could try to serve seasonal produce, teaching children that strawberries grow in real conditions outside and do not appear magically in supermarkets in January from the supermarket storerooms. Some countries do actively promote their indigenous food culture in schools; for example, Japan has the *Shokuiko Kihon Ho* system or Basic Law of Food (Takano, 2013). This makes the education system responsible for promotion of healthy diet and maintenance of Japanese food culture, and is partly a response to the penetration by US fast food multinationals, such as McDonald's into Japanese culture and schools.

Schools can be an important 'nutritional refuge' for pupils who may be served less-wholesome foods at home, and healthy eating in schools may feed back into the home environment. It is not unknown for pupils to turn up at school having had no breakfast, and some even have no supper to go home to. Lunchboxes provided by less-affluent parents may be unhealthy too, with contents reported as processed cheese, chicken nuggets, cold toast or even last night's cold chips. Some children don't know how to handle a knife and fork, a sign that they are eating takeaways and sandwiches that can be eaten with the hands directly. Meanwhile, doctors are seeing Victorian dietary diseases such as rickets reappearing amongst deprived schoolchildren (Chakrabortty, 2018). Poor nutrition, hunger and an excess of sugary processed food also make children badly behaved and less likely to learn anything. It has even been suggested that schools should remain open as lunch centres for 365 days a year, including the 175 non-school days, weekends and school holidays. Alternatively, other council premises such as leisure or community centres could serve school lunches to the poorer pupils, an initiative known as 'Food 365'(Brooks, 2018) currently being implemented in North Lanarkshire, a deprived part of Scotland. Of course, this only works if the food is both nutritious and appealing. Birds Eye found that 11% of adults claimed that memories of bad school dinners had put them off green vegetables for life.

Parents, though, are not always appreciative of schools' efforts to improve the diet of their pupils. Priestlands School in Lymington, Hampshire, was forced to return two pigs donated by a local farmer after protests by vegan parents; the pigs were to be reared by the pupils and then slaughtered for meat to teach the children where meat really comes from, which is not a plastic pack in the supermarket chiller (Gibbons, 2018). In other towns, this initiative might have raised protests from Jewish or Muslim parents too. In another social setting, the celebrity chef Jamie Oliver took on school nutrition in the deprived town of Rotherham, South Yorkshire. Pupils were forbidden from leaving the school grounds at lunchtime to buy burgers, as they were accustomed to; the canteen under Jamie Oliver's direction produced healthy food (which was not immediately appreciated by the children themselves). The parents also significantly undermined this initiative by taking 'orders' from the school gate at break time and turning up at lunchtime with what the children really wanted: burgers, sandwiches, chips and fizzy drinks (Shaw, 2014: 151). Significantly, the parents had three major objections to Jamie Oliver's programme. Firstly, "why is this middle-class guy from Hampstead (a wealthy London suburb) turning up to tell us what to eat". Secondly, if children did change their tastes and want his food, parents would be unable to afford it and lack the knowledge to cook it. Cheap sugary processed food is always cheaper than healthy foodstuffs. Thirdly, these healthy foods would be unobtainable in the local shops on less-affluent housing estates in Rotherham anyway; purchasing them would require a long and expensive trip to a large supermarket, and if the parents tried to grow, for example, basil, in window boxes or in their gardens, they risked social ostracism by their less nutritionally conscious neighbours. School nutritional improvement programmes, therefore, need to bring in the parents, too, and perhaps move gradually, introducing some fresh vegetables to go with the less-healthy meals to begin with, and even hosting simple cookery lessons for the parents as well as the children, maybe also include 'nudge' factors, such as the health impact of better foods on children's life prospects, and even reach out to include local shops to incentivize them to provide the foods that parents should be buying. This could include government- or health service–funded vouchers for the shops so that ordering and stocking fresh produce that spoils quickly is less risky for them.

Similar nutritional efforts could be made in other arenas of state food provision such as prisons and the military. Although there is obvious societal resistance to the idea of providing 'nice' food for offenders, a good diet can reduce prison rioting, violence and security costs, much as healthy eating curbs hyperactivity and misbehaviour amongst school children. The punishment of prison is loss of liberty, not poor feeding as well. In the US prison system, however, 'penal food'—that is, a deliberate reduction in the quality of food provided, is very much a part of the prison system. The Florida Department of Corrections "recommends a basic mix of carrots, spinach, dried beans, vegetable oil, tomato paste, water, grits and oatmeal" (The Economist, 2013b: 55), which is baked into a 'nutraloaf'. This 'nutraloaf' meets basic nutritional requirements and can be served without utensils, an obvious advantage for the prison staff; however, it looks disgusting, tastes bland and is said to cause severe constipation. In some young offender institutions, as little as £2.50 a day was being spent per day per inmate on food in 2011 and very little on fresh fruit and vegetables, leading to inmates bullying each other for fresh fruit (Shaw, 2014: 30). A poor prison diet can also worsen some pre-existing medical conditions, such as diabetes. Conversely, well-behaved prison inmates are easier to rehabilitate and to teach skills to that will enable them to gain employment on release (London Development

Agency, 2005: 39). Prison could also be used for 'dietary rehabilitation'; since prisoners come from the more deprived sections of society and are likely to have a poor diet on release also, prisoners near their release date could be given some nutritional coaching on how to eat cheaply but more healthily. There would be objections from the political right, but society would benefit in terms of reduced healthcare and better post release conduct and employment prospects.

Hyperactivity and disobedience are not problems widely reported amongst military recruits, but the armed forces have been aware of the importance of a good diet for maintaining fighting capability since before the time of the Boer War and World War One, when many British volunteers had to be turned away for physical unfitness because of their poor diet. Today, the Institute of Naval Medicine (2016) has produced a 48-page report detailing the importance of good nutrition amongst recruits. However, if one visits many Ministry of Defence bases across Britain, army, air force or naval, one finds many of the on-base shops stock very little fresh produce. Military recruits are often from less-affluent social backgrounds, and the affordability and knowledge aspects of fresh vegetable preparation means these recruits may be less inclined than, say, Jamie Oliver, towards healthy eating. Yet the absence of demand for fresh produce (which is why these base shops often do not stock it) points to a nutritional educational need amongst the armed forces, thwarting the best intentions of the Institute of Naval Medicine. Once again, the benefits of a good diet are being lost, both within the military and in terms of life skills and health after these recruits leave the services.

7.2 Hospitals and Care Homes

Obesity impacts on the functioning in the finance of hospitals in many ways, directly and indirectly. As noted earlier, obesity predisposes to many illnesses that are long-term and expensive to treat and provide care for, including diabetes, blindness, amputations, cancer and liver disease; this increases the loading on health services. Obese staff also function less well, and the low pay of nursing staff makes them liable to a poor diet and consequent weight gain. In the UK, hospital beds and ambulances have required modifications for morbidly obese patients (Shaw, 2014: 30). Very importantly, the nutritional content and palatability of food served to patients has a major bearing on the speed and quality of their recovery. Bed-blocking is a common problem for hospitals, with patients having technically recovered from whatever ailment they were admitted for in the first place, yet not fit enough to be discharged into independent home living. These arguments for better quality food also apply to care homes for the elderly, which are becoming a major feature of society in many developed countries where life expectancy has lengthened, often meaning more years spent in partial incapacity, just as the pressure for working-age people to put in more hours to make ends meet is also intensifying due to high house prices, austerity, real wage stagnation and other factors. Yet old-age care is a Cinderella service, often underfunded, and food for care recipients and hospital patients is often one of the first costs to be cut.

The amount allocated by hospitals per day per patient on food varies widely, with some medical facilities spending as little as £2.61 per day (Lay, 2018). This may lead to bizarre situations such as the former NHS hospital cook now working as a minicab driver to bring these pre-prepared meals to hospital (Pemberton, 2018). Even more strangely, hospital patient food wars for fruit, similar to those in prisons noted earlier, resulted from shortages of bananas. In one dementia ward, a patient protested that a fellow patient had stolen her banana. The consultant assured her that she would get another one; however, this was not financially possible with the 15 patients on the ward allowed just 3 bananas per day between them. The nurses either had to cut them up so everyone got a piece or have a rota as to who got a banana that day. The result was that one patient had stolen another's banana and hidden it under her pillow, so prized and scarce was fruit in that ward. Yet this was Britain in the 21st century, not some 1940s wartime situation with fruit rationing.

Hospital accountants complain that drug prices are rising, yet the cost of a chef could more than pay for itself in shortened patient recovery times. Some patients refuse hospital food because it is so unappetizing, becoming undernourished. Visitors too might be more attracted to a hospital with a good-quality canteen, and frequent visiting is a psychological boost to patient's well-being. In other instances, visitors have felt the need to bring in supplemental food themselves for the patient. This can confound doctor's dietary monitoring, is inequitable with poorer families less able to afford this extra food and places an extra financial burden on families who may be scarcely able to afford good food themselves. The nutritional health of the visitors themselves, however, can be put at risk in some medical establishments, with the hospital raking in considerable income from unhealthy fizzy drinks vending machines. Great Ormond Street Hospital, London, was reportedly earning £8,000 a week from its Coca Cola vending machines in 2017, which was also the cost of a child's stay in Great Ormond Street for three days. These same visitors, and the general public, may become complacent about diet because the NHS is always there as a safety net, seemingly free because it is not charged for at point of use. A woman in Doncaster was heard to say, as she ate a sugary cake, "I'm on statins; it's OK", whilst patients with mobility problems exasperate their physiotherapists because they don't stick to boring exercise routines at home; they expect the physiotherapist to fix them in a 30 minute session (Turner, 2017).

The NHS, and doctor's surgeries, could gain long-term cost savings by making us more aware of the health implications of the food we eat; as

Hippocrates famously said, "let your food be your medicine and your medicine be your food". This could be especially useful for mildly obese people who have not yet presented with more serious obesity-related illnesses, such as diabetes. In Liverpool, 2000, GP surgeries gave out vouchers redeemable for fresh fruit and vegetables from local Co-op stores; although adult consumption levels of these foods returned to previous levels once the scheme ended, some schoolchildren did continue with eating more portions per day than before (Shaw & Shaw, 2009: 94). Taking the diet issue a stage further back, the issue was probably not accessibility to fresh produce but knowledge of how to prepare vegetables. In 2018, the NHS is running cookery classes for the overweight. Sixty-six thousand people have been referred to the diabetes prevention programme, offering 16 hours of both exercise coaching and healthy cooking lessons. Participants go on to lose an average 3.5 kg weight. The target is to enrol 200,000 people by 2019, and the National Institute for Health and Care Excellence estimates that two million UK citizens could benefit from these classes (Smyth, 2018b).

Meanwhile, in the US, similar schemes have been trialled with health services in the most deprived areas linking up with food banks and food pantries to 'prescribe' fruit and vegetables. Additionally, six Chicago health clinics have, from 2015, hosted 26 'Fresh Truck' visits to food banks by 3,200 households by the Greater Chicago Food Depository, whilst Idaho doctors host food pantries with fresh produce. The supermarket industry has not yet linked in with this initiative, because these 'Fresh Trucks' are serving deprived areas where no retailer has deemed it worthwhile to set up shop. Of course, it is a very different commitment to set up and run a store as opposed to visits by a mobile lorry-based retailer, and there are sound financial reasons why fresh produce retailers have not entered some urban neighbourhoods: lack of demand for fruit and vegetables, security costs, low local spending power and a market spilt amongst varied ethnic groups who all have their own local shops to cater for their national food tastes. Nevertheless, one may suspect that the main supermarkets are not all that interested in trying to market low-volume sales of less-profitable fresh produce to a deprived community when the real profits lie elsewhere in selling processed food to more affluent consumers.

7.3 Television and Other Advertising

Semi-state entities, such as the British Broadcasting Corporation or Raidió Teilifís Éireann in Ireland, although they do not directly advertise commercial products, do influence the dietary habits of children through their programming. What responsibility do these organizations have for ensuring their food messages, even indirectly, are healthy ones? The example of TV shows such as *Blue Planet II* shows how a TV show can galvanize public opinion and achieve a major change in consumer behaviour to improve the environment. TV soap stars can set an example (Bennett, 2016) with characters in popular soap operas shown eating healthy fruit and vegetables, not junk food. In the UK, there are currently some controls on the TV advertising of unhealthy food, with its promotion outlawed in advertising breaks in shows whose audience contains over 25% of those under 16, although many children also watch programmes such as *The X Factor* or *Britain's Got Talent*, which do not fall under this ban because, overall, they have a higher proportion of adult viewers. Overall, the Institute for Fiscal Studies in Britain estimated that half the TV adverts seen by children in 2015 were for unhealthy sugary food and drink. Cancer Research UK has estimated that junk food advertisements on TV are causing UK teenagers to consume an extra 18,000 calories a year, equivalent to 2kg extra bodyweight a year, or a (literally) staggering 3.5 stone weight gain per decade. There are also as yet no controls on the portrayal of food within programmes, which can constitute a form of advertising known as product placement.

Advertisers of unhealthy food often adopt a Janus-like stance. Janus was the Roman god of gateways and transitions (hence our name for the month of January), and had two faces, each looking in opposite directions. Food advertisers, with their 'healthy' face, claim they are not responsible for the growing obesity crisis because they only inform people about food choices, they do not force anybody to eat sugary, fatty, processed foods. However, we can be sure they do not make this claim with their 'financial' face turned towards their food-industry clients, who in the UK in 2016 spent £143 million on the advertising of unhealthy foods. This figure compares with the £5.2 million spent in 2016 by the UK government on its Change4Life campaign.

Janus is familiar with the theory of evolution. The history of advertising of unhealthy products, such as alcohol and cigarettes, is generally one of a cat and mouse game between government regulation seeking to curb such advertising and the advertisers getting cleverer and more ingenious at using the channels they still have open, as well as finding new channels, to continue promoting their (socially undesirable) product and so ensuring their commercial survival. The Guinness adverts were a classic example of this, with the 'black and white' elements of the product, a glass of black Guinness with its white head, emphasized in images that made almost no mention of alcohol, or even the name 'Guinness' at all. Likewise, Marlboro cigarettes used their iconic macho Western cowboy image to good effect, again barely mentioning the actual product at all.

The junk food advertising industry has increasingly turned to neuromarketing, the study of how consumers' brains respond to (often subtle) stimuli, as opposed to more traditional methods of marketing which simply communicated the presence and attributes of the product to the potential customer. The term 'neuromarketing' was first used in 2002, although one might say that the classical Marlboro arid US Midwest images were early examples of neuromarketing; the Marlboro brand was so strong that simply seeing a billboard image of a cowboy on horseback amongst the desert mesas might conjure up a desire to buy that particular brand of cigarettes. The HFSS (High Fat Sugar Salt) food industry is entering the social media field to attempt to instil brand awareness of certain junk foods in children's brains, aware that 'training' of people's brains to expect a reward from a particular brand can persist for years afterwards. For example, consumers of Cheetos cheese puffs derived a guilty pleasure from having their fingers coated with orange dust from the product, which led to an advertising campaign called the Orange Underground. This featured 'snack food anarchists' who covered their faces with scarves made of Cheetos (Boseley, 2018; YouTube, 2010). Hence the Cheeto snack acquires a brand aura of qualities such as rebelliousness, untidiness, sabotage, anti-establishment. The Cheeto advertisements (the name sounds like 'cheat') features adults performing acts of sabotage, from messing up a bossy woman's neat white blouse to messing with an obsessively tidy work colleague's desk, but children are most likely to find these videos, and hence the food product, very appealing. The Coca Cola Christmas Lorry advertisements are also very appealing to children, with many features that will attract them. They have a catchy jingle *"Holidays Are Coming"*, with a procession of brightly lit red, white and green Coca Cola lorries that are so close together they more resemble a festive train, with emphasis on Christmas lights and all the rest of the festive panoply, along with frequent images of amazed children gawping at the bright lights show (YouTube, 2006). These examples show that tackling TV advertising alone will only be a partial solution; we live in an increasingly multimedia society, and Internet channels such as YouTube must be included in any healthier advertising initiative. The issue of multimedia advertising of unhealthy food has begun to be tackled; from July 2017, the Committee of Advertising Practice has banned junk food advertising aimed at children in social media and online, also print and cinema,

Overall, the issue of food marketing via the ever-growing and ever-changing array of social media and mass media is one where healthy food campaigners will always be one step behind the adept junk food advertisers. Regulation, law making, tends to be responsive and reactive not proactive because of the fast pace of change in the electronic media industry. However, the utilization of fiscal measures, such as taxation, might pre-form the financial landscape in which junk food retailers, manufacturers and their advertising agencies anticipate operating in. Well-formulated fiscal measures have a significant role to play in promoting healthy eating.

7.4 Taxation

The potential for utilizing fiscal measures to promote a healthy diet—for example, through 'fat taxes'—has been widely discussed, as has the use of state sponsored 'nudges', such as the images of unhealthy lungs on cigarette packets. In April 2018, the UK implemented a 'sugar tax' of 18p/litre on soft drinks with over 5g sugar per 100ml, and 24p/litre for those exceeding 8g per 100 ml. Taxes on meat have also been proposed, on environmental rather than health grounds, with the proviso that the threshold turnover at which these taxes become payable would be high so as to protect smaller local farm shops, whilst the large supermarkets would pay. However, reducing meat consumption and substituting with vegetables would bring some health benefits too. A danger with taxing fat or sugar is that the tax burden would fall disproportionately on the poor; besides the social justice issue, there is a risk that impoverishing further the already deprived might make high-calorie, low-nutrient foods behave as Giffen Goods. A Giffen Good is an inferior good whose demand rises as its price rises, along with a general price level rise (or consumer spending power falls), because there are no readily available substitutes, and other higher quality goods are even more unaffordable. In 19th-century impoverished areas of Ireland, potatoes were a Giffen Good; the demand for them rose as their relative price increased, because meat was then even more unaffordable. Sugar taxes could, therefore, be counter-productive, raising the consumption of unhealthy foods amongst the least affluent consumers. Perhaps the overall fiscal burden of food taxes should be made neutral by having small negative sales taxes on healthy food to encourage shops to sell these more competitively.

In 2016, the major UK supermarkets actually asked Prime Minister Theresa May to intervene more to "force them to sell healthy food". The rationale was that without compulsory legislation, the major supermarkets might try and sell healthier food but would always be at risk of being undermined on price or flavour (sweetness) by smaller competitors. Legislation to cut salt, saturated fat or sugar, or curb junk food (especially that aimed at children) would be welcomed by the larger supermarkets—who could then claim social responsibility for having made this move, protected by the rules from smaller cheaters as a 'level playing field' was guaranteed.

In summary, achieving a real improvement in diet should be a primary goal of supermarket CSR, but the supermarkets cannot act alone here. A holistic approach by the government must include a wide range of other agencies, many of which are already wholly or partly under national control, including schools, hospitals, prisons, the military and the media. It is not enough to aim for better sales or marketing of healthy food; consumer tastes must also be nudged in a healthier direction, in a similar manner to how the government has achieved major shifts in public opinion of and demand for things like smoking, road safety and alcohol consumption. Nevertheless, the supermarkets, which as we saw in Chapter 1 have an oligopoly of food sales in many countries, developed and middle income, must bear a significant responsibility for diet and health, as well as the many other externalities associated with the food they sell: environmental, economic, social and the effects of large-scale food retailing on the local communities they are a part of. The final chapter concludes with a review of existing supermarket CSR initiatives and assesses where these CSR programmes are adequate and where they fall short of societal needs. It also summarizes the future directions supermarket CSR could take so as to tackle the current obesity epidemic and help achieve a sustainable global food system.

8 Supermarket CSR Initiatives Now and Change for Future Health and Sustainability

8.1 A Classification of Current Supermarket CSR Initiatives

As we saw in earlier chapters, the major supermarkets maintain a very large range of CSR initiatives in areas ranging from pollution and the environment through the conditions of suppliers and their employees to co-existing and supporting the local community and the healthiness of the food we buy from them. As we saw in Chapter 1, in Britain, the largest four supermarkets possess about 70% of the retail groceries market; the next four control a further 23% of the market. This oligopoly is replicated across most of the developed world and is rapidly being replicated elsewhere too. Yet obesity rates in most developing countries remain high and are rising in the Global South too. The supermarkets exist to sell their customers what food they choose to buy, or are persuaded to buy through marketing initiatives; they are not public health agencies or educators. However, with such a hold on the market, they must be held responsible for the societal and medical consequences of the products they sell, just as we hold the vendors of other 'hazardous' goods responsible for the safety consequences of what they sell, the vendors of alcohol, tobacco and motor cars, for example.

CSR can be classified by aim: environmental, educational, social and so on; it can also be classed by the balance of altruism versus reward it produces for the corporation. Some CSR creates very little obvious reward for the company—for example, the programme by Paribas to send educational books to children in African countries (Shaw, 2007: 14). Conversely, an environmental CSR initiative to use less energy does benefit the environment but is also doing what the company would be doing financially anyway: minimizing its costs in terms of energy use. Whilst the Paribas initiative has been very little publicized, supermarket initiatives to use less energy, vehicle fuel, water and packaging tend to be well trumpeted and form a key part of their CSR publicity pages on the Internet. In 2012, M&S, with its catchily named Plan A ("because there is no Plan B"), saved £22 million from energy-use reduction; £6.3 million from creating less waste, saving on disposal charges; £16.3 million on packaging materials not used; and £2.1 million in fuel economies on its transport fleet, a tidy sum of £46.7 million in total (Chandler & Werther, 2014: 155). Sometimes, the 'bottom line' gain is concealed somewhat, as in "we send zero waste to landfill"; it is seldom mentioned that companies, unlike the private individuals who shop there, have to pay to deposit waste at landfills. One might debate whether such initiatives should count as CSR at all, even though they do benefit the environment and the planet. At the other extreme, charitable CSR—for example, educating Romanian children on road safety—as Lidl has done, imposes extra costs on the company and often does little or nothing, directly, to increase revenue or profits. However, there is still good publicity from these initiatives, so arguably even this CSR is not totally 100% altruistic.

CSR initiatives may also be reactive or proactive. Proactive initiatives are designed to steal a march on competitor companies and 'shame' them into following suit; the leader gets most of the credit for starting the programme; however, the laggard companies cannot afford not to follow on, even though they get less benefit from being 'shown up' as reluctant, slow or unimaginative in this aspect of CSR. They would come off even worse, in publicity terms, from not following suit at all. Proactive CSR carries the danger, for the initiator, that competitors may not follow; they may judge that if the CSR initiative is expensive and carries little immediate benefit to the bottom line, then shoppers may prefer lower prices and pay no heed to any diffuse environmental or societal benefit. In times of austerity, squeezed wages and tight household incomes, this may be a viable, if rather cynical, strategy, especially for the discount or lower market end grocers. This may create a dilemma for upper market end grocers, who cannot afford to alienate their customers by being seen as socially irresponsible, but who fear losing customers to cheaper rivals. Even Waitrose has lost trade to the hard discounters Aldi and Lidl. In this case, a variant of proactive CSR may be deployed, which is to approach the government and ask for rules demanding that all grocers follow this CSR improvement in corporate operations. In the previous chapter, it was noted that the large UK supermarkets have asked the current prime minister, Theresa May, to "force them to sell healthier food"; such legislation would prevent undercutting by cheaper less-healthy retailers.

Very recently, in summer 2018, after revelations emerged in the UK media that the 'Red Tractor' certification did not guarantee human treatment of farm animals because in almost all cases, the farm had advance warning of the inspectors calling, the British Retail Consortium (which includes UK supermarkets) has called for more unannounced inspection visits to agricultural businesses (Webster, 2018c). Under this 'proactive CSR', the initiating company still gets credit for being the motivator of a government policy change but has also ensured that it cannot be undermined by cut-price 'defectors'.

8.2 The Feel-Good Factor of CSR

In a low profit-margin environment, with many consumers still cash squeezed after a decade of austerity, not just in the UK but also in many countries where real wage growth has been stagnant, it is perhaps not surprising that supermarkets have tended to prioritize the 'environmental/resource use' CSR whilst rather less progress has been made on healthy food, as attested to by growing waistlines across the world. As Dibb notes (2004: 39),

> None of Tesco's 27 CSR Key Performance Indicator targets for 2004/5, covering the company's impacts on society, the economy and the environment, refer to targets in support of nutrition and public health, though that is not to say that Tesco does not have policies relating to nutrition and health.

The supermarkets want to appear as purveyors of healthy rather than obesogenic food, hence the initiatives on sweets at the checkout, for example, and the presence of abundant fresh produce near the supermarket entrance, sometimes embellished into a faux 'street market' as in the case of Morrison's Market Street initiative, or the Tesco programme of free fruit for children in the aisles. Penetrate a little deeper into the store, however, and much of the produce on the shelves is rather less than nutritionally sound.

Supermarket consumers are made to feel good by a range of local community initiatives, from Asda's "Your Square Mile" to the Waitrose "Community Matters" scheme. However, the famous question in the Good Samaritan parable, "Who is my neighbour?" is intended to illustrate that our neighbour isn't just those physically proximate to us, but any fellow human in need of assistance; the ethical issues of 'neighbourliness' in CSR have been explicated in Chapter 2 of this book. The global food system means that we are ever more closely connected to, in the sense of "their sudden absence would affect our lives", cash-squeezed farmers many countries away, poorly remunerated labourers in remote corners of the Fens, fishermen on the high seas and even African and Asian workers paid a dollar or two a day in "far off countries we know nothing about", to paraphrase a certain 1930s British politician. Then we have the farm animals herded into huge steel sheds, or the wildlife in distant rainforests. Meanwhile, supermarket CSR tends to focus on just a stage or two back in the supply chain, ostensibly monitoring the employment conditions and environmental responsibility of their suppliers—whilst making such supplier CSR ever harder by squeezing the wholesale price so that the supermarket can maintain the illusion of cheap food. It is an illusion indeed, once the social and environmental costs of that 'cheap' food are factored in.

8.3 Refocussing CSR Towards Health and Sustainability

How could supermarket CSR be refocussed to promote a more environmentally and socially sustainable food system? Firstly, the 'environmental' focus could be extended from less resource use to the sustainability of the food itself. This may not necessarily mean 'buying British'; as we saw earlier, growing warm-climate food in Spain and then flying it into the UK may use less energy than growing it in hothouses in Britain. Meat can be an efficient means of feeding people if the animals are reared on crops not suitable for human consumption; pigs and chickens can be fed on waste food, goats can be farmed in arid mountainous areas unsuitable for crops and grass-eating animals fed from steppe lands. This may mean a return to smaller-scale suppliers and hence more expensive, scarcer meat—a small price to pay for saving the planet and one that would actually make many people healthier.

More use should be made of the old strong brown paper bags for food—the paper bags being made of recycled material and biodegradable. Some plastic packaging is inevitable, but this can be reduced if supermarkets promoted a shift to consumption of more fresh vegetables and fruit, rather than processed pre-packaged foods, and the plastic itself should be made biodegradable. Store layouts could become part of CSR initiatives if fresh produce were also sold in the ready-meal areas, so as to promote consumption of these, with those fatty, salty, cheesy ready-made pasta dishes, for example. Also have cooking utensils, sieves and chopping boards, with the fresh produce (and ready meals section) to promote home vegetable preparation, just as supermarkets now insert corkscrews and glasses in or near the wine section.

Supermarket offers could also be more oriented to healthy food, and this could then be part of their CSR in a sort of 'healthy race to the top'; who has the healthiest offers on this week? Many supermarkets have free taster samples, but these are frequently sugary drinks or puddings or cheese or meat. Perhaps copy Tesco and have more free fresh fruit samples, even more exotic fruit that some consumers may be less familiar with, papayas, kiwis and so on. Extend these offers in a free supermarket in-house magazine, much as Waitrose already does; their *Waitrose Food* journal has many healthy dishes, although quite a few sugary puddings appear in there too. Maybe even employ some 'nutritional advisor' staff who can assist with healthy meal planning. Ensure that all meal recipe leaflets, already present in many supermarkets, are nutritionally optimized with at least two servings of vegetables and have instructions for preparing less-familiar vegetables. Consumers could be made more aware of which vegetables are in season, in which parts of the world, thereby encouraging both healthier and more environmental eating, and extending these campaigns to the public media, newspapers, TV and social media advertising. Very few TV adverts at present are for fresh produce, but if a non-food product was consumed as little, relatively speaking, as fresh fruit and vegetables, it would be heavily promoted to raise demand.

Supermarket loyalty-point schemes, such as Sainsbury's Nectar or Tesco Clubcard, could be made into a readily quantifiable CSR tool by giving extra points for purchases of healthier foodstuffs. So-called meal deals could also be refocussed; at present, they are subtly aimed at couples—for example, romantic Valentines dinners with wine and an upmarket dessert. Instead, aim these at families, without the wine but with more fruit and vegetable focussed food, to encourage children to eat with their parents. Family eating with the children at the same table as the adults, eating the same food can reduce child obesity (Kime, 2008). In specific product categories where the consumer market tends to be more affluent, and there are smaller higher-price niche retailers, such as Whole Foods or Wild Oats Natural Foods, for groceries, Aguirre (2005: 17) suggests the "environmental gains for higher prices" trade-off could be kick-started by persuading these retailers, with a more price-inelastic consumer base, to set the trend for environmental initiatives. This could then 'shame' retailers further down the social affluence scale into following suit. After Whole Foods, Waitrose would follow and then hopefully Tesco and Asda. This tactic, instituting a 'race to the top' would be appropriate in the case of encouraging greater fisheries sustainability or environmentally sustainable farming methods, soil conservation or rare species preservation.

As noted earlier, other organizations should join in promoting healthier food alongside supermarket CSR policies. A range of organizations, from the BBC to major tourist attractions, have joined in the fight against plastic pollution by, for example, ditching plastic straws and cutlery. Perhaps this could be joined into a holistic effort at healthier food generally, allied with the supermarkets who would be providing this food. The principle of promoting healthy food in schools along with supermarket vendors could be extended to hospitals and the military; "this supermarket promotes healthy defence of the nation", or "this supermarket wants you to get healthy and well again soon" might make good CSR. Even with prisons, some effort along the lines of prisoner rehabilitation and reduction in reoffending rates might be adaptable to a CSR initiative.

8.4 Keeping the Supermarkets Intact, Candid, Responsible and Responsive

It has been suggested that supermarkets be broken up, but this might be counter-productive to a healthy sustainable diet. Food prices will probably rise as economies of scale are lost (possibly pushing some less-affluent consumers into a poorer diet), and takeovers may mean the corporation reassembles itself over time anyway. However, the trend towards further concentration within the supermarket industry has reasserted itself with a vengeance recently, and this should be resisted. In 2018, we have seen, firstly, the merger between the British chains Asda and Sainsbury's, and, secondly, the announcement that Tesco of Britain and Carrefour of France are to form what is effectively a cross-channel buying group with a customer base of around 30 million consumers in their domestic markets alone, with £80 billion spending power. These moves will be politically popular, offering more choice and lower prices for the consumer. Analysts at Jefferies estimate that Tesco and Carrefour will save £400 million via this alliance (Kollewe, 2018), but what is less open to discussion is where these 'savings' will come from. In fact, we already know the answer: the suppliers. Some of the squeeze will be on big businesses with less public sympathy; Tesco anticipates large savings on the fuel bill for its lorry fleet, for example. However, smaller suppliers are likely to face even tougher times, and Asda has already been rated as "the worst of the big four supermarkets in terms of its treatment of suppliers" (Hurley, 2018). Whilst breaking up the existing oligopolies of supermarkets in countries like the UK and France may be undesirable, we may not want to progress to the duopolistic situation currently prevailing in Australia. To protect smaller retailers and smaller suppliers, councils should have the power to veto planning applications not just 'on the day' but for a set period of perhaps three or five years. This would prevent supermarkets 'wearing down' councils with repeated applications; alternatively, central government could indemnify councils against the cost of repeated supermarket applications. Legislation would be required to prevent supermarkets making repeated applications under different 'front company' names, as Tesco did in Bristol under names like Jesters. To prevent sites lying empty because of planning obstacles, firstly, perhaps give local people a chance to vote on what they want done with sites that have remained empty for a year or more: housing, retail, leisure or some other use.

Supermarkets should be more open with their environmental and social CSR policies. They are often secretive because they don't want to help the competition by giving out commercially sensitive information, such as the amount of packaging they use or recycle. Supermarkets may be giants, but size may actually increase vulnerability. Sixty-five million years ago when Earth's climate radically changed, it was the huge dinosaurs that became extinct, not the tiny mammals and insects. Today's supermarkets sometimes behave as if they had the same vulnerabilities. Walmart discovered that a US town of population just 4,500 was big enough to support a large out-of-town store, just so long as most of the competition was eliminated (Monbiot, 2000: 200). This policy is usually seen as ruthless aggression towards small shops; it could also be seen as fearfulness of the other supermarket competition that would be encountered in larger towns. As companies get larger, they get often more risk averse, despite having the resources to weather mistakes and unexpected events.

In a welcome contrasting move to this culture of secrecy, in 2013, Tesco took the 'bold step' of 'airing its dirty laundry in public' by publicizing that it threw away 28,500 tonnes of food, UK£ 12.5 billion worth, in the previous 12 months (Owens, 2013). This disclosure was intended to galvanize the entire supermarket sector into reducing food waste; for Tesco, it showed that the corporation was attempting to be more honest in its CSR reporting, not just greenwashing. In 2016, Sainsbury became the second UK supermarket chain to call for all UK supermarkets to have to publish food waste data by law (Cohen, 2016). This might cast the large four chains in the UK in a more favourable light compared to the relatively new and fast-growing entrants Aldi and Lidl who are encroaching on the Big Four's market share in the UK and similarly gaining from the incumbent dominant supermarkets in other countries.

Mobilizing public opinion through the media is the key to achieving fair, open and sustainable CSR policies that produce real benefits for people, society and the planet. The recent example of how the TV programme *Blue Planet II* galvanized society, how it spurred people, corporations, governments and NGOs into action over the menace of plastic pollution, is a textbook example of how CSR policies are set from the base of public opinion upwards, with the adept usage of media messages to reach the widest audience possible, not from the corporation or government downwards. In conclusion, we may do well to keep in mind the words of Pierre Bourdieu:

> Successful demonstrations are not necessarily those which mobilise the greatest number of people, but those which attract the greatest interest among journalists. Exaggerating only slightly, one might say that if fifty shrewd people (who can make a successful 'happening') get five minutes of television airtime, they can have as much political effect as half a million demonstrators.
>
> (Bourdieu & Haacke, 1995: 23)

Supermarkets may be able to weather the occasional demonstration by disgruntled farmers, or shoppers overburdened with plastic waste. Such demonstrations may soon be forgotten anyway, but it would be beneficial for society and the planet if the CEOs of Walmart and Tesco would turn on the television in the evening, not just expecting some light entertainment, but with a tiny sense of trepidation too. Their increased heart rate should then translate, soon enough, into our enhanced healthfulness.

Bibliography

ActionAid. (2011) www.actionaid.org.uk/sites/default/files/doc_lib/the_real_asda_price.pdf, accessed 20 March 2018.

Adjoian, T., Dannefer, R., Willingham, C., Braithwaite, C. and Franklin, S. (2017) 'Healthy Checkout Lines: A Study in Urban Supermarkets', *Journal of Nutrition Education and Behaviour*, 49(8): 615–22.

Aguinis, H. and Glavas, A. (2012) 'What We Know and Don't Know About Corporate Social Responsibility: A Review and Research Agenda', *Journal of Management*, 38(4): 932–68.

Aguirre, T. (2005) *'Sustainable Seafood and Corporate Social Responsibility'*, Report Published by the Graduate School of International Relations and Pacific Studies University of California, San Diego.

Aldhous, P. and McKenna, P. (2010) 'Hey Green Spender', *New Scientist*, 6–9.

Allen, P. (2008) 'Mining for Justice in the Food System: Perceptions, Practices and Possibilities', *Agriculture and Human Values*, 25(2): 157–61.

Australian Government. (2016) *'Inquiry Into Trolley Collection Services Procurement by Woolworths Limited, A Report by the Fair Work Ombudsman Under the Fair Work Act 2009'*, Report Published by the Commonwealth of Australia.

Bakan, J. (2005) *The Corporation: The Pathological Pursuit of Profit and Power*, London: Constable.

Barnard, H. (2018) *Poverty in Wales*, York: Joseph Rowntree Foundation, www.jrf.org.uk/file/51053/Briefing, accessed 10 August 2018.

Barnett, C., Cloke, P., Clarke, N. and Malpass, A. (2005) 'Consuming Ethics: Articulating the Subjects and Spaces of Ethical Consumption', *Antipode*, 37(1): 23–45.

Bartky, S.L. (1990) 'Narcissism, Femininity and Alienation', in Bartky, S.L. (ed.), *Femininity and Domination: Studies in the Phenomenology of Oppression*, New York: Routledge, 33–44.

Bell, R. and Cuthbertson, R. (2004) 'Collaboration in the Retail Supply Chain', in Reynolds, J. and Cuthbertson, C. (eds.), *Retail Strategy*, Oxford: Elsevier.

Bellon, T. (2018) 'Monsanto Ordered to pay $289 Million in World's First Roundup Cancer Trial', 10/8/2018, https://uk.reuters.com/article/uk-monsanto-cancer-lawsuit/monsanto-ordered-to-pay-289-million-in-worlds-first-round up-cancer-trial-idUKKBN1KV2HF, accessed 18 August 2018.

Bennett, R. (2016) 'Healthy-Eating Soap Stars to Set an Example', *The Times*, 26/2/2016: 4.

BEPA. (2009) '*Functional Uses of Egg Products in Food Production*', Published by the British Egg Products Association, London, www.bepa.org.uk/about-us/contact-us/, accessed 2 May 2018.

Berger-Walliser, G. and Scott, I. (2018) 'Redefining Corporate Social Responsibility in an Era of Globalization and Regulatory Hardening', *American Business Law Journal*, 55(1): 167–218.

Bierce, A. (1911) *The Devil's Dictionary*, London: Bloomsbury.

Blythman, J. (2004) *Shopped: The Shocking Power of British Supermarkets*, London: Harper Collins.

Boffey, D. (2017) 'Eggs Contaminated with Insecticide May Have Entered UK, EU Warns', *The Guardian*, 7/8/2017, www.theguardian.com/world/2017/aug/07/eggs-contaminated-with-insecticide-may-have-entered-uk-eu-warns, accessed 8 March 2018.

Bohstedt, J. (2010) *The Politics of Provisions: Food Riots, Moral Economy, and Market Transition in England, c.1550–1850*, Farnham, Surrey: Ashgate.

Bonner, F. (2011) 'Lifestyle Television', in Lewis, T. and Potter, E. (eds.), *Ethical Consumption*, Abingdon: Routledge.

Boswell, J. (2008) *Life of Johnson (Oxford World Classics)*, Chapman, R.W. and Rogers, P. (eds.), Oxford: Oxford University Press.

Bourdieu, P. (1984) *Distinction: A Social Critique of the Judgment of Taste*, Cambridge, MA: Harvard University Press.

Bourdieu, P. and Haacke, H. (1995) *Free Exchange*, Cambridge, MA: Polity Press.

Boseley, S. (2018) 'Food Firms Could Be Sued If Ads Found to Hijack Children's Brains', *The Times*, 26/5/2018: 7.

Bradford, A. (2012) 'The Brussels Effect', *Northwestern University Law Review*, 107(1): 1–66.

Brooks, L. (2018) 'Council Plans Free School Meals All Year to Tackle Holiday Hunger', *The Guardian*, 16/2/2018, www.theguardian.com/education/2018/feb/16/council-free-school-meals-year-holiday-hunger-north-lanarkshire, accessed 23 April 2018.

Business Respect. (2006) 'The Big Supermarkets—Now Competing on Price, Quality . . . and Trust', 21/5/2006, www.businessrespect.net/page.php?Story_ID=1635, accessed 28 February 2018.

Butler, S. (2018) 'Sainsbury's Accused of Breaking Promise on Welfare of Its Chickens', *The Guardian*, 21/4/2018: 44.

Cambridge Leadership Development. (2013) '*Quadruple Bottom Line for Sustainable Prosperity*', Published by Cambridge Leadership Development, St John's Innovation Centre, Cambridge.

Cameron, N., Amrhein, C.G., Smoyer-Tomic, K.E., Raine, K.D. and Chong, L.Y. (2010) 'Cornering the Market: Restriction of Retail Supermarket Location', *Environment and Planning C*, 28: 905–22.

Carroll, B. (1991) 'The Pyramid of CSR: Towards the Moral Management of Organizational Stakeholders', *Business Horizons*, 34(4): 39–48.

Chakrabortty, A. (2018) 'Where Food Is the First Lesson', *The Guardian*, 25/4/2018: 10–11.

Chandler, D. and Werther, W.B. (2014) *Strategic Corporate Social Responsibility*, Thousand Oaks, CA: Sage.

Childs, M. (2015) 'Harry Hyams: Property Developer Who Built Up an Empire But Found Notoriety with His Centrepoint Skyscraper', *The Independent*, 22/12/2015, www.independent.co.uk/news/obituaries/harry-hyams-property-developer-who-built-up-an-empire-but-found-notoriety-with-his-centrepoint-a6783571.html, accessed 2 May 2018.

Clements, L. (2018) 'Energy Drinks Ban for Cardiff School Children', *The Cardiffian*, 6/3/2018, http://jomec.co.uk/thecardiffian/2018/03/06/energy-drinks-ban-cardiff-school-children/, accessed 8 May 2018.

Cohen, D. (2016) 'Sainsbury's Boss Says Supermarkets Must Be Made to Publish Food Waste Data', *London Evening Standard*, 4/10/2016, www.standard.co.uk/news/foodforlondon/supermarkets-must-be-made-to-publish-food-waste-data-says-sainsbury-s-boss-a3360856.html, accessed 5 March 2018.

Colls, R. and Evans, B. (2008) 'Embodying Responsibility: Children's Health and Supermarket Initiatives', *Environment and Planning A*, 40(3): 615–31.

CORE. (2018) *Putting People and the Planet at the Core of Business*, http://corporate-responsibility.org/issues/corporate-crime/, accessed 18 August 2018.

Croker, H., Lucas, R. and Wardle, J. (2012) 'Cluster-Randomised Trial to Evaluate the 'Change for Life' Mass Media/Social Marketing Campaign in the UK', *BMC Public Health*, 12(1): 404.

Cruickshank, J. (2012) 'Positioning Positivism, Critical Realism and Social Constructionism in the Health Sciences: A Philosophical Orientation', *Nursing Inquiry*, 19(1): 71–82.

Daneshku, S. (2014) 'UK Supermarkets Aim to Burnish Image on Promoting Health', *Financial Times*, www.ft.com/content/c0f4a98e-86ab-11e3-885c-00144feab7de, accessed 28 February 2018.

Daniels, N. (2001) 'Justice, Health and Healthcare', *The American Journal of Bioethics*, 1(2): 2–16.

Daniels, N. (2008) *Just Health: Meeting Health Needs Fairly*, New York: Cambridge University Press.

Davies, R. (2004) 'Planning Policy for Retailing', in Reynolds, J. and Cuthbertson, C. (eds.), *Retail Strategy: The View from the Bridge*, Oxford: Elsevier.

Davies, R. (2018) 'We'll Replace Your 'Copycat' Waitrose Bar for Free, Says Chocolatier', *The Guardian*, 19/5/2018: 21.

Davis, D. (1966) *A History of Shopping*, London: Routledge and Keegan.

Defra. (2006) *Food Industry Sustainability Strategy*, London: Department for Environment, Food and Rural Affairs.

Demmerling, T. (2014) *Corporate Social Responsibility Overload*, Hamburg, Germany: Anchor Academic Publishing.

Department of Health. (2008) *Healthy Weight, Healthy Lives: Consumer Insight Summary*, London: Central Office of Information.

Department of Health. (2009) *Change4Life Marketing Strategy*, London: Central Office of Information.

Devinney, T.M., Auger, P., Eckhardt, G. and Birtchnell, T. (2006) *The Other CSR: Consumer Social Responsibility*, www.ssireview.org/issue/fall_2006, accessed 4 April 2018.

Devlin, H. (2014) 'Supermarket Foods Contain Far More Fat Than Advertised', *The Times*, 7/4/2014: 17.

Dibb, S. (2004) *Rating Retailers for Health*, Published by the National Consumer Council, London.

Digital Spy. (2018) *The City & The City Explained*, www.digitalspy.com/tv/feature/a854138/the-city-and-the-city-episode-1-explained-confusing-bbc-tv-review/, accessed 18 May 2018.

Doane, D. (2005) 'The Myth of CSR', *Stanford Social Innovation Review*, Fall: 23–9.

Doward, J. (2014) 'Milk Price Row: Booths Says Stores Have Duty to Pay Farmers Fairly', *The Observer*, 2/5/2014: 22.

Dube, A., William, L.T. and Eidlin, B. (2007) *A Downward Push: The Impact of Wal-Mart Stores On Retail Wages And Benefits*, UC Berkeley Department of City and Regional Planning, http://laborcenter.berkeley.edu/retail/walmart_downward_push07.pdf, accessed 3 April 2018.

The Economist. (2013a) '*Welcome to the Capital*', 28/7/2013: 38.

The Economist. (2013b) '*How Bad Can It Be?*', 23/12/2013: 55.

The Economist. (2015) '*Buying Up the Shelves*', 20/6/2015: 66.

The Economist. (2016) '*High Expectations*', 30/1/2016: 22.

Edmondson, J., Davies, Z., Gaston, K. and Leake, J. (2014) 'Urban Cultivation in Allotments Maintains Soil Qualities', *Journal of Applied Ecology*, 51: 880–9.

Edwards, F. and Mercer, D. (2012) 'Food Waste in Australia: The Freegan Response', *The Sociological Review*, 60(S2): 174–91.

Ekelund, L., Hunter, E., Spendrup, S. and Tjärnemo, H. (2014) 'Communication GHG Mitigating Food Consumption In-Store', *British Food Journal*, 116(10): 1618–35.

Elkington, J. (1997) *Cannibals with Forks*, Mankato, MN: Capstone.

Ezeala-Harrison, F. and Baffoe-Bonnie, J. (2016) 'Market Concentration in the Grocery Retail Industry: Application of the Basic Prisoners' Dilemma Model', *Advances in Management & Applied Economics*, 6(1): 47–67.

Felsted, A. (2013) 'Changing Times See Tesco Shelve Landbanks', *Financial Times*, 17/4/2013, www.ft.com/content/478ca30a-a73e-11e2-bfcd-00144feabdc0, accessed 12 May 2018.

Fitzpatrick, I. and Young, R. (2017) *The Hidden Cost of UK Food*, Bristol, UK: Sustainable Food Trust.

Flora Supermarkets. (2018) www.mykonos-flora.gr/en/mykonos-history/, accessed 28 February 2018.

Fox, T. (2013) *Global Food, Waste Not Want Not*, London: Institute of Mechanical Engineers.

Fox, T. and Vorley, B. (2004) *Stakeholder Accountability in the UK Supermarket Sector, Final Report of the 'Race to the Top' project*, London: International Institute for Environment and Development.

Fox, T. and Vorley, B. (2006) 'Small Producers: Constraints and Challenges in the Global Food System', in Barrientos, S. and Dolan, C. (eds.), *Ethical Sourcing in the Global Food System*, London: Earthscan.

Friedman, M. (1970) 'The Social Responsibility of Business Is to Increase Its Profits', *New York Times Magazine*, 13/9: 122–6.

Friends of the Earth. (2017) '40 Handy Bread Tips—and What to Do with Stale Bread', https://friendsoftheearth.uk/food/40-handy-bread-tips-and-what-do-stale-bread, accessed 2 May 2018.

Garbero, A. and Sanderson, C. (2014) 'Appendix 2', in Lutz, W., Butz, W. and Samir, K. (eds.), *World Population and Human Capital in the Twenty First Century*, Oxford: Oxford University Press.

Geyer, R., Jambeck, J.R. and Law, K.L. (2017) 'Production, Use, and Fate of All Plastics Ever Made', *Science Advances, American Association for the Advancement of Science*, www.ncbi.nlm.nih.gov/pmc/articles/PMC5517107/, accessed 28 January 2018.

Gibbons, K. (2018) 'School Gives Away Its Pigs After Vegan Parent Protests', *The Times*, 23/1/2018: 24.

GMB. (2005) '*Asda Wal Mart; The Alternative Report*', Published in Conjunction with War on Want, https://waronwant.org/sites/default/files/Asda%20Wal-Mart%20-%20The%20Alternative%20Report.pdf, accessed 20 March 2018.

Good Shopping Guide. (2018) www.thegoodshoppingguide.com/supermarkets/, accessed 2 March 2018.

Gouldson, A., Sullivan, R. and Afionis, S. (2013) 'The Governance of Corporate Responsibility, Centre for Climate Change Economics and Policy', Working Paper No. 137, Centre for Climate Change Economics and Policy, Sustainability Research Institute, University of Leeds.

Government of Canada. (2017) '*Little Known Uses for Eggs*', Published by Agriculture and Agri-Food Canada, www.agr.gc.ca/eng/industry-markets-and-trade/market-information-by-sector/poultry-and-eggs/poultry-and-egg-market-information/sub-sector-reports/table-and-processed-eggs/little-known-uses-for-eggs/?id=1384971854397, accessed 2 May 2018.

GRAIN. (2014) '*FOR SALE; Supermarkets Are Undermining People's Control Over Food and Farming in Asia*', Published by GRAIN, 17/9/2014, www.grain.org/article/entries/5010-food-sovereignty-for-sale-supermarkets-are-undermining-people-s-control-over-food-and-farming-in-asia, accessed 13 April 2018.

Griggin, M., Sobal, J. and Lyson, T.A. (2009) 'An Analysis of a Community Food Waste Stream', *Agriculture and Human Values*, 76(1 / 2): 67–81.

The Guardian. (2014a) '*Revealed: Tesco Hoarding Land That Could Build 15,000 Homes*', 24/6/2014, www.theguardian.com/business/2014/jun/26/tesco-hoarding-land-that-could-build-15000-homes-supermarket, accessed 12 May 2018.

The Guardian. (2014b) '*Tesco Scoops Carbuncle Cup for "Inept, Arrogant, Oppressive" Woolwich Store*', www.theguardian.com/artanddesign/2014/sep/03/tesco-woolwich-carbuncle-cup-architectural-prize, accessed 12 May 2018.

The Guardian, anon. (2018) '*A Million Slices of Bread Thrown Away Every Hour*', 17/3/2018: 59.

Hall, G.M. (2016) 'Corporate Social Responsibility on the Food Processing Industry', in Ortenblad, A. (ed.), *Research Handbook on Corporate Social Responsibility in Context*, Cheltenham, UK: Edward Elgar.

Harvey, F. (2017) 'M&S First to Detail How Drugs Used', *The Guardian*, 20/12/2017: 7.

Hebuch, S. (2010) 'Corporate Social Responsibility in the Creation of Shareholder Value', in Aras, G. and Crowther, D. (eds.), *A Handbook of Corporate Governance and Social Responsibility*, Aldershot, UK: Gower.

The Herald. (1997) '*Store Ordered to Stay Open; Judge Rules That Closure of Anchor Operation Would Jeopardise Future of Shopping Centre*', 9/12/1997, www.heraldscotland.com/news/12349607.Store_ordered_to_stay_open_Judge_rules_that_closure_of_anchor_operation_would_jeopardise_future_of_shopping_centre/, accessed 21 February 2018.

Hereford Times. (2015) '*New £5 Million Primary School in Hay-On-Wye School Could Bring Community Together*', 28/10/2015, www.herefordtimes.com/news/13902527.New___5_million_primary_school_in_Hay_on_Wye_school_could_bring_community_together/, accessed 12 May 2018.

Hipwell, D. (2017a) 'Tesco Failed to Honour Its Promises on Merger', *The Times*, 21/3/2017: 33.

Hipwell, D. (2017b) 'Waitrose Lorries to Be Fuelled by Gas from Rotting Food', *The Times*, 9/2/2017: 14.

Hipwell, D. (2018) 'Homes Are Where Heart Is in Lidl's Plans', *The Times*, 31/7/2018: 35.

Humphries, W. (2017) 'Waitrose Comes Clean Over 'British' Lamb', *The Times*, 14/2/2017: 21.

Hurley, J. (2018) 'Asda Is the Worst Big Grocer, Say Suppliers', *The Times*, 26/6/2018: 41.

Imamura, F., Micha, R., Khatibzadeh, S., Fahimi, S., Shi, P., Powles, J. and Mozaffarian, D. (2015) 'Dietary Quality Among Men and Women in 187 Countries in 1990 and 2010: A Systematic Assessment', *The Lancet*, 3(3): 132–42.

Institute of Naval Medicine. (2016) *Nutrition and Healthy Eating*, Published by the Institute of Naval Medicine, Portsmouth. https://assets.publishing.service. gov.uk/government/uploads/system/uploads/attachment_data/file/576093/05_JSP_456_DCM_Pt_2_Vol_1_-_Ch_4_Nutrition_Amndt_008.pdf, accessed 6 March 2018.

Intermarche. (2014) http://itm.marcelww.com/inglorious/, accessed 5 March 2018.

Jones, P., Comfort, D. and Hillier, D. (2005) 'Corporate Social Responsibility and the UK's Top Ten Retailers', *International Journal of Retail & Distribution Management*, 33(12): 882–92.

Jones, P., Wynn, M., Comfort, D. and Hillier, D. (2007) 'Corporate Social Responsibility and UK Retailers', *Issues in Social and Environmental Accounting*, 1(2): 243–57.

Kaye, L. (2012) 'Costco, the Genuine Retail CSR Leader?', *Triple Pundit*, 14/8/2012, www.triplepundit.com/2012/08/costco-genuine-retail-csr-leader/, accessed 7 March 2018.

Keith, S. (2012) 'Coles Woolworths and the Local', *The Australasian—Pacific Journal of Regional Food Studies*, 2: 48–81.

Kenney, S. (2009) *'The Fourth Bottom Line of Sustainability: Perspective'*, www. triplepundit.com/2009/11/the-fourth-bottom-line-of-sustainability-perspective/, accessed 18 April 2018.

Khan, N. and Kakabadse, N.K. (2014) 'CSR: The CoEvolution of Grocery Multiples in the UK (20052010)', *Social Responsibility Journal*, 10(1): 137–60.

Kierkegaard, S. (1998) *Works of Love*, H.V. Hong and E.H. Hong (eds. and trans.), Princeton, NJ: Princeton University Press.

Kime, N. (2008) 'Children's Eating Behaviours: The Importance of the Family Setting', *Area*, 40(3): 315–22.

Kollewe, J. (2018) 'Tesco and Carrefour Team Up to Reduce Costs', *The Guardian*, 3/7/2018: 23.

Korten, D.C. (2015) *When Corporations Rule the World*, Oakland, CA: Berrett-Koehler Publishers, Inc.

Lambie-Mumford, H. and Dowler, E. (2014) 'Rising Use of Food Aid in the United Kingdom', *British Food Journal*, 116(9): 1418–25.

Laville, S. (2018) 'British Supermarkets Create Estimated 800,000 Tonnes of Plastic Waste Each Year', *The Guardian*, 18/1/2018: 10.

Lavin, M. (2005) 'Supermarket Access and Consumer Well-Being', *International Journal of Retail and Distribution Management*, 33(5): 388–98.

Lay, K. (2018) 'Hospital Meals Cost Less than £3 a Day', *The Times*, 12/4/2018: 9.

Lawrence, F. (2008) *Eat Your Heart Out*, London: Penguin.

Leach, E. (2016) *'Corporate Reputation: Why It's Not Completely Stacking Up for Supermarkets'*, Report by Gather, London, http://gather.london/

corporate-reputation-why-its-not-completely-stacking-up-for-supermarkets/, accessed 28 February 2018.

Lever, J. and Evans, A. (2017) 'Corporate Social Responsibility and Farm Animal Welfare: Towards Sustainable Development in the Food Industry?', in Idowu, S. and Vertigans, S. (eds.), *Stages of Corporate Social Responsibility. CSR, Sustainability, Ethics & Governance*, Basingstoke: Springer.

Lévinas, E. (1969) *Totality and Infinity*, trans. Lingis, A., The Hague: Martinus Nijhoff.

Lidl. (2017) *Corporate Social Responsibility*, https://careers.lidl.co.uk/en/corporate-social-responsibility-1824.htm, accessed 18 April 2018.

Lister, R. (2015) 'To Count for Nothing: Poverty Beyond the Statistics', *Journal of the British Academy*, 3(1): 139–65.

Living Wage Foundation. (2017) www.livingwage.org.uk/what-real-living-wage, accessed 15 May 2018.

Lloyd, D. (2013) *SkillSmart*, www.retailmanagementskills.org/skillsmart/, accessed 9 March 2018.

Lord, S. (2014) '*Tesco and the Myth of Corporate Social Responsibility*', Published by Feminist Ire, 30/7/2014, https://feministire.com/2014/07/30/tesco-and-the-myth-of-corporate-social-responsibility/, accessed 13 April 2018.

London Development Agency. (2005) *Better Food for London: The Mayor's Draft Strategy*, London: London Development Agency.

Lowder, S.K., Skoet, J. and Singh, S. (2014) 'What Do We Really Know About the Number and Distribution of Farms and Family Farms in the World?' ESA Working Paper No. 14–0, Published by the Food and Agriculture Organization of the United Nations.

Macfadyen, S., Tylianakis, J.M., Letourneau, D.K., Bentone, T.G., Tittonell, P., Perring, M.P., Gómez-Creutzberg, C., Báldi, A., Holland, J.M., Broadhurst, L., Okabel, K., Renwick, A.R., Gemmill-Herren, B. and Smith, H.G. (2015) 'The Role of Food Retailers in Improving Resilience in Global Food Supply', *Global Food Security*, 7: 1–8.

Massey, D. (2005) *For Space*, London: Sage.

Marine Stewardship Council. (2013) '*German Retailer Kaufland Donates EUR 100,000 to the Gambian Artisanal Tonguesole Fishery for Social Projects and Upcoming MSC Assessment*', Report Published 23/4/2013, www.msc.org/newsroom/news/german-retailer-kaufland-donates-eur-100-000-to-the-gambian-artisanal-tonguesole-fishery-for-social-projects-and-upcoming-msc-assessment/%3Fsearchterm%3Dkaufland, accessed 8 March 2018.

Mc Hardy, A. (2001) 'Surprises in store', *The Guardian*, 11/7/2001, www.theguardian.com/society/2001/jul/11/guardiansocietysupplement8, accessed 15 May 2018.

Miller, A. (2014) *A School Trip . . . to Tesco*, Sustainable Food Trust, http://sustainablefoodtrust.org/articles/trip-to-tesco/, accessed 6 March 2018.

Mohezar, S., Nazri, M., Kader, M., Ali, R. and Yunus, N. (2016) 'Corporate Social Responsibility in the Malaysian Food Retailing Industry: An Exploratory Study', *International Academic Research Journal of Social Science*, 2(1): 66–72.

Monbiot, G. (2000) *Captive State*, London: Palgrave Macmillan.

Moneybox. (2013) '*Why Don't Corporations Give to Charity?*', 8/8/2013, www.slate.com/articles/business/moneybox/2013/08/corporations_don_t_

give_to_charity_why_the_most_profitable_companies_are.html, accessed 22 February 2018.

Moon, J. and Vogel, D. (2008) 'Corporate Social Responsibility, Government, and Civil Society', in Crane, A., McWilliams, A., Matten, D., Moon, J. and Siegel, D. (eds.), *The Oxford Handbook of Corporate Social Responsibility*, Oxford: Oxford University Press, 303–23.

Moore, M. (2018) 'Palm Oil Lobby Smears Store Boss', *The Times*, 20/4/2018: 3.

Morrison's. (2018) *Supermarket CSR*, www.morrisons-corporate.com/cr/, accessed 28 February 2018.

Moses, K. (2010) 'Lidl Supermarket Tuna Contains Fish Species Not on the Label', *The Ecologist*, 24/11/2010, https://theecologist.org/2010/nov/24/lidl-supermarket-tuna-contains-fish-species-not-label, accessed 8 March 2018.

Moulds, J. (2017) 'Supermarkets Certify Exploitative Fishing', *The Times*, 20/11/2017: 18.

Mullerat, R. (2013) '*Corporate Social Responsibility: A European Perspective*', The Jean Monnet/Robert Schuman Paper Series, 13(6), June, Published with the Support of the European Commission.

Musaddique, S. (2018) 'Waitrose to Become First UK Supermarket to Ban Energy Drinks for Under 16s', *The Independent*, 4/1/2018, www.independent.co.uk/news/business/news/waitrose-energy-drink-ban-under-16s-uk-supermarket-red-bull-stores-march-5-a8141806.html, accessed 6 March 2018.

Narain, J. and Powell, M. (2018) 'Supermarket Sellout on Teen Energy Drink Crackdown', *The Mail on Sunday*, 6/5/2018: 17.

Neate, R. (2018) 'Anger Over Glut of 'Posh Ghost Towers' Planned for London', *The Observer*, 4/2/2018: 3.

New Scientist. (2018) '*What You Can Do*', 19/5/2018: 31.

NFU. (2014) '*NFU Review of Grocery Retailer CSR Policies*', www.farminguk.com/content/knowledge/nfusupermarkets.pdf, accessed 2 March 2018.

Nicholson, C. and Young, B. (2012) '*The Relationship Between Supermarkets and Suppliers: What Are the Implications for Consumers?*', Report by Consumers International, London.

Niebuhr, N. (1961) *Moral Man and Immoral Society: A study in ethics and politics*, Louisville, Kentucky: Westminster John Knox Press.

Nussbaum, M.C. (1992) 'Human Functioning and Social Justice: In Defense of Aristotelian Essentialism', *Political Theory*, 20(2): 202–46.

Oram, J., Conisbee, M. and Simms, A. (2003) *Ghost Town Britain II Death on the High Street*, London: New Economics Foundation.

Owens, J. (2013) 'News Analysis: Tesco's Transparency on Food Waste Is a CSR Wake-Up Call for the City', *PR Week*, 15/11/2013, www.prweek.com/article/1220637/news-analysis-tescos-transparency-food-waste-csr-wake-up-call-city, accessed 5 March 2018.

Parish, R. (1996) 'Health Promotion: Rhetoric and Reality', in Bunton, R., Nettleton, S. and Burrows, R. (eds.), *The Sociology of Health Promotion*, London: Routledge.

Patel, R. (2012) *Stuffed and Starved*, London: Portobello Books.

Paton, G. (2015) 'Food Waste Scandal of the Calais Stowaways', *The Times*, 13/6/2015: 1.

Pearce, F. (2009) 'Supermarkets Get Slippery Over Green Palm Oil Promises', *The Guardian*, 4/12/2009, www.theguardian.com/environment/2009/dec/04/sustainable-palm-oil-failure-greenwash, accessed 28 February 2018.

Pemberton, M. (2018) 'Hospitals Need Real Food that's Cooked by Real Chefs', *Daily Mail*, 14/4/2018: 46.

Peng, M.W. (2009) *Global Strategy*, Ohio: South West Cengage Learning.

Pidd, H. (2018) 'Housing Crisis: 15,000 New Manchester Homes and Not a Single One 'Affordable', *The Guardian*, 5/3/2018: 15.

Pilkington, E. (2017) 'We All Cried When Walmart Closed Down', *The Guardian*, 2, 10/7/2017: 4–5.

Porter, M.E. and Kramer, M.R. (2006) 'Strategy and Society: The Link Between Competitive Advantage and Corporate Social Responsibility', *Harvard Business Review*, 84(12): 78–92.

Prieto-Carron, M. (2006) 'Central American Banana Production: Women Workers and Chiquita's Ethical Sourcing from Plantations', in Barrientos, S. and Dolan, C. (eds.), *Ethical Sourcing in the Global Food System*, London: Earthscan.

PR Newswire. (2013) 'Lidl Wins "National Retailer of the Year" for Green Credentials', www.prnewswire.co.uk/news-releases/lidl-wins-national-retailer-of-the-year-for-green-credentials-225809241.html, accessed 9 April 2018.

Pollard, D. (2006) 'The Gangmaster System in the UK: Perspective of a Trade Unionist', in Barrientos, S. and Dolan, C. (eds.), *Ethical Sourcing in the Global Food System*, London: Earthscan.

Public Health England. (2018) '*Fast Food Outlets: Density by Local Authority in England*', www.gov.uk/government/publications/fast-food-outlets-density-by-local-authority-in-england, accessed 20 July 2018.

Quartz. (2017) *The World's Plastic Problem, in Two Charts*, https://qz.com/1033477/the-worlds-plastic-problem-in-two-charts/, accessed 28 January 2018.

Rani, N. and Ramachandra, K. (2015) 'Growth in Grocery Retailing in India-Competitive Landscape of Modern vis-à-vis Traditional Grocers', *SDMIMD Journal of Management*, 6(2): 9–18.

Raskin, P. (2018) *Corporate 20/20*, Boston, MA: Tellus Institute, www.corporation2020.org/, accessed 28 July 2018.

Rawls, J. (1971) *A Theory of Justice*, Cambridge, MA: Harvard University Press.

Rawls, J. (2001) *Justice as Fairness: A Restatement*, Kelly, E. (ed.), Cambridge, MA: Harvard University Press.

Reardon, T. and Gulati, A. (2008) '*The Rise of Supermarkets and Their Development Implications; International Experience Relevant for India*', IFPRI Discussion Paper 00752 February 2008, Published by the International Food Policy Research Institute, University of Michigan.

Riley, M. (2014) '*ASDA Pure Organics*', Social Film, produced by LionEyes for Asda, www.lioneyestv.co.uk/portfolio-item/asda-pure-organics/, accessed 20 March 2018.

Roberts, F. (2017) *Migros Brings Sustainability to Swiss Supermarket Supply Chains*, www.supplychaindigital.com/company/migros-brings-sustainability-swiss-supermarket-supply-chains#, accessed 16 April 2018.

Roy, M. (2016) *Supermarket Weep: Woolies' Share Continues to Fall and Coles and Aldi Split the Proceeds*, www.roymorgan.com/findings/7021-woolworths-coles-aldi-iga-supermarket-market-shares-australia-september-2016--201610241542, accessed 5 March 2018.

RSPO. (2018) www.rspo.org/, accessed 28 February 2018.

Schaffner, D.J., Bokal, B., Fink, S., Rawls, K. and Schweiger, J. (2005) 'Food Retail-Price Comparison in Thailand', *Journal of Food Distribution Research*, 36(1): 167–71.

Sempergreen. (2017) *Lidl Is Leading the Way*, www.sempergreen.com/en/about-us/news/lidl-is-leading-the-way, accessed 9 April 2018.

Seth, A. and Randall, R. (1999) *The Grocers*, London: Kogan Page.

Seymour, J. and Girardet, H. (1986) *Far From Paradise*, London: British Broadcasting Corporation.

Shaw, H.J. (2003) 'The Ecology of Food Deserts', PhD, University of Leeds.

Shaw, H.J. (2007) 'The Role of CSR in Re-Empowering Local Communities', *Social Responsibility Journal*, 3(2): 11–21.

Shaw, H.J. (2008) 'Resisting the Hallucination of the Hypermarket', *International Journal of Baudrillard Studies*, 5(1): 1–30.

Shaw, H.J. (2014) *The Consuming Geographies of Food: Diet, Food Deserts and Obesity*, London: Routledge.

Shaw, H.J. (2017) 'The Food Desert Phenomenon', in Kateman, B. (ed.), *The Reducetarian Solution*, New York: Penguin Random House.

Shaw, J.J.A. (2019) *Law and the Passions: Narratives of Feeling in the Administration of Justice*, Oxford: Routledge.

Shaw, J.J.A. and Shaw, H.J. (2009) 'Corporate Social Responsibility and "Little Fleas": Small Is Beautiful', in Aras, G. and Crowther, D. (eds.), *Corporate Social Responsibility in SMEs*, Research Series: Issues in Corporate Behaviour and Sustainability, Social Responsibility Research Network.

Shaw, J.J.A. and Shaw, H.J. (2015) 'The Politics and Poetics of Spaces and Places: Mapping the Multiple Geographies of Identity in a Cultural Posthuman Era', *Journal of Organisational Transformation & Social Change*, 12(3): 234–56.

Shaw, J.J.A. and Shaw, H.J. (2016) 'Mapping the Technologies of Spatial (in) Justice in the Anthropocene', *Information and Communications Technology Law*, 25(1): 32–49.

Shildrick, T. and MacDonald, R. (2013) 'Poverty Talk: How People Experiencing Poverty Deny Their Poverty and Why They Blame "The Poor"', *The Sociological Review*, 61(2): 285–303.

Simms, A. (2007) *Tescopoly*, London: Constable.

Smith, A. (1981) *An Inquiry into the Nature and Causes of the Wealth of Nations*, Campbell, R.H. and Skinner, A.S. (eds.), Indianapolis, IN: Liberty Classics.

Smith, A. (2002) *The Theory of Moral Sentiments*, Haakonssen, K. (ed.), Cambridge: Cambridge University Press.

Smith, J.M. (2004) *Seeds of Deception*, Totnes: Green Books.

Smith, J.M. and Jehlicka, P. (2007) 'Stories Around Food, Politics and Change in Poland and the Czech Republic', *Transactions*, 32(3): 395–410.

Smithers, R. (2016) 'Lidl Follows Asda in Plan to Buy All Bananas from Sustainable Sources', *The Guardian*, 1/2/2016, www.theguardian.com/business/2016/feb/01/lidl-promises-stock-only-bananas-sustainable-sources, accessed 7 March 2018.

Smithers, R. (2018) 'Raise a Toast! New Beers Made from Leftover Breads Help to Cut Food Waste', *The Observer*, 29/4/2018: 25.

Smyth, C. (2018a) 'Ban on Junk Food Deals as Obesity Drive Unites MPs', *The Times*, 25/4/2018: 1–2.

Smyth, C. (2018b) 'NHS Cookery Classes Serve to Cut Obesity', *The Times*, 14/3/2018: 12.

Sodano, V. and Hingley, M. (2013) 'The Food System, Climate Change and CSR: From Business to Government Case', *British Food Journal*, 115(1): 75–91.

Spittles, D. (2017) 'Supermarket Sweep: Thousands of New London Homes Could Be Built Above Stores, and Tesco Is Leading the Charge', *Homes and Property*, 10/10/2017, www.homesandproperty.co.uk/property-news/buying/new-homes/thousands-of-new-london-homes-could-be-built-above-stores-and-tesco-is-leading-the-charge-a114431.html, accessed 14 May 2018.

Starkey, J. (2018) 'Cow's 450 Mile Round Trip to Die', *The Times*, 12/3/2018: 19.

Sustain. (2001) '*Eating Oil—Food in a Changing Climate*', Sustain/Elm Farm Research Centre Report, December.

Sutcliffe, J. (1816) *A Treatise on Canals and Reservoirs*, London: Hartley.

Takano, K. (2013) 'Business Opportunity and Food Education in Japan', *Social Responsibility Journal*, 9(4): 516–33.

Taylor, D. (2013) 'Fast-Food Staff Go on Strike Over Wages that Leave Them Unable to Feed Their Families', *The Times*, 7/12/2013: 54.

Temby, S. (2016) *The Six Things You Need to Know About ACCC v Woolworths*, Consumer Markets & Franchising, www.maddocks.com.au/6-things-need-know-accc-v-woolworths/, accessed 11 April.

Temple, N. (2018) *Best Before*, London: Bloomsbury.

Tesco. (2014) *Eat Happy Project*, www.ourtesco.com/2014/01/26/introducing-the-tesco-eat-happy-project-and-our-farm-to-fork-initiative/, accessed 6 March 2018.

Tesco Clubcard. (2017) '*Privacy and Cookies Policy*', updated 10 October 2017, www.tesco.com/help/privacy-and-cookies/privacy-centre/privacy-policy-information/privacy-policy/, accessed 20 March 2018.

Tibbett, J. (2013) 'Freegans risk the hazards of dumpster diving', *Canadian Medical Association Journal*, April 185(7): 281–2.

Tukker, A. and Jansen, B. (2008) 'Environmental Impacts of Products: A Detailed Review of Studies', *Journal of Industrial Ecology*, 10(3): 159–82.

Turner, J. (2017) 'Exercise Needs to Become Our Drug of Choice', *The Times*, 26/8/2017: 29.

Turns, A. (2017) *Tesco School Trips: What The Fork?*, http://blog.foodassembly.com/2017/06/07/uk-tesco-school-trips-fork/, accessed 6 March 2018.

UK Government. (2017) '*Health Matters: Obesity and the Food Environment*', Published by Public Health England, 31/3/2017, www.gov.uk/government/publications/health-matters-obesity-and-the-food-environment/health-matters-obesity-and-the-food-environment--2, accessed 16 April 2018.

UN General Assembly Resolution. (2015) 'Transforming Our World: The 2030 Agenda for Sustainable Development A/RES/70/1', www.un.org/ga/search/view_doc.asp?symbol=A/RES/70/1&Lang=E, accessed 19 July 2018.

Verdonk, R & Shakel, O. (2016) '*Citrus Report—Israel 2016*', Published by USDA Foreign Agricultural Service, https://gain.fas.usda.gov/Recent%20GAIN%20Publications/Citrus%20report%20-%20Israel%202016_Tel%20Aviv_Israel_12-22-2016.pdf, accessed 16 May 2018.

Von Vark, C. (2016) 'Behind the Label: Is Certification Working?', *The Guardian*, 10/3/2016: 26.

Wacquant, L. (2008) 'Pierre Bourdieu', in Stones, R. (ed.), *Key Sociological Thinkers*, 2nd edition, London and New York: Palgrave Macmillan, 215–29.

Waitrose. (2018) *Supermarket CSR*, www.johnlewispartnership.co.uk/content/dam/cws/pdfs/our-responsibilities/2017files/JLP-Human-Rights-Report-2016 17-Final.pdf, accessed 28 February 2018.

Watts, B. (2014) 'Homelessness, Empowerment and Self-Reliance in Scotland and Ireland: The Impact of Legal Rights to Housing for Homeless People', *Journal of Social Policy*, 43(4): 793–810.

Watts, J. (2018) 'Nairobi Feels the Force of World's Most Draconian Plastic Bag Ban', *The Guardian*, 26/4/2018: 11.

Webster, B. (2017a) 'Tesco to stop selling disposable plastic bags', *The Times*, 8/8/2017: 1.

Webster, B. (2017b) 'Scrap Use-By Dates on Milk to End Waste of 100 Million Pints', *The Times*, 27/2/2017: 1.

Webster, B. (2018a) 'Idyllic Meat Wrappers Hide Harsh Reality of Modern Mass Farming', *The Times*, 10/3/2018: 4–5.

Webster, B. (2018b) 'Workers at Farm Supplying Tesco Laughed While They Kicked Pigs', *The Times*, 24/5/2018: 13.

Webster, B. (2018c) 'Supermarkets Call for More Surprise Checks on Farms', *The Times*, 31/7/2018: 16.

Wilshaw, R. (2016) '*Supplier Treatment: Why Tesco and Other Supermarkets Should Integrate Business and Ethics*', 3/2/2016, Published by Oxfam, https://policy-practice.oxfam.org.uk/blog/2016/02/why-tesco-and-other-supermarkets-should-integrate-business-and-ethics, accessed 13 April 2018.

Wilson, H. (2018) 'Sainsbury's Tie-Up Under New Scrutiny', *The Times*, 22/5/2018: 37.

Wilson, L. (2011) 'Coles Cut Supermarket Milk Price 'To Help Families', *The Australian*, 30/3/2011, www.theaustralian.com.au/news/nation/coles-cut-supermarket-milk-price-to-help-families/news-story/ac722e250ec00029d6ad3bdc2106cb58, accessed 7 March 2018.

Wind-Cowie, M. (2010) *Civic Streets: The Big Society in Action*, London: Demos.

Woolworths. (2014) '*Response to Competition Review Issues Paper*', June, http://competitionpolicyreview.gov.au/files/2014/06/Woolworths.pdf, accessed 11 April 2018.

World Bank. (2001) *World Development Report 2000/2001*, New York: Oxford University Press.

World Food Programme. (2018) *Zero Hunger*, www.wfp.org/hunger/stats, accessed 17 July 2018.

World Growth. (2011) *Coles, Woolies Socially Irresponsible*, https://worldgrowth.org/2011/05/coles-woolies-socially-irresponsible/, accessed 11 April 2018.

Wrigley, N. and Lowe, M. (2002) *Reading Retail*, London: Arnold.

Wrigley, N., Lambiri, D. and Cudworth, K. (2010) '*Revisiting the Impact of Large Foodstores on Market Towns and District Centres*', Published by The University of Southampton.

Wrigley, N., Lowe, M., Guy, C., Woods, S. and Shaw, H.J. (2007) '*Relocalising Food Shopping*', Published by The University of Southampton.

YouTube. (2006) www.youtube.com/watch?v=ogetBqMgau0, accessed 10 May 2018.

YouTube. (2010) www.youtube.com/watch?v=vW-Th9tldcs, accessed 10 May 2018.

YouTube. (2012) www.youtube.com/watch?v=NYndyqp1gDU, accessed 10 May 2018.

Younge, G. (2005) 'McDonald's Grabs a Piece of the Apple Pie: 'Healthy' Menu Changes Threaten the Health of Biodiversity in Apples', *The Guardian*, 7/4: 15.

Zhen, Y. (2007) *Globalization and the Chinese Retailing Revolution*, Oxford: Chandos.

Index

Printed in Great Britain
by Amazon

35961200R00117